Virgil's Iliad

VIRGIL'S ILIAD
An essay on epic narrative

K. W. GRANSDEN
UNIVERSITY OF WARWICK

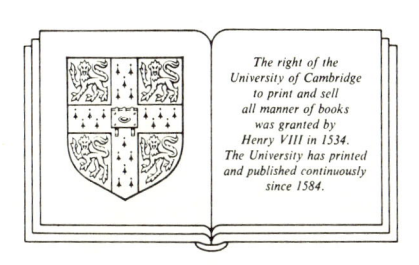

CAMBRIDGE UNIVERSITY PRESS
CAMBRIDGE
LONDON   NEW YORK   NEW ROCHELLE
MELBOURNE   SYDNEY

Published by the Press Syndicate of the University of Cambridge
The Pitt Building, Trumpington Street, Cambridge CB2 IRP
32 East 57th Street, New York, NY 10022, USA
296 Beaconsfield Parade, Middle Park, Melbourne 3206, Australia

© Cambridge University Press 1984

First published 1984

Printed in Great Britain at the University Press, Cambridge

Library of Congress catalogue card number: 84-4236

British Library Cataloguing in Publication Data
Gransden, K.W.
Virgil's Iliad.
1. Virgil. Aeneid. Books 6–12—Sources
2. Homer. Iliad   3. Homer—Influences
—Virgil
I. Title
873'.01   PA6825

ISBN 0 521 24504 4 hard covers
ISBN 0 521 28756 1 paperback

AMICIS

CONTENTS

Preface ix
Introduction 1
Prologue: Homer's *Iliad* 9

Part I: Peace
1 Transition 31
2 Invocation 39
3 Homecoming 44
4 Dynastic 57
5 Juno 67
6 Catalogue 81
7 Diplomatic 87

Part II: War
1 Absence 97
2 Nisus and Euryalus 102
3 Siege 119
4 The council of the gods 126
5 The return of Aeneas 138
6 The funeral of Pallas 154
7 The council of war 174
8 Camilla's last stand 183
9 War and peace 192

Bibliography 218
Indexes 220

PREFACE

In 1965 I began to think about the European epic tradition, which was being established as a core course for first-year undergraduates reading English and Comparative Literature at the new University of Warwick. For the first time I began to look at the *Aeneid* in relation to its Homeric exemplars on one side, and to its successors, *The Divine Comedy* and *Paradise Lost* on the other. For someone with a traditional classical education, accustomed to look at works of literature more or less in isolation, this was an exciting and fruitful adventure, and my first debt must be to Professor G. K. Hunter, from whose original inspiration the course evolved and is, I hope, still evolving.

During this period there has also been a significant shift in the direction and emphasis of literary criticism itself. There has been a steadily growing interest in narrative and in the ways in which the reader himself constructs and manipulates narrative; in the 'voice' of the 'implied author' of a narrative; in the structure and articulation of long texts. At the same time there has been a tendency to move away from close analysis of isolated words and phrases, and to become more concerned with larger sense-units and the importance of recurring themes and motifs.

Nevertheless, readers of difficult texts, especially those in foreign languages, will continue to need annotated editions. Some years ago Professor E. J. Kenney invited me to edit *Aeneid* VIII for the series of Cambridge Greek and Latin Classics of which he and Mrs P. E. Easterling are general editors. This undertaking gave me the opportunity of trying to keep in mind the ways of looking at narrative to which I have referred, while not (I hope) quite losing sight of the traditional needs and expectations of the student of Latin poetry. I do not know how successfully I solved that problem, but Professor Kenney subsequently invited me to edit *Aeneid* XI, and it was while pondering my Introduction to that text that I realised how much preliminary work I needed to do on the second half of the poem. That preliminary work has led to this book, the scope and intention of which are described in the Introduction.

I should like to thank all those colleagues and students, past and present, with whom I have been fortunate enough to be able to discuss epic poetry in general and Virgil in particular. From such discussions, as much as from reading, I have been able to get some beginnings of an understanding of the fascinations and complexities of narrative. In addition, my thanks are due to Susan Moore, of Cambridge University Press, who read the book in manuscript and saved me from many errors and imperfections, and to Elizabeth Hannay, who read the proofs and saved me from some more. For those which doubtless remain I am solely responsible.

INTRODUCTION

The first six books of the *Aeneid* have generally received more attention than the last six. This may be partly due to the comparative inaccessibility of books VII–XII in good modern editions, and partly also to the popularity of books II, IV and VI, each of which may be easily isolated. All of this is bound to have contributed to a persistent judgement of the poem. My main purpose in this essay is to try to re-establish the paramount value of books VII–XII as epic narrative. They represent, after all, Virgil's Iliad.[1] It is commonly agreed that Homer's *Iliad* surpasses his *Odyssey* in tragic intensity and in the power of its narrative. If this is so, and if *Aeneid* VII–XII is less successful than *Aeneid* I–VI, then Virgil must be judged to have proven inadequate to the greater artistic challenge when he came to it, and the *maius opus* becomes an empty rhetorical gesture. It seemed worth writing something which would argue the contrary case: that, far from constituting a falling off, *Aeneid* VII–XII is a continuous epic narrative of sustained power and grandeur, planned and executed on the largest scale and offering a structural unity which matches that of its great model.

I shall also argue that any reading of *Aeneid* VII–XII involves not only a reconsideration of the first half of the poem – thus, although book VI is a complete piece of narrative, the reader who has never gone on to book VII will make something quite different out of it from what will be made by a reader who is going on, or who has already gone on – but also a reconsideration of Homer's *Iliad*. To achieve a true sense of the meaning of the *Aeneid*, the reader must have a sense – it need

---

[1] The terms 'Odyssean' *Aeneid* and 'Iliadic' *Aeneid* are familiar from Brooks Otis, *Virgil: a Study in Civilised Poetry* (Oxford 1964) chs. vi, vii.

not, probably will not, be complete or precise – of what Homer's *Iliad* meant to the implied reader of the *Aeneid* and to Virgil himself.

No book in the second half of the poem can be satisfactorily detached from the continuous texture of the narrative whole. At no point until the last sentence of book XII can we reach a complete reading of the poem and make sense of it as a history of human experience. And it is through this sense of significant unity which the Virgilian Iliad elicits from the reader that he is finally able to construct a significance not just for the last six books but retrospectively for the whole epic. The tragic tensions, the loftily overarching historical suspensions and resolutions of Virgil's Iliad should strike the reader with a force which extends back to the now distant earlier books and to the first days of the hero's trials and sufferings, *multum . . . et terris iactatus et alto*, when he stood on the north African littoral and gazed in Juno's temple at the murals of the Trojan war, the heroic conflict which he had, albeit traumatically, come through. There he saw himself depicted in the thick of battle, in close combat with the Achaian chieftains, *se quoque principibus permixtum agnouit Achiuis*. Aeneas did not know then that he would soon be again at war. And in book VIII, when he gazed in wonder and surmise at the scenes depicted on the shield, he could not still, and would not ever, complete the significance of what he saw. That he leaves to the reader. His own renewed conflict lay immediately ahead, the conflicts on the shield in a different order of temporality.

The murals in Juno's temple in the first 'Odyssean' book constitute one of the poem's most important motifs. Everything Aeneas sees there as over and done with – slaughter, sacrilege, destruction – he will live through again: first in his own retrospective narrative of the last days of Troy, the tragic power of which is secured by the shift into a first-person narrative and the interposition of a reader–hearer who is herself emotionally involved with the narrator and waiting to play a tragic role herself inside the temporality of the poem's primary narrative scheme; and then again in the poem's Iliadic closing books, the narrative of the Italian campaign. The reader's sense and recollection of book I will be transformed in memory and become part of his final sense of the whole epic, the perspectives of which extend from the hero, focus of all the poem's temporalities, and from all the other characters, the *mezzi* and *impedimenti*,[2] the facilitators and impediments of his mission, Creusa, Anchises, Dido, Latinus, Evander, Mezentius, Camilla, Nisus, Euryalus, Turnus.

A whole new cast of characters, new locations, a new start, are signalled by the narrator in book VII – *maius opus moueo* – yet the reader does not start all over again, for the same hero unites the whole, and in the huge transition bridging the two halves moves out of the sixth book, with its dreams of past and future, its rivers of fantasy, into the seventh, with its massive build-up of local realities beside the Tiber. Among the new characters, slipping in at the very end of VII, is Camilla, who will dominate XI: she will recall to the reader not only Dido and Cleopatra, heroic, doomed and deceived, but also the virgin huntress, the Amazon Penthesilea who came to help the Trojans after Hector's death and was killed by Achilles. Thus the reader of VII–XII looks back as Aeneas looked back; the experience of reading VII–XII will modify his sense of I–VI.

Virgil must have known Homer by heart. He thought deeply and philosophically about the meaning of history and the life and suffering of humanity. He saw the past, as his readers must, not only diachronically but also synchronically. An epic poem is temporal and dynamic; yet it is also spatial, the reader moves through it as through a location, turning back and retracing his steps when he wishes as Aeneas retraced his steps on that last fatal night in Troy. But all the time, the momentum of the reading of any long narrative must be forward, must be towards the end. We must want to get to the end as much as Aeneas did.

>hic labor extremus, longarum haec meta uiarum.

[2] See Tasso, *Discorso . . . del Poema Eroico*.

And though the end comes last, we may infer it any moment not only from previous readings of the poem, if any, but from a continual awareness that Virgil is not merely alluding to the *Iliad*, but redeploying it, almost, in a sense, overlaying it with his own visionary misreading or (at the least) recension of it.[3] For the modern reader, to try to make sense of the *Aeneid* without continual recourse to Homer is like trying to read a code whose secret is lost. 'The meaning of a text depends upon other texts which it absorbs and transforms.'[4]

Virgil might have treated the official Augustan myth of Aeneas as a piece of Callimachean aitiology. He decided not to do so, but to attempt a recension of both the Homeric epics, with Aeneas replaying the roles of Achilles, Hector and Odysseus. He thus ensured the survival of heroic epic as a serious form for another millennium and a half. Charming though it is, one cannot take the *Argonautica* of Apollonius seriously as an essential anterior text to the *Aeneid*. Virgil obliged the sophisticated reader to take heroic epic seriously, he obliged Europe to go on reckoning with Homer even when most of Europe could not read him. The *Aeneid* casts a retrospective light on the structural and metaphorical achievements of the *Iliad* and the *Odyssey*. Matthew Arnold's view of poetry, in which Homer is great not because he is *naïf* or primitive but because he is an artist of high seriousness, is directly derived from his reading of Virgil, who may indeed be seen to have rescued his great model, with true vatic foresight, from the fallacies of primitivism and historicism which, many centuries later, clouded a proper reading of Homer and caused foolish scholastic distinctions to be drawn between Homer and Virgil, obscuring even for the enlightened the true nature and scope of Virgil's *imitatio*.[5]

No one writing about Virgil can fail to be conscious of the weight of past scholarship, criticism and exegesis. Yet anyone

---

[3] 'Each poet must slay his poetic father.' Harold Bloom, quoted in J. Culler, *The Pursuit of Signs* (London 1981) 13.
[4] Culler, *Pursuit* 104.
[5] For these we may go back to Quintilian, *I.O.* l. 46–51, 85–6. 'Virgil comes second to Homer, but nearer first than third.'

who allowed himself to be too much aware of this would never write about Virgil at all. My chief debt will be obvious. I have tried to follow the work of Knauer[6] by producing a study of *Aeneid* VII–XII as a seamless whole, the second half of a *carmen perpetuum*. Most recent studies of the *Aeneid* have concentrated on key passages and drawn from them sets of interpretative principles, a 'reading'. I have sought no such principles. I start, and end, with a single ungainsayable fact, that the *Aeneid* is an *imitatio* of the two epics of Homer, the most notable instance, probably, in European literature of 'intertextuality'.[7] I have not been able wholly to resist the temptation, which nearly all writers on Virgil have found irresistible, to indulge in a little speculation in my final pages, but I hope I have kept this self-indulgence to an acceptable minimum. Antiquarian and allegorical exegesis have also been reduced to the minimum.

I have, however, been indebted to work done on narrative by critics outside the field of classical study. Some of these ideas have produced shifts of emphasis which are stimulating and perhaps valuable to readers of any long narrative text. I see no reason why any narrative should be exempt from such scrutiny (however imperfect) just because it is written in Latin.

Commentators on ancient texts have traditionally concentrated on explaining the meanings of words and sentences: understandably, since only a few people know much Latin or Greek and because so much of the pagan past must remain strange and remote to us. But the emphasis on words and phrases is bound to slow the reader down to walking pace, is bound to stress the difficulties of the language. A reader of the *Aeneid* can be detained for ages (and pages) by notes on words like *enim* which, while models of learning, impede the reader's sense of the narrative. Anyone who has tried to teach long narrative texts in Latin will, I believe, confirm that many pupils cannot see the wood for the trees and often fail to reach

[6] G. N. Knauer, *Die Aeneis und Homer* (Göttingen 1964).
[7] Culler, *Pursuit* 101–18.

any sense of the structure and movement of narrative. They lose all sense of what is happening and of the processes by which what is happening is presented. In the words of a recent writer, 'without complementing the verbal by a wider structural approach, how can one explain such features as constellations of personae, juxtaposition of larger narrative sections . . . the possible effects of narrative pace?'[8] The 'presented world' of the narrative must be realised by the reader through the process of presentation, the author's techniques – e.g., in epic, the juxtaposition and relationship of speeches, narrative and descriptive ecphrasis. The reader sees – and what do we mean when we say that we 'see' something in a literary narrative? – parallels and correspondences between articulated sections of the whole, formal arrangements such as triadic or chiastic structures, all of them non-verbal phenomena. 'Granted our discussion of these phenomena must be verbal. But we do not derive them immediately from the given string of words, and although we may verbalise our findings, we are rarely able to discover specific concrete evidence in the text for such large-scale inferences.' And in the words of another critic, 'the most significant level where the mind lingers, is not the verbal but the ideational: *the final response is to events imaginatively recreated, not to word-meanings*'.[9] Anyone who considers for a moment what is meant by 'reading' the *Aeneid*, and the effect of the poem when read, will probably admit that what stays in the mind is a sense of the whole, and particularly of how it starts and ends, and of the movements which span these points. Nor is anyone familiar with the poem always able to extrapolate any single reading from the totality of all readings and from a larger, less definite sense of the poem which is more than the sum of all readings.

Any teacher of the *Aeneid* knows how few students nowadays get to the end of it. Yet only when one has done this can a retrospective overview be imposed upon the reading

---

[8] H. Ruthrof, *The Reader's Construction of Narrative* (London 1981) 40.
[9] S. L. Bethell, *Essays on Literary Criticism and the English Tradition* (London 1969) 45, quoted in Ruthrof, *Reader's Construction* 38.

process, the making of the work. In each several re-reading, the making of the work will be modified by, and will modify, previous readings. How else, if at all, can we grasp it all? There are moments in reading any long work when one has a familiar, all too fleeting sense of having grasped the whole. Such moments may be illusory, but they are a persistent phenomenon which the traditional commentaries seldom account for.

As to the translations, Lattimore's *Iliad* has set a standard which is incomparable, and all extensive quotations are from his version.[10] I have made my own translations of short extracts quoted only in order to isolate some word or phrase relevant to Virgil. The translations from the *Aeneid* are my own. I have preserved the distinction between Virgil's Aeneas and Homer's Aineias; otherwise, I have not thought it necessary to use the Greek spelling of names of Homeric heroes familiar in the *Aeneid*. And though Lattimore prefers Achilleus, Aias, etc., I have taken the liberty of changing some of his spellings in order to achieve uniformity.

[10] *The Iliad*, translated by Richmond Lattimore, copyright 1951 by the University of Chicago.

PROLOGUE: HOMER'S *ILIAD*

Homer's *Iliad* remains a work of peculiar and unique interest because it is the oldest surviving example of a long complete piece of narrative fiction in our literary tradition; and still completely accessible to us after two and a half millennia. It is fascinating to discover that Homer does not, as we might have expected, merely 'tell a story', transmit an account of events; he presents a discourse, a set of codes displayed with (for us) the pride and excitement of novelty as well as (for him) the strength and confidence bestowed by an already rich tradition. The Muses, the descriptive epithets, the whole stylistic apparatus we were once excited to discover to have depended on an oral narrative technique, may now excite us for other and quite different reasons. The oral excitement generated by Parry has worn off, but we are only now beginning to think how to read the text as a piece of narrative.

To take two examples: the phrase 'Priam and the people of Priam of the good ash spear' denotes the entire nation of Troy but is used only in the context of the inevitable doom being prophesied for the city, so that we realise that the good ash spear is in fact not going to be good enough (no more destiny-proof than Wotan's), and that the formulaic phrase operates as a signifier to which readers will respond as to dramatic irony. Again, it has sometimes been said that these adjectives are primarily there for metrical and syntactical convenience, so that (for instance) Achilles is called swift-footed when he is not moving (l.489), 'but that could mark the contrast between his normal state and his present inactivity'.[1] Since most people read the poem in English, the metrical

---

[1] C. M. Bowra, *Homer* (London 1972) 24.

reason for a particular choice of descriptive phrase is the least interesting thing about it: and in any case, so rich is Homer's repertoire, there are some alternatives which are metrically identical. After reading a few hundred lines, we are aware that Homer is presenting a hero with a number of recurrent and insisted-on qualities and characteristics. The value of the accumulations, choices and repetitions lies in the gradual build-up the reader makes, and not in any individual isolated metrical phoneme.

If reading the *Iliad* poses problems different from those encountered when reading *War and Peace*, can these problems be identified, and if so can they be solved? Or is their uniqueness and their insolubility the essential mystery of the *Iliad* which persists long after the excitement generated by Parry and Wolf has worn off?

> Who was it wrote the *Iliad*? What a laugh!
> Why Homer, all the world knows. Of his life
> Doubtless some facts exist. It's everywhere.
> We have not settled, though, his date of birth.
> Until . . . 'What's this, the Germans say is fact
> That Wolf found out first? It's unpleasant work,
> Their chop and change, unsettling one's belief.
> All the same, while we live, we learn, that's sure.'
> . . . And after Wolf, a dozen of his like
> Proved there was never any Troy at all,
> Neither besiegers nor besieged. Nay, worse,
> No actual Homer, no authentic text,
> No warrant for the fiction I as fact
> Had treasured in my heart and soul so long,
> Ay mark you, and as fact held still, still hold,
> Spite of new knowledge, in my heart of hearts
> And soul of souls, fact's essence freed and fixed.

For Browning,[2] modern in this as in so many of his insights,

---

[2] Browning, *Development* (included first in his late collection *Asolando: Facts and Fancies*).

the 'authentic text' of Homer's *Iliad* remained inviolate and unassailable, for it belongs to the reader.

One might posit an innocent or first-time reader of the *Iliad* who had never heard of Zeus or Troy. This seems more likely, though perhaps not much more likely, than a reader of *War and Peace* who had never heard of Napoleon and the retreat from Moscow. Or one might have 'heard of' Troy or Moscow, Zeus or Napoleon, and still not be sure of their place in these particular narratives. Napoleon is as much a character in *War and Peace* as Prince Andrew, and Tolstoi presents him in exactly the same way, as we can see in book x; before the battle for the Shevardino redoubt Napoleon sees the war as a game; afterwards he could not cope with the terrible spectacle of the battlefield of the dead until he could rationalise it as his doing, his will. Napoleon, riding over the battlefield, rationalising the war, is part of the same narrative discourse which has just isolated the wounding of Prince Andrew, presented in Homeric fashion with two epic similes;[3] and beyond all this, the author as the retrospective total consciousness of the historical process offers the reader a remoter perspective in which the great commanders appear as pawns of destiny.

In the *Iliad* the Olympian deities, of which the naive or first-time reader may have heard, are so real to the heroes that they speak to them and see them and even wound them. Yet behind even Zeus's view of the battle, as he sits apart, Homer himself presents a display of events of which Zeus too is only part.

The *Iliad* is the narrative of a siege in which the Achaians (Greeks) are the attackers and ultimate victors, the Trojans the defenders and ultimate losers. But the narrative begins by saying nothing of ultimate victory for the Achaians.

> Sing, goddess, the anger of Peleus' son Achilles
> and its devastation, which put pain thousandfold
> upon the Achaians,

[3] 'Like a bird whirring in rapid flight and alighting on the ground, a shell dropped with little noise . . . the smoking shell spun like a top between him and the prostrate adjutant . . .' (*War and Peace* x.xxxvi).

> hurled in their multitudes to the house of Hades strong souls
> of heroes, but gave their bodies to be the delicate feasting
> of dogs, of all birds, and the will of Zeus was accomplished
> since that time when first there stood in division of conflict
> Atreus' son the lord of men and brilliant Achilles.

The poet announces that he will treat of the anger of Achilles, and that this wrought havoc upon his own side: the surprise word for the naive reader is 'Achaians'. The narrative gradually emerges, as background and hereafter are filled in, though there is always a single temporality and no flashbacks as such, until we are aware of a time 'before the wrath' as well as after it. What emerges as our text is a self-contained tale which is also part of a missing larger tale which we don't have but can construct in a sketchy outline quite different in texture from the immensely packed, detailed story Homer himself gives us. The excitement and mysteriousness which continues to attend readings of the *Iliad* – and not just first-time readings, which may indeed be poorer in those qualities because the reader does not yet know how to place what he can read in the context of what he cannot read, but all readings – is due largely to our sense that what is displayed includes fragments of and references to a missing text, which is both essential and at the same time superfluous. This missing tale confers on the told tale, the tale of Achilles' anger, the actual text, a larger and grander significance which the reader finds access to, saying in effect 'this wrath might seem trivial were it not part of a larger structure'. Achilles' anger is a stratagem whereby Homer can turn Achilles into the star of his narrative, which has a very large cast of characters, many of whom are really part of the missing Troy tale.

There is thus an ambiguity at the very outset of any confrontation with the *Iliad*: an ambiguity codified in the simple and obvious fact that the title of the poem and its opening are at variance. The old analysts solved this problem by saying that there were really two, or several, poems, behind the monumental *Iliad*. Yet there is only one text, the monumental *Iliad* itself, substantially, to the best of our knowledge, the text that Virgil read; and the challenge of this text to the modern reader is that he must try to make sense of it (not that it does not already 'make sense') by the act of reading it. This is difficult for any long work, which tends to become fragmented in our consciousness until we have read it many times (more times than most readers of the poem will probably ever read it). Eventually we shall impose on our reading of that opening invocation our sense of how the poem will end and of all that has to happen for that ending to occur. Any first 'naive' reading of the text must be unique. Reading in progress and retrospective reading (that is, awareness as we read of what we have not yet read this time) are very different activities.[4] Once you know the end, on any subsequent reading, however fragmented, however much you choose to isolate specific passages for various purposes (sheer pleasure, critical complexity, 'crucialness' to the story) you will be imposing a retrospective sense of the whole work which could not have entered your mind when you were first reading it, and which, now, any passage you choose to isolate can be made to – indeed will be bound to – illustrate and confirm.

'Who then among the gods set Achilles and Agamemnon at strife?' asks the narrator, with the air of one presenting a mystery and a surprise, the hidden cause, at once to be revealed, for his grand narrative effect. Apollo is angry at the dishonouring of his priest, whose daughter Chryseis Agamemnon has carried off from an earlier siege: the first 'piece of pastness' in the narrative. In narrative, effect frequently precedes cause, in that we encounter it first: a clear example of the mimetic effect. Lewis Carroll was making a serious point about narrative when the White Queen pricked

[4] Cf. H. Ruthrof, *Reader's Construction* 75.

her finger. 'That accounts for the bleeding, you see. Now you understand the way things happen here.'

Agamemnon refused to return the priest's daughter, so Apollo sent a plague upon the Achaians, an intimation or foreshadowing of the disasters which the narrator has already announced will be the consequence of Achilles' anger. That anger has not yet erupted. It does so now. Achilles seems to provoke a confrontation with Agamemnon when he summons an assembly on the tenth day of the pestilence and wonders aloud at the cause of the god's displeasure. The reader knows this already, so that a kind of irony is operating: 'Come let us enquire of some soothsayer who should tell us why Apollo is angry.' Agamemnon says nothing. The whole of this opening is a stratagem by which the narrator brings into existence the wrath promised in the opening line.

The soothsayer demands protection before he speaks. 'For I shall provoke one who rules all the Argives and whom the Achaians obey.' The reader is now waiting for the narrative to catch him up. He can relax; he is already ahead. Achilles speaks again provocatively, bringing the inevitable wrath promised by the narrator nearer. 'No man while I live shall lay violent hands upon you, not even if you mean Agamemnon . . .'

Effect precedes cause. Behind the events narrated there lies a cause for the reader to elicit. Why did Achilles deliberately provoke Agamemnon? So that Achilles would be angry and make good the narrator's proclaimed theme; and for that to work psychologically, Achilles must be a certain kind of character, touchy, jealous of Agamemnon, while aware, as the reader has got to become, that he himself is the better soldier.

When Achilles is obliged by Agamemnon to surrender Briseis as a replacement for Chryseis he loses face. His mother Thetis pleads to Zeus for recompense for her son. Zeus promises a run of Trojan victories until the Achaians 'do Achilles honour and exalt him with recompense'. Homer invents a debt owed by Zeus to Thetis in order to manipulate the narrative; again he creates a cause for an effect already pre-empted as necessary: exactly as the episode of Chryseis

PROLOGUE: HOMER'S *ILIAD*

and the subsequent taking by Agamemnon of Briseis creates a cause for the effect already pre-empted by the narrator as essential to his story, namely the wrath theme itself. Now the story requires a run of Trojan victories led by Hector, culminating in the death of Patroclus during the absence of his friend Achilles from the battlefield. Since the death of Patroclus and the subsequent death of Hector at the hand of Achilles, now returned to the fight, are the climax of the *Iliad*, the narrator must create causes to explain how such events occur. The reader must not supply alternative explanations to those in the discourse itself. None of these events, and especially not the death of Patroclus wearing the armour of Achilles, in a sense masquerading as, mirroring, Achilles himself, could occur without Achilles' absence. So absent he must be: therefore angry; therefore dishonoured. Thus we work back to a situation in which so great a hero can be dishonoured; we work back to the beginning.

Is Zeus's interference to be understood as the cause of the Trojan victories? Would Achilles' absence by itself have been insufficient cause? After nine years in which so many of the principal heroes are still alive an indecisive pattern of swaying fortunes must have obtained. Are events which we think of as brought about by various combinations of management and chance, equally well presented in a narrative as the products of a kind of divine fiddling with human affairs? Such questions are asked frequently by narrators of later fictions, and especially by Tolstoi in *War and Peace*; he will not let the great leaders have credit or discredit for events which they suppose to have been brought about by their wills, but which the narrator, in his role as the total consciousness of history, sees as the working out of historical necessity.

The *Iliad* is a tragic poem. The run of Trojan victories is cruelly delusive not only in terms of a story in which Hector is doomed to die (the fear so touchingly faced by Andromache in the scene of their parting in book VI) but in terms also of the larger, missing yet omnipresent story of the destruction of Troy itself, of which Hector is the presented symbol. Achilles loses his shield when Patroclus dies and his body is stripped of his friend's armour; but his shield is replaced by divine intervention. When Hector dies Troy loses its irreplaceable shield.

The fall of Troy is continually put into the reader's mind by Homer through the words of Hector and Agamemnon, who both say

> For I know well this thing in my heart and mind:
> The day will come when holy Ilium shall be destroyed
> and Priam and the people of Priam of the good ash spear.[5]

That recurrent phrase, to which I have already drawn attention, is used also by Zeus in a quarrel with Hera in book IV. Zeus wishes that the war might end with the return of Helen and the sparing of Troy. Hera bursts out in angry protest. Zeus asks her what the Trojans have done to her to make her hate them so.

> For of all the cities beneath the sun and starry heaven
> dwelt in by men who live on the earth,
> dear to my heart was holy Ilium
> and Priam and the people of Priam of the good ash spear.[6]

Again, those words must be decoded in terms of the ultimate fall of the Trojans despite the success of their present counter-attack.

Zeus reluctantly assents to the city's doom, but warns Hera: 'Don't try to stop me when I wish to destroy another city.' Hera replies that Argos, Sparta and Mycenae are dearest to her heart. Zeus may destroy them whenever they are hateful to him. Here we are carried forward beyond even Troy's fall to the destruction of Mycenae itself, Agamemnon's citadel,

[5] *Iliad* 4.163–5, 6.447–9.   [6] *Iliad* 4.44–7.

proudest and richest creation of bronze age civilisation. Thus history casts a long proleptic shadow over the brief moment of Achilles' wrath and its consequences, to the point where the reader, for all his wonder at the magnificent age of heroes, may almost see them with the retrospective eye of Tolstoi, as strutting dinosaurs. If they behaved like this, no wonder they and their culture fell, and this may become part of our own reading of the *Iliad*.

The capriciousness and collective instability of divine motivation and divine interference form a *donnée* of the narrative of the *Iliad*. What might be expected to emerge for the reader is a sense of randomness, yet the narrator operates a total consciousness of how things are, a control of events both before the *Iliad* and beyond it, which has the effect of subsuming randomness within inevitability. The will of Zeus, least unstable element in the divine order, is that which is accomplished, and is not that which is not accomplished: hence the narrator's opening promise about the anger of Achilles

> and its devastation which put pains thousandfold
> upon the Achaians
> ... and the will of Zeus was accomplished

The correlative of the will of Zeus is the ordered, coherent and logical narrative of the *Iliad*, a poem containing, and contained by, history.

Reading the *Iliad*, reading *War and Peace*, the reader senses the ultimate powerlessness of great heroes and at the same time their belief in their own power to control events.

The presented world of the *Iliad* is one in which chance is never the reason for anything, yet might be deduced as the reason for everything. The gods nullify, or render superfluous, the concept of chance, yet the patterns of causality their presence in the narrative creates may be seen as random in that what determines them is Homer's own unpredictable narrative. If he wants a god, he puts one there, as he does at the deaths of Patroclus (Apollo) and Hector (Athene). If he does not want a god there, he removes them, as in the final confrontation between Achilles and Priam when Hermes, having escorted Priam to Achilles' tent, says he will leave 'for it would anger others for immortal gods to be entertained face to face by mortals'. The problem of getting rid of Hermes is a problem of narrative not of theology.[7] Tolstoi says of chance that it only denotes a certain stage in understanding phenomena. The author of the *Iliad* has constructed a discourse in which the concept of chance is not required for the reader to understand what he reads.

The effect of reading the *Iliad* is a sense that time stands still, that the fighting seems always to have been going on, yet in the total consciousness of the narrator there is a before and an after. Thus at the opening of *Iliad* XII we are told that

> when in the tenth year the city of Priam was taken
> and the Argives gone in their ships to the beloved
>   land of their fathers,
> then at last Poseidon and Apollo took counsel
> to wreck the wall, letting loose the strength of rivers
>   upon it . . . and Zeus rained
> incessantly, to break the wall faster and wash it
>   seaward.
> . . .
> Thus, afterwards, Poseidon and Apollo were
>   minded
> to put things in place, but at this time battle and
>   clamour were blazing

and the reader returns to the 'meanwhile' of the presented world of the narrative, in which these things have not yet taken their due place in the chain of temporality. 'Troy has fallen' and 'Troy has not yet fallen' are both in their different modes simultaneously true. Thus, although the destruction of holy Ilion does not occur within the temporality of the chain of

---

[7] *Iliad* 24.463–4. Macleod's note ((ed.), *Homer: Iliad Book XXIV* (Cambridge 1982)) seems rather to miss the point. Gods do appear to men, albeit disguised, and show them favour, as Aphrodite does to Helen in *Iliad* III. There is no question but that Helen knows who she is.

events dependent on the wrath of Achilles, far from lying beyond Homer's imagining, it has in fact already, for Homer and his reader, taken place. *fuimus Troes, fuit Ilium et ingens gloria Teucrorum*[8] does not become true for the first time in *Aeneid* II. The legend that the gods deserted the doomed city, so powerfully evoked by Virgil,[9] could be deduced from the *Iliad* itself, even though we lack the *Iliou Persis* on which Virgil probably modelled his own account of the city's last hours.

Why was Troy doomed? The obvious answer is that Paris ran off with Helen, whose recovery is the ostensible motive and object of the campaign. Ferrucci, in his book *The Poetics of Disguise*, says that she represents the dream of happiness both sides pursue and neither can relinquish. For the Trojans, to give her back is unthinkable, and for the Greeks, not to get her back is unthinkable. Hence the abortive duel, in book III, between Paris and Menelaus. Far from being absurd, as the commentators often invite us to think, this duel is the narrative enactment of a focused stalemate, of equally balanced forces and wills. The war is past the stage when it could be settled by Helen's men alone; they take on here a symbolism which belongs to the missing Troy tale. So with another famous scene, the 'Teichoskopia', when Helen identifies the Greek leaders for Priam. Again, the commentators assume there is a problem here,[10] yet since the episode is admitted to be one of the most touching and effective in the poem, it must be the case that we read the passage with quite different narrative expectations from those of documentary realism, and that the sense we all of us make without difficulty of the passage has nothing to do with what is 'likely'. To quote Barthes's *Introduction to the Structural Analysis of Narrative*

> the imitation of life is a contingent quality; the function of the narrative is not to 'represent', it is to provide a display which is still an enigma to us but which can only be of a mimetic order. The 'reality' of a sequence does not lie in the 'natural' succession of the

---

[8] *Aeneid* 2.325–6.   [9] *Aeneid* 2.601–33.
[10] But not M. M. Willcock, *Companion to the Iliad* (Chicago 1976) 39–40. There is a good discussion in G. S. Kirk, *Homer and the Oral Tradition* (Cambridge 1976) 81–5.

actions of which it is composed, but in the logic which is revealed in it, is risked and satisfied.

In the same essay Barthes discusses the way narrative often tries to introduce devices which pretend to give it a 'natural' cause of existence: the epistolary device for instance, supposedly discovered manuscripts, films which start before the credits. 'Reluctance to display its codes is a mark of bourgeois society and the mass culture which has developed from it.' Helen on the walls of Troy, the abortive duel between Paris and Menelaus, must be read in terms of the narrative code of the *Iliad*, which is extremely sophisticated and self-displaying. The effect of the scene on the wall as Homer presents it is quite different from the effect a 'flashback' would have had. This is happening now. It is a display of the Greek leaders, of Helen herself, of the author's narrative technique. It is really Helen, not the Greek leaders, who are on show. We see her as the old men see her, as Priam sees her, and later as Aphrodite and Paris see her. Our first sight of her was earlier in that third book, when she was alone, stitching her tapestry of war, and was led forth by Iris away from her quiet representation of war to take part in another representation for which the narrator required her presence. It is her war. And her most famous appearance in the *Iliad* shows her talking to Hector, in the presence of Paris, wishing she had died before these things happened 'but since the gods had brought it about that these bad things should be so, then I wish I could have been the bed-mate of a better man than this'. There follow the famous lines referring to herself and Paris as two

> on whom Zeus set a vile destiny so that hereafter
> we shall be made into things of song for the men
> of the future.[11]

Helen foresees the *Iliad*, which (of course) Homer imagines to be as yet unwritten.

[11] *Iliad* 6.357–8.

Yet the true subject of the *Iliad* is not after all Helen, who appears in only three of its twenty-four books, but Achilles, whom we also see alone, 'singing of men's fame'.[12] What Helen foresees is the larger 'missing' Troy tale within which the *Iliad* as the tale of Achilles' wrath makes sense. Both Helen and Achilles are shown as self-conscious, self-aware, aware of their role in the narrative which they enact. Helen, herself inactive in the war, is a presenter of the war to Priam, a recorder of the war in pictures, a prophet of the *Iliad*. Achilles, during his own period of inaction, articulates action in the figure of the artist, the singer of heroic song. When he returns to the fight, and has killed Hector and agreed to give back his body and so to bring the tale and the discourse to their end, Achilles presents the parable of the two urns of Zeus and the good and evil he allots to men. The artist is also the philosopher; it is not merely men's fame and their deeds, good or bad, which shall form the song on the lips of men, but an attempt to understand will be part of the song and of the singer's function. From its beginning, narrative was seen by the narrator himself not only as record or chronicle, not only as presented world, but as discourse, speculative commentary. By the end of the *Iliad*, the reader too is ready to moralise on that presented world. We know how; we may still wonder why.

Both Helen and Achilles confront themselves and their roles. Achilles in particular is forced into self-confrontation by his awareness of an existential choice imposed on him by destiny: to choose a short glorious life and to die in Troy, or to return home to a safe but inglorious old age. When Achilles in his wrath withdraws from the fight he only withdraws to the ships, he does not, though he threatens to, leave Troy for good (and thus effect the second choice). When in book XXIV he voluntarily returns Hector's body, the mirror image of book I (when he refused to return Briseis) is typical of the poem's narrative structure, which reflects back on itself and reverses

[12] *Iliad* 9.189.

its own images. In the same way, Achilles' decision to withdraw (the war is futile) and his decision to return (the war is inevitable) reflecting on each other enact the poem. When Achilles confronts Hector in book XXII for the last duel, Hector is wearing Achilles' armour, stripped from Patroclus's body. Achilles confronts himself. Their last exchange emphasises the common destiny of death. If it be not now, yet it will come.

Helen regrets running away with Paris, Achilles regrets Patroclus's death, yet both felt they had free will when they performed their actions. Tolstoi in book IX ch. i of *War and Peace* (the famous passage which contains the statement that 'a king is history's slave') says

> Each man lives for himself, using his freedom to attain his personal aims, and feels with his whole being that he can now abstain from doing this or that action. But as soon as he has done it, that action performed at a certain moment in time becomes irrevocable and belongs to history, which has not a free but a predestined significance.

The action performed freely at a certain moment in time is the narrative of the *Iliad*. But the author of the *Iliad*, Homer, requires the reader to reflect on the presented world of the narrative and on the causes of events whose logic for the reader is that they are the narrative of the *Iliad*.

Let us consider how Homer presents the actions of Achilles in the *Iliad*. Patroclus's death shakes him profoundly. We are told by the narrator several times in XVIII that he is disturbed (*ochthesas*), greatly disturbed (*meg' ochthesas*), heavily sighing. Achilles moreover shows an awareness and self-consciousness about his own actions, for example in the great speech to his Myrmidons delivered 'groaning deeply' at 18.324–42.

> Ah me. It was an empty word I cast forth on that day
> when in his halls I tried to comfort the hero Menoitios.

PROLOGUE: HOMER'S *ILIAD*

I told him I would bring back his son in glory to
  Opous
with Ilium sacked, and bringing his share of war
  spoils allotted.
But Zeus does not bring to accomplishment all
  thoughts in men's minds.
Thus it is destiny for us both to stain the same soil
here in Troy, since I shall never come home, and
  my father
Peleus, the aged rider, will not welcome me in his
  great house,
nor Thetis my mother, but in this place the earth
  will receive me.
But seeing that it is I, Patroclus, who follow you
  underground,
I will not bury you till I bring to this place the
  armour
and the head of Hector, since he was your
  great-hearted murderer.
Before your burning pyre I shall behead twelve
  glorious
children of the Trojans for my anger over your
  slaying.
Until then you shall lie where you are in front of
  my curved ships
and beside you women of Troy and deep-girdled
  Dardanian women
shall sorrow for you night and day and shed tears
  for you, those whom
you and I worked hard to capture by force and the
  long spear
in days when we were storming the rich cities of
  mortals.

After Achilles has said this Zeus says to Hera

> So you have acted then, lady Hera of the ox eyes.
> You have roused up Achilles of the swift feet.

To which Hera replies

> Majesty, son of Cronos, what sort of thing have you spoken?
> Even one who is mortal will try to accomplish his purpose
> for another, though he be a man and knows not such wisdom as we do.

Homer presents an effect; then a cause. The hero performs a free act of his own will, as Napoleon did at Borodino. Yet that act is, without his understanding how, part of the process of history. Napoleon on the battlefield 'awaited the end of this action . . . which he was unable to arrest'. The narrator as the total consciousness of history places the hero's actions within the larger structure of his own retrospective awareness of the consequences as well as the causes of the actions. But whereas Tolstoi, a child of the nineteenth century, speculates about the nature of historical necessity and sees the will of the gods as merely 'the most primitive approximation'[13] to an intelligible cause, Homer, using the gods as an element in the narrative itself, can make speculation about cause itself take on the texture of narrative discourse. The exchange between Zeus and Hera follows Achilles' speech in the diachronic presentation of the narrative, yet is seen also as the cause of the displayed heroic effect, a cause of which Achilles himself remained ignorant; as Napoleon continued to suppose that the events of Borodino came about through his will.

In the reconciliation between Achilles and Agamemnon in book XIX, the necessary narrative end of the wrath which must separate and unite the deaths of Patroclus and Hector, it is Agamemnon who claims to have been deluded and that Zeus and Destiny and the Fury that walks in the mist have bereft him of his wits. Agamemnon's long speech is framed by two short ones from Achilles. In neither does he mention Delusion (*Ate*). First he dwells on himself and his wrath

[13] *War and Peace* XIII.i.

> ... I think
> the Achaians will too long remember this quarrel
> between us.

Then, after Agamemnon's long speech, he says

> ... But now let us remember our joy in warcraft
> ...
> nor delay, since there is still a big work to be done.
> So can a man see once more Achilles among the
> front fighters.

The contrast between the two presentations is striking. It is not that Achilles cannot speculate about causes; we know he can, and does. After the reconciliation, he says

> Father Zeus, great are the delusions you visit on
> men.
> Without you the son of Atreus could never have
> stirred so
> the heart inside my breast, nor taken the girl away
> from me
> against my will, and me in helplessness. No, but
> Zeus somehow
> wished that death should befall great numbers of
> the Achaians.

Achilles remains self-regarding; Homer's presentation of him is closer to that of Helen than to the figure and behaviour of Agamemnon. He refers to himself in the third person; he retains a kind of monstrous pride in the consequences of his wrath. He even ends by telling Agamemnon that he would never have got away with taking Briseis if Zeus had not willed destruction on the Achaians. In fact, as Homer presented the events of book 1, Zeus's intervention followed, but did not cause, the quarrel.

Homer presents Achilles as Tolstoi presents Napoleon: 'He alone, with his ideas of glory and grandeur, his insane self-adulation – he alone could justify what had to be done.'[14] Achilles likewise, after the cruelly delusive run of Trojan victories, becomes the only hero who can justify as well as accomplish what has to be done, the killing of Hector, the challenge to Apollo and destiny when he nearly scales the walls and enters Troy single-handed, and the fight with the river god: all of this motivated and justified by the death of his *alter ego* Patroclus, who fought in his armour, and foreshadowed his own death.

In the second Epilogue to *War and Peace* Tolstoi seems to express the two polarities within which the story of Achilles is turned into narrative discourse.

> (1) To imagine a man's actions entirely subject to the laws of inevitability, without any freedom, we must assume the knowledge of an infinite number of space relations, an infinitely long period of time, and an infinite series of causes.
> (2) To imagine a man perfectly free and *not* subject to the laws of inevitability, we must imagine him all alone, beyond space, beyond time, and free from dependence on cause.[15]

At times Achilles comes near to being presented by Homer as though he thought himself all alone. Yet Homer binds him into a nexus of causes, through his mother, through Patroclus, through the actions of Hector. But those causes, those dependences, are not infinite. Homer himself selects them and links them into a logic of narrative which, starting from the quarrel and the wrath, proceeds to an end which the reader, once he has got to it, understands to be the only end he *could* have got to. Yet all the time, Achilles is seen, and sees himself, as free to act or not to act.

For the modern reader as, I believe, for Virgil, Homer is a presence in the discourse of the *Iliad* of whom we remain continually aware, as he was aware of himself and of the world he was bringing into being. Any discussion of narrative must include the narrator: and how should Homer be any more an exception to this rule than Virgil? When Homer introduced

[14] *War and Peace*, first epilogue, iii.
[15] *War and Peace*, second epilogue, x.

the Muses we must assume that for him they signified something about the creation of literature. They are often invoked before catalogues or complicated passages in which indiscriminate fighting must be sorted out; or as a ritual gesture before the most complicated undertaking of all, the *Iliad* itself. 'Sing, goddess, the wrath of Achilles . . .' Yet they are not invoked before some of the greatest climaxes of the narrative, the deaths of Patroclus or Hector, or book XXIV. The Homer who addresses the Muses clearly distinguishes the role of the composer:

> Tell me now, you Muses who have your homes on Olympus.
> For you, who are goddesses, are there, and you know all things,
> and we have heard only the rumour of it and know nothing.

The composer's task is clear: it is one of selection and presentation, not omniscience. No artist can know everything, nor perhaps does he want to. Narrative is choice. Thus Homer says he cannot provide a complete documentation of the troops in book II, only the Muses can remember everything. 'I will give the leaders and the totals of the ships.' From traditional material like the Troy cycle it is clear that any composer will have to select: the wrath of one hero, the return of another. In the great climaxes Homer makes his narrative, as we say, 'speak for itself', not in literal chronicle or documentary but as display. Nowhere is this more strikingly evident than in the death of Patroclus, the most important single element in the narrative of the wrath. Only in that it brings Achilles back into the fighting is the Patrocleia important; in that it does this, it is the most important passage in the poem. Here, and here only, does Homer address Patroclus in the second person. Clearly, like all apostrophe, this one operates as an intensifier,[16] but its function inside the

[16] J. Culler, *Pursuit* 138. Homer addresses Achilles at the beginning of his *aristeia* (20.1–2).

narrative cannot be confined within that definition. Homer addresses Patroclus as Patroclus addresses Hector.

> Then did the end of life appear to you, Patroclus
> (Homer to Patroclus)
> Death and powerful destiny are standing beside you
> (Patroclus to Hector)

Homer does not merely recount; he tells us that he is recounting. And he is concerned to ensure that the implied reader understands his role at precisely the most personal and significant passages in the poem. 'Then dying you answered him, rider Patroclus' must be read as 'I, Homer, know this, for this discourse is mine.' Homer is not the old impersonal bard, nor the voice and record of an illiterate people. He is the first composer, the first man to be aware of what writing narrative involves, aware that it can be done and that he is doing it. In this way and in no other can he have been a great poet for Virgil and his other classical imitators, all of whom were ignorant of orality. Homer addresses Patroclus alone; but he comments on Achilles. 'Now *although* he [Hector] was a dead man[17] brilliant Achilles spoke to him.' Homer speaks from his overview-point as the total consciousness of the narrative; the tone of admiring yet critical wonder is unmistakably Homer's and seems to be associated particularly with his creation and treatment of Achilles' character as displayed in the narrative. The fact that Hector is dead turns Achilles' two-line speech into a soliloquy, another instance of his enormous self-regard, his sense of himself as set apart.

> Die; and I will take my own death at whatever time
> Zeus and the rest of the immortals choose to accomplish it.

The sequence of events in any narrative has to be seen by the implied reader as though it could be independent of its actual

---

[17] *Iliad* 22.364 τὸν καὶ τεθνηῶτα.

treatment, not necessarily as though it had actually happened already (as the battle of Borodino actually had, and as the siege of Troy, in some way remote from the *Iliad*, may have happened), but in another sense: that such events might have been codified into other texts than ours using different insights, different rhetorical stratagems – even, conceivably, a different cause of Achilles' anger which would have had different narrative consequences yet might still have reached the end stated by Homer at the beginning of the *Iliad*.

When Homer addresses Patroclus, when he presents Achilles in soliloquy and self-regard as the mirror of a single self-consciousness reflecting upon events, then in doing this he draws the reader not just into the presented world of the events and their causes, but into his own presentational mode. We are to suppose that the events narrated took place long ago, in a world without writers. In the greatest passages of the poem, Homer fully assumes the new and masterful role of independent narrator, a narrator who is both teller of the tale and the total consciousness of the events which comprise the tale as he has chosen to tell it. He is also the composer, excited by the new and immense technical problems he has set himself, problems of codification which will give his narrative an internal logic able to work for the naive first-time reader and also teleologically, for the sophisticated reader who must make sense of an ending the poet's opening remarks did not reveal. Somehow from the wrath of Achilles and the woes visited on the Achaians, who won the war, we come to the death of Hector, the symbol of Troy. The reason for the poet's intensified and intensifying apostrophe of Patroclus is that in this episode the wrath theme must be changed into a symbolical prefiguration of Troy's fall. There is nothing of the symbolic in Achilles' wrath and withdrawal, nothing of the missing larger Troy-tale. Only when Patroclus's death, the last and most terrible effect of the wrath, becomes the cause of Hector's death, does the poet operate a different code of narrative, a brilliant and wholly original shift into a symbolic mode whose momentum was powerful enough to provide a dramatic structure for Virgil. It is then that the reader understands that the missing Troy tale is not missing at all but is in the text before him.

PART I: PEACE

1. Transition

Aeneid VI, and the poem's first half, ended with Aeneas's ascent from the underworld and his departure from Cumae, whence the Trojans sailed round the gulf of Caieta to the modern Gaeta:

> Then he sailed straight to the harbour of Caieta,
> And dropped anchor; the ships were beached.

The reader will pause here, not merely because he has reached the end of a book, although this is itself a significant landmark in a long narrative, whence the use of spatial metaphors (from racing, voyaging, etc.) at the ends of books.

> Sed nos immensum spatiis confecimus aequor
> et iam tempus equum fumantia soluere colla.
> (*Georg.* 2.541–2)

This figure is not found in the *Aeneid*: Virgil no longer needs to be so self-conscious, he does not need to dramatise his poetic progress in this way. But Spenser in the *Faerie Queene* ends book III with 'wilest here I do respire' and book IV canto v with a direct echo of Virgil:

> But here my weary team nigh over spent
> Shall breathe itself awhile, after so long a went.

The end of a book of an epic or chapter of a novel has always been significant. The space, the turning of the page, the break in transmission, articulate an interval in which the reader will have the sense both of an ending and of a fresh start. He has a choice: to go on, or to pause. The end of *Aeneid* VI marks a particularly significant moment in the narrative. Aeneas must move from the underworld to Latium. Fraenkel was surely right to argue that this transition could not have been made at the end of VI (where it might at first sight have belonged) without 'doing violence to the moving and exalted ending of the nekuia'.[1]

But as the reader moves into book VII he finds that the mood of remoteness and alienation which had pervaded book VI has not yet been dissipated. The poet knows that the reader needs time to rub his eyes free of dreams and for those dreams to 'fade into the light of common day'. Neither the reader nor the Trojans and the action of the epic, have quite left behind the experiences and insights of the world of shadows.

> You also, nurse of Aeneas, Caieta, gave this coast of ours,
> Dying there, eternal fame. If there's a thing called glory,
> This place is marked with your honour, and the name
> Commemorates your bones in the great country of the west.
> But now the good[2] Aeneas, all rites duly performed,
> The deep sea falling calm, sailed from the harbour
> . . .

Structurally, book VI is the pivot of the entire *Aeneid*. For Aeneas now, there is no going back, as there was at the end of book I, when in his narrative to Dido he returned to the burning ruins of Troy in search of the past. The way now is forward and clear, into the future inescapably revealed by his father.

The opening of VII, the aitiology of Caieta (death of the nurse) recalls and balances the end of V, the aitiology of Palinuro (death of the pilot), completed in VI when Aeneas

[1] 'Some Aspects of the Structure of *Aeneid* VII', *JRS* 35 (1945) 1–14.
[2] The denotative *pius* is here associated with a religious rite duly performed by Aeneas. His first appearance in the second half of the poem is appropriately marked. So in book I, after the storm, lamenting the loss of his comrades, he presents himself to his (disguised) mother: *sum pius Aeneas* . . . (1.378).

encountered Palinurus's shade wandering unburied, as the shade of Patroclus had wandered. This second brief piece of aitiology, in no way developed into a full narrative as the death of Palinurus was, acts as a bridge to the magical voyage to the mouth of the Tiber. There follows one of Virgil's most extraordinary paragraphs. We are still half in an Odyssean world of the marvellous, where nothing seems quite real, a world of fantastic impressionism. In an unearthly moonlight which recalls the descent into the underworld *sub luce maligna*, Aeneas sails past Circe's island, here located off the coast of Latium. Groans and roars of beasts are heard, of beasts once men, transformed by witchcraft, a weirdly parodic refraction of the visit to the underworld. The phrase *hic exaudiri gemitus*, 'from this place came groans', links the beast-men with the cries of the damned in Tartarus, heard but not visited by Aeneas. Nor is he here drawn into contact with evil. Neptune sends a favouring wind: a structural and thematic correspondence with the opening of book 1, when Neptune rescued the Trojans from Juno's storm. This is Aeneas's last trial by water. The flickering moonlit scene recalls the colour-drained landscape of the underworld.

> Night falls. Winds breathe. A white moon on their track,
> Under a wavering light the sea shines . . .

But then, as the lurid but ineffectual terrors of the night give way to rosy dawn, the Odyssean world of fantasy disperses like a dream and with the dawn come calm seas and smooth landfall at the mouth of the Tiber. The atmosphere becomes Italian, pastoral, geographically familiar. It is perhaps the most extraordinary transition in the poem. Father Tiber, with his yellow sand, bursts abruptly into the sea and into the poem (*prorumpit*) as Aeneas gazes for the first time on a scene so familiar to the implied reader. (Virgil exploits this contrast between what Aeneas sees for the first time, with wonder or incomprehension, and what the reader recognises as familiar, at several crucial points in the poem, and particularly in book

VIII.) Birds native to the estuary (*adsuetae ripis*) fly and sing, in contrast to the paranormal noises of the night, and Aeneas beaches his ships in a mood of joy which he sustains – although the reader does not – until the end of book VIII, for Aeneas is spared the grim events which will shortly be narrated.

It is only now that the poet is ready for his second invocation. The need to withhold it for 36 lines has been scrupulously judged. A transition was needed, and indeed the first paragraph of VII constitutes the first part of a much larger transition, the first arch of a bridge spanning the whole of books VII and VIII, which need to be taken together. The Odyssean world of marvels, travels, adventures, prophecies, miraculous insights, begins slowly to recede, as we enter the processes of history. The arrival in Latium takes us into a new order of time as well as place.

That opening of VII, with its nocturnal voyage and its pastoral daybreak on the still marvellous yet familiar Tiber, is repeated at the beginning of VIII, the two books together constituting a prelude to the Virgilian Iliad as well as a postlude to the Virgilian Odyssey. The rumblings of coming war begin soon to be heard in an atmosphere of Italian peace, order and tradition. Book VIII ends with Aeneas's shield, an 'Iliadic' object yet also the marvellous object and end of a quest, a golden fleece, and the Trojans are like Argonauts sailing along uncharted waterways; yet for the implied reader they are not the sea roads of a mythical voyage but the home river: the allusion to Catullus 64 in the passage in book VIII emphasises Virgil's use of an important motif, 'the familiar was once marvellous', as the *Argo* was to the sea gods:

> *mirantur* et undae,
> *miratur* nemus *insuetum* fulgentia longe
> scuta uirum fluuio pictasque innare carinas
> . . . uiridisque secant placido aequore siluas[3]

---

[3] *Aen.* 8.91–6. The wonder caused by the *Argo*, the first ship, is recalled by Dante at the end of the *Paradiso* (33.96) in a striking simile which accompanies the poet's ultimate vision of the Eternal Light: 'che fe' Nettuno ammirar l'ombra d'Argo'. Cf. also Catullus 64.12–15.

TRANSITION

> *Wonderful and strange to waters and woods*
> *Are the gleam of heroes' shields, the painted ships*
> *. . . and they glide through easy water in a green shade.*

Book VII brings Aeneas to the mouth of the Tiber, near Ostia, book VIII brings him upstream to the site of Rome and brings the reader to his journey's end and the teleological end of the poem.

There is a difference between a reader's progress through a long narrative composition and the retrospective explanatory overview of the whole attempted by critics, who tend to overschematise the structure of the *Aeneid*. There is certainly a correspondence between books I and VII which the reader of VII, if he has read and remembers I, will accommodate to what for him is the more exciting dynamic aspect of the narrative of VII. The second invocation is the author's reminder of structure; it has no narrative function; the author is here in his role as antiquarian and historiographer:

> Nunc age, qui reges, Erato, quae tempora rerum,[4]
> quis Latio antiquo fuerit status, aduena classem
> cum primum Ausoniis exercitus appulit oris,
> expediam . . .

> *Come now, Muse, Erato: what kings, what times, what*
>   *circumstances*
> *Prevailed in old Latium when first*
> *That foreign army reached the Italian shore*
> *Shall I unfold. . .*

The formula *nunc age . . . expediam* is that of doctrinal exposition, and belongs to didactic epic: it is Lucretian, and occurs again in *Aeneid* VI at the beginning of the *Heldenschau*. It

---

[4] The O.C.T. punctuates *quae tempora, rerum quis fuerit status*. But as Fordyce points out (ed.), *Aeneid VII–VIII* (Oxford 1977), n. ad loc.), although *status rerum* is good Latin, the Lucretian echo (5.1276, *sic uoluenda aetas commutat tempora rerum*) surely guarantees the reading known to Servius, though he explained it curiously by reference to L.'s theory of time (see Conington on 7.37).

also belongs to cyclic epic, whereas the appeal to the Muse is Homeric. Virgil characteristically combines both modes.[5]

The correspondence between I and VII is also a reminder to the reader that book I (the beginning of the so-called 'Odyssean' *Aeneid*) is strongly Iliadic. Both books contain invocations; that in book I is modelled on the invocation of the Odyssey but with the significant inclusion, in the fifth line, of the word *bello*, 'war'. The role of Juno in the two books is also strikingly similar. First she summons Aeolus to try to destroy Aeneas. In VII she summons the fury Allecto. Her two great monologues in these books have their germ in some lines spoken in soliloquy by Poseidon in *Odyssey* V (from which book is also taken Aeneas's first oration, 'thrice and four times blessed are they who died at Troy'), but her implacable determination to oppose the Trojans takes its primary motivation from the *Iliad*. Her hatred becomes in the *Aeneid* positively Satanic; indeed her 'sense of injured merit' (Milton's phrase about Satan is a translation of Virgil's *spretae iniuria formae*) over the judgement of Paris (not mentioned in the *Iliad* until book XXIV) is mentioned by Virgil early in his first book. Satan's resentment in *Paradise Lost* over God's exaltation of the Messiah is a largely unnoticed parody of the judgement of Paris.

Venus's plea to Jupiter in book I after Aeneas's suffering in the storm, and Jupiter's great prophecy of reassurance, are strongly Iliadic, for in the mother's plea on behalf of her son is recalled the plea of Thetis to Zeus on behalf of the dishonoured Achilles. In both episodes the father of gods and men must, in order to satisfy the hero's mother, oppose the will of Hera/Juno. Zeus's will (*boule*) is mentioned by Homer in the opening invocation of the *Iliad*: 'and the will of Zeus was accomplished'. The will of Jupiter is accomplished in the *Aeneid*. That will is co-ordinate with history, and is set out in the great 30-line prophecy in *Aeneid* I. Upon this speech the whole structure of the poem rests: *manent immota tuorum fata*

---

[5] Thus Erato is from the second invocation of the *Argonautica* (3.1, εἰ δ'ἄγε νῦν, Ἐρατώ . . . .)

tibi, 'your family's destiny remains, as you wish, fixed'. This allusion both to the Roman nation and the *gens Iulia* (Augustus's family) introduces the poem's first great prophetic guarantee.

Not only does VII echo I, but I anticipates and is completed in XII exactly as *Iliad* XXIV completes, and is prepared for in, *Iliad* I. The smile with which Jupiter reassures Venus in I is the smile with which he reassures Juno in XII and reconciles her to a future in which the poem's implied reader already lives, in which Juno is honoured in Rome and the Troy she hated exists only in the past: *Troia fuit*.

olli subridens hominum sator atque deorum

olli subridens hominum rerumque repertor

Virgil's sense of the end being in the beginning and the beginning in the end is clearly stated in book I, with its repetition of a key word, *finis*. This word, occurring in the first book (where it seems least appropriate) looks forward to the 'end' of book XII, the poem's end, to Jupiter's last question to the defeated Juno, *quae iam finis erit, coniunx?* (12.793), and beyond that to ends which lie outside the limits of the poem as narrative, beyond even the apocalypses of the 'implied author'.[6]

In both *Iliad* I and *Aeneid* I the death of the hero is prophesied. Thetis sadly foresees that Achilles' life will be brief and tragic; in contrast, Jupiter reaffirms to Aeneas's mother that she shall bear her son to heaven. His triumphant 'end' seems wholly unpredicated in the fresh toils and trials imposed by Juno in book I, and this opposition between the

[6] For the 'implied author' see Wayne Booth, *The Rhetoric of Fiction* (Chicago 1961) 70–7 *et passim*. It is used to refer to the author's 'second self'. This is not to be identified with the narrator, but is created by the author as he writes the work. Booth observes that 'it is a curious fact that we have no terms either for this created "second self" or for our relationship with him (i.e. as readers)'. The implied author of the *Aeneid* is not the narrating 'I' (*maius opus moueo*, etc.), 'who is only one of the elements created by the implied author and who may be separated from him by large ironies', but is that which persists in the reader's mind after he has finished reading the work quite independently of the story.

'end' of apotheosis and the seemingly unending sufferings must be felt and understood by the reader as it cannot be by the hero. Aeneas's famous words in his first speech, *deus dabit his quoque finem*, 'to these things also god will bring an end', are Odyssean but they are transposed into an Iliadic context when they are re-echoed in the Venus–Jupiter scene a few lines later. But before this, Virgil uses *finis* again in a curious connective formula; after the storm is over and the Trojans make landfall he writes *et iam finis erat*, 'and that was the end of that'.

But that end was a beginning, the beginning of a new episode in the story. The end which Aeneas assures his men the god will bring can be read as a proclamation of faith, but only because the reader himself can bring the end, knows indeed that it already exists even if he never reads the rest of the poem. 'Narrative presumes that events precede the discourse which reports them.'[7]

In Venus's prayer to Jupiter, *quem das finem, rex magne, laborum?*, 'What end do you give, great king, to his labours?', the answer, again, will not surprise the reader, and is not meant to, though a naive reader who does not know the story of Aeneas's deification might be able to reproduce the proclaimed fears and subsequent comfort supposed to be felt by Venus. Rhetoric is precisely a way of drawing the reader into emotions he did not feel at the beginning. But the key word *labores* ought to signal a link in the reader's mind between Aeneas and Hercules, even though the latter's role as a paradigm in the poem does not emerge until later. Thus, any second and subsequent reading of the poem will enable the reader to understand that Aeneas will be deified, like Hercules. In 6.801–5 Virgil refers to the labours of another hero, Augustus, who is there said to have excelled Hercules in the extent of his civilising mission. Only a few lines further on Venus's question, 'What end?', is directly answered. Jupiter says *imperium sine fine dedi*, 'I have given them empire without end'. The labours of Aeneas, of which Venus complains, will

---

[7] Culler, *Pursuit* 172; F. Kermode, *The Sense of an Ending* (Oxford 1967) 67–89.

end in the hero's death and transfiguration, an event which existed before the poem but which the poem does not reach; yet in another sense, for his descendants, the Aeneidae, they had not ended when Virgil wrote the poem, a thousand years after the events supposedly narrated. And a thousand years after that, Beatrice said to Dante: 'You shall be with me, without end (*senza fine*) a citizen of that Rome of which Christ is a Roman.'[8]

In the last book Jupiter asks Juno, returning to the rhetorical question he had been asked in book I, *quae iam finis erit, coniunx?*, 'What now shall be the end, wife?' The whole speech echoes that first speech to Venus.

> You know, and you admit you know, that Aeneas is
> Destined for divinity.

The reader knows this by now, even if he did not in book I. The poem's end is in its beginning and its beginning in its end. The Iliadic conflict finally resolved in XII is announced in Jupiter's first speech in book I: *bellum ingens geret Italia*, 'he will wage a great war in Italy'. Throughout the 'Odyssean' opening book of the *Aeneid* we never forget the poem's overriding Iliadic theme and structure. By placing his Iliad after his Odyssey, reversing the Homeric sequence, Virgil holds back the known and proclaimed end until the narrative itself is ready to reach it.

2. Invocation

> Come now, Muse, Erato: what kings, what times, what circumstances
> Prevailed in old Latium when first
> That foreign army reached the Italian shore

---

[8] *Purgatorio* 32.101–2.

> Shall I unfold, recall how the battle first began.
> Goddess, instruct your poet. I shall tell of dreadful war,
> Of the front line and kings high courage led to death,
> Etruria's forces, all Italy compelled to arms.
> For me there arises a greater order of things.
> I start the greater work.

'All Italy compelled to arms': these words from the second invocation of the *Aeneid* would have stirred in the heart of the Augustan reader an uneasy sense of *déjà vu*, memories of the civil war so newly ended; a meaning which would be encouraged by *reuocabo*, I shall recall, a conventional narrative signal (the poet makes things happen again when he narrates them) here taking on the dark colour of actual experience. Against this stirring of the grim memories of civil war Virgil sets words from a quite different semantic field: lofty, philosophical, the apocalyptic diction of the cosmic cycles. The 'greater order of things' echoes words from the poet's fourth *Eclogue* in which is announced the cyclic return of the golden age, the *Saturnia regna* in terms of the Platonic great year and the Sibylline prophecies.

> *magnus* ab integro saeclorum *nascitur ordo*
>
> *the great order of the ages starts afresh*

This allusion is relevant to *Aeneid* VII because the poet is about to describe the point in the historical cycle (*tempora rerum*) reached in Latium, where a direct descendant of Saturn (the god who was exiled by his usurping son Jupiter to take refuge in Latium and there inaugurate a new order of things, a golden age) presides over a peaceful (if precariously peaceful) régime which is now to be disrupted by the coming of the Trojans. The 'time' which the poet will tell of is not just chronicle-time but significant time.[9] With the Iliadic epic now begun Virgil

---

[9] On 'temporality' and 'chronicity', and the difference between successive time (χρόνος) and meaningful time (καιρός) see F. Kermode, *The Sense* chs. ii, iii.

himself invokes and inaugurates the new order of history which starts with Aeneas and culminates in Augustus. *maius opus moueo*, 'I start the greater work', echoes Jupiter's own prophecy in book I: *uoluens fatorum arcana mouebo*, 'I will unroll the book of destiny and reveal its secrets.' Virgil, guided by the advising Muse, will unroll the secret cause and dire results of war, will chronicle in epic narrative the origins and course of Roman *imperium*; just as, in VI, guided by the spirits of the underworld, he had revealed the chthonic mysteries, 'things unattempted yet in prose or rhyme',[10] *res alta terra et caligine mersas*. The greater order of things which the poet now sets himself to unfold is, for the implied reader, the story of how modern civilisation began and reached its zenith under Augustus. The random shooting of a pet animal, the *furor* of a discarded suitor, the need of immigrant exiles to settle and build, lead to the triple triumph on the Shield of Aeneas in book VIII. 'Actions performed at a certain moment in time become irrevocable and belong to history, in which they have not a free but a predestined significance.'[11]

The word *ordo* occurs in another prophetic passage, in III, when Helenus reveals to the Trojans the extent of their further wanderings before they reach the promised land in accordance with destiny as revealed by Jupiter:

> sic fata deum rex
> sortitur uoluitque uices, is uertitur ordo
>
> *So the king of the gods apportions*
> *Destiny, turning the wheel. This is the order of things.*

uates is used by Virgil of himself in the second invocation, but nowhere else thus in the poem. He and Horace deliberately revived the word to replace the fashionable Grecism *poeta* and to restore to the role of the poet something of the bardic and prophetic dignity of the Italian past.[12] Throughout the *Aeneid*,

---

[10] Milton, *Paradise Lost* 1.16.   [11] Tolstoi, *War and Peace* IX.i.
[12] On *uates* see J. K. Newman, *Augustus and the New Poetry* (1967) 109ff., K. W. Gransden, *Aeneid VIII* (Cambridge 1976) on *Aen.* 8.340–1.

uates is frequently used in its meaning of 'prophet': thus in VIII, on the Shield of Aeneas Vulcan

>   res Italas Romanorumque triumphos
> haud uatum ignarus uenturique inscius aeui
> fecerat ignipotens, illic genus omne futurae
> stirpis ab Ascanio pugnataque in ordine bella.
>
>   *There had the master of fire*
> *Not ignorant of the prophets or of the future unaware*
> *Set forth the state of Italy and the triumphs of the*
>   *Romans,*
> *There the whole nation that will be*
> *Descended from Ascanius and all its wars in order.*

Now in book VII Virgil, about to embark on the expatiation of all these prophecies, becomes himself vatic, like Jupiter, Helenus, the Sibyl, Vulcan. He is about to describe how Latinus king of Latium was prophetically warned by the indigenous Italian god Faunus that his daughter Lavinia was not destined to marry the local chief, Turnus, to whom she was then betrothed, but a stranger, an immigrant who would exalt the Latin name to the stars. Thus in the second invocation Virgil is not only the servant of the Muses, invoking their aid in the traditional Greek style, but the instructed bard, himself gifted like Vulcan with insight into the 'future'. The Shield of Aeneas, on which Vulcan has portrayed the history of Rome from Romulus to Augustus, is a visual metaphor for epic narrative. The wars are set forth on the shield *in ordine*, in order, in the manner of annalistic chronicle, but the description of them in the *Aeneid* is in the grandest epic style.

The vatic function became an obsession with Milton, long before *Paradise Lost*. In *Lycidas* he had already meditated on the relation between art and the fame of the artist. In lamenting Edward King's death, he had shown himself aware that the sacred task and burden of writing poetry might cut short the poet's career before he had crowned his achievement and ensured immortality, by making his due progress through the genres, as Virgil had done, from pastoral (the poem he was actually writing) up to the highest genre, epic. In *Lycidas* Milton invokes the figure of Orpheus, the type of the supreme bard, Homer's equal, but destroyed untimely:

> What could the Muse herself, that Orpheus bore,
> The Muse herself, for her enchanting son . . .

Milton brings back the figure of Orpheus in his epic, in the second invocation, placed, just like Virgil's, early in his seventh book; he too asks the Muse to instruct him in the task still remaining: 'still govern thou my song' (cf. 'Goddess, instruct your poet'). But he then prays, with a *frisson* of fear, and perhaps recollecting the fate of King which had inspired his own greatest pastoral, to be spared the doom of Orpheus:

> nor could the Muse defend
> Her son. So fail not thou who thee implores . . .

After the ecphrasis of the shield at the end of VIII, the 'prophetic' future virtually vanishes from the *Aeneid*. There remain only 9.641–4, 10.11–15, 10.241–5, 12.832–40. But several times in the last books of the poem Virgil claims that the tragic and heroic story he is narrating will triumph over time: *prisca fides, sed fama perennis*, old legend perpetually renewed. The poet guarantees, as it were, both the validity of his narrative and its exemplary value as the first evidence of Roman greatness, born out of the wicked discord of Trojans and Latins. The *aristeia* of the Greek Pallas and the Italian Lausus alike contribute to a new meaning of *uirtus*. Virgil's intense involvement in his Iliad is not a poet's detached yet willed involvement in a story of battles long ago, but a personal involvement in the recent past, of which, in a cyclic view of history, the war between Trojans and Rutuli is a paradigm.

3. Homecoming

Immediately after the second invocation Virgil embarks on a new order of narrative. The structure of the opening words is striking. They occur after the caesura in a verse whose first part is the declaration of the 'greater work'.

maius opus moueo. Rex arua Latinus et urbes

Thus the structure of this line signifies the importance and immediacy of the greater work, and identifies it, somewhat unexpectedly, in the introduction of a new character, a historical presentation of the pastoral and local world of the eponymous king of the Latins, with his totemistic 'woodpecker' grandfather, his nymph-mother and his descent from Saturn himself, who (we shall learn in book VIII from another local king with a nymph mother and pastoral associations) came to Italy as an exile after the usurpation of his throne by Jupiter, named the people Latins, brought in laws, tradition and civilisation, and ruled in peace.

This immediate and emphatic presentation of Latinus is achieved by juxtaposition with the *maius opus* assertion inside the same hexameter, and by the further use of the figures of 'enclosing word order', making him king of the land (*rex arua Latinus*), and epexegesis (*et urbes*), which extends his power to cities, for his is no backwoods settlement. Indeed, we are told in XI that he is *praediues*, a king of the old bronze age, an Italian Agamemnon.

Saturn's peace has on the whole been maintained under Latinus although, as we shall learn, not without local disturbances. Latinus has no male heir, but his daughter is betrothed to a local chieftain, Turnus, king of the Rutuli. The fairy-tale motif of the rival suitors assimilates allusions to both the Homeric epics: Lavinia as Penelope, Aeneas as the homecoming Odysseus, a Trojan Ulysses redeemed of all the treason of the wooden horse; Lavinia as Helen, with a more complex variation of the Paris–Menelaus story, in which Turnus must be seen as the wrongly betrothed, Aeneas as the lawful partner coming from over the sea to claim his own.

Nevertheless, the first mention of Turnus in the poem carries no hint of the disgraceful. On the contrary, he is *ante alios pulcherrimus omnis*, and Latinus's queen Amata is on his side. So far the environment seems placid. But

> sed uariis portenta deum terroribus obstant.

As we read of these portents, this divine opposition to the alliance with Turnus, the adjective *pulcherrimus* rings a faint knell of trouble in our memory. In book I (and here is another correspondence between the opening books of the poem's two halves) Dido was introduced to the reader with that same superlative adjective: *forma pulcherrima Dido*. Dido was the chief of the *impedimenti* which beset Aeneas's Odyssey: Turnus is to be the chief of the *impedimenti* which will beset his Iliad. The reader must respond to, and emphasise, the parallels between the two daemonic heroes as the epic unfolds.

The portents which stand in the way of the betrothal are common features of Roman divination: the swarm of bees which settled on the top of the laurel sacred to Apollo (the god who guided the destiny of the Trojans and who was the tutelary deity of Augustus himself) are declared by an unnamed *uates* (the seer is also the figure of the poet-narrator) to signify that a hero will come and settle on the citadel of Latinus: the verses

> aduentare uirum et partis petere agmen easdem
> partibus ex isdem et summa dominarier arce

place their emphasis on the opening and concluding words: *aduentare uirum*, a hero is coming (cf. 8.201, *aduentum dei*, when Hercules saved the settlers on the site of Rome from the monster Cacus, and thereby became a forerunner of Aeneas), and *summa dominarier arce*, in which the word *arce* would carry for the implied reader all the majesty of the Roman Capitol, symbol of Rome's eternal dominion.

The crown of fire round Lavinia's head is also a traditional sign of greatness (the phenomenon is variously associated by Virgil with Iulus–Ascanius, Aeneas himself, and Romulus), but one which will end the nation's peace. The paragraph's last word is an emphatic and menacing one, *bellum*:

> The prophets sang that Lavinia would be illustrious in fame and fate,
> Yes, but for the nation it meant a great war.

The next paragraph tells of the confirmation of these prophetic warnings. Latinus, sleeping in a grove sacred to a local and ancestral deity, receives the oracle (the ritual of *incubatio*[13]):

> Seek not to join your daughter in wedlock to a Latin,
> Child of my blood, heed not that arranged marriage.
> Sons-in-law you shall have, who coming from abroad shall with their blood our
> Name glorify to the stars, and from that stock shall spring
> Those who shall see the whole world, wherever the sun
> On his daily journey from ocean to ocean looks down,
> Under their feet in perpetual obedience move.

From this prophecy, and from Latinus, Virgil now effects a transition to Aeneas, who in a brief interlude presides over the Trojans' first meal on Latin soil and himself receives a portent of settlement and colonisation. This is Aeneas's only appearance in book VII.

The art of epic narrative depends to a considerable degree on the linking and juxtaposition of episodes and on the way the reader effects transitions, building as he does so a larger and

---

[13] On *incubatio* see P. T. Eden (ed.), *Aeneid VII* (Leiden 1975) on 7.81ff. and Fordyce, *Aen. VII–VIII* on 7.81, 87.

unbroken (for epic is a *carmen perpetuum*) sense of movement. Virgil's mastery of the art of transition in epic narrative is underrated, if not ignored, by most commentators. I want here to digress briefly to book IV, one of the most often read and most widely admired parts of the poem, to try to show how Virgil's narrative technique actually works for the reader. I shall look at lines 129–278. The action of this short passage is swift and dramatic, the set pieces cosmic in their grandeur. We start with the celebrated 'royal hunt and storm', when the heroes ride forth in the early morning. The scene is one of colour, movement and excitement. But the reader's excitement and anticipation is different from that of the actors – they are living for the moment, for the thrills of the chase, and the only anticipation is that of young Ascanius, hoping for a wild boar or, perhaps, a mountain lion. But the reader has just moved from the scene between Venus and Juno in Olympus. He knows that the glorious dawn is at once and unexpectedly to be interrupted by the engineered hailstorm. Our excitement and anticipation as readers is directed towards that dramatic new paragraph beginning with onomatopoeic insistence

> *In*terea *m*agno *m*isceri *m*urmure caelum
> *in*cipit, *in*sequitur co*mm*ixta grand*in*e n*im*bus

In the very centre of this crucial paragraph Virgil has embedded the strange episode of the 'rigged wedding', with its heavy, menacing spondees and its sense of impending doom

> speluncam Dido dux et Troianus eandem
> deueniunt. prima et Tellus et pronuba Iuno
> dant signum; fulsere ignes et conscius aether
> conubiis . . .

> *To the same cave Dido and the Trojan chief*
> *Came. And primal Earth and bride-attending Juno*
> *Gave the signal. Lightning flashed, the sky itself*
> *Witnessed their union.*

This brilliant and highly charged descriptive passage is followed by four lines of authorial moral discourse:

> The day was the start of death and woe, the start
> And cause; careless of what men saw or said
> Dido no longer kept her love a secret;
> She hid behind the pretence of being married.

Immediately after this comment, the narrative of action is rapidly resumed with the account of Rumour, personified as a monster out of fantasy or science-fiction, getting bigger and stronger as it moves faster, beginning as a wisp of fear, feeding on itself till its head touches the sky while its feet touch the ground, feathered with eyes, tongues, mouths, and ears. It flies through the twilight and broods all day on roof-tops like the ill-omened bird which appears as a portent to Dido before she dies, a little further on in book IV.[14] Again, Virgil inserts some authorial moral comment into a highly pictorial piece of allegorical description, and, as so often with his authorial moral comment, he uses the figure of epiphonema, reducing and abstracting the grandly baroque and extravagant description to an epigrammatic and generalising summary:

> tam ficti prauique tenax quam nuntia ueri
>
> *Messenger alike of wicked lies and truth*

Virgil here uses a different kind of diction from that in which his great descriptive set pieces are written: they are all colour and movement, highly visual even when most fantastic, the moral summaries are pointed *sententiae*, abstract digests.

Now the narrative of action is swiftly resumed: Rumour appears to Iarbas, rather as Allecto appears to Turnus in VII, and his response is psychologically presented: he behaves as any man would on hearing a rumour that his former lover has rejected him for another man.

Jupiter hears Iarbas's prayer, and turning his eyes sees Dido and Aeneas *oblitos famae melioris amantes*: 'forgetting in their

[14] *Aen.* 4.184–7, 460–3.

love their nobler fame'. Virgil effects this transition entirely through syntax:

> Talibus orantem dictis . . .
> audiit omnipotens, oculosque . . . torsit
>   . . . oblitos famae melioris amantes.
> tum sic Mercurium adloquitur . . .

The sequence of transitions is handled with a sweep and confidence in the grand design of the narrative (the successive episodes spotlighted and 'held', yet articulating the larger structure) which is both particularly notable and wholly characteristic of the poem: if I dwell on it here a little, it is in the hope of encouraging the reader to gain a technique of reading the *Aeneid* through, and particularly its last six books, which are relatively unfamiliar, by first considering one of the most accessible passages in the earlier books.

The transitional sequence runs as follows: Dido wanders distraught through her city; she is observed by Juno, whose dialogue with Venus follows. Then comes the working out of that plot in the hunt, storm and marriage in the cave. Now Rumour stalks fantastically through the north African cities, alighting on Iarbas's house; he prays to Jupiter, who, regarding the lovers, sends Mercury down to earth to remind Aeneas of his neglected mission.

The flight of Mercury, coming as it does so soon after the weird march of Rumour, offers an obvious parallel; the good messenger is contrasted with the bad; Rumour's journey is motiveless and indiscriminate, without regard for truth or lies, Mercury's is purposeful, its function is that of Jupiter's will itself, *nostri nuntius*, historical necessity, which can be delayed but never changed.[15]

The key lines contrasting the functions of the bad and good messengers take the form of epigrammatic 'epiphonemata':

---

[15] For Jupiter as the 'understander' of history, 'the ultimate rationality of the processes of history', see further part II ch. 4 below and cf. C. H. Wilson, 'Jupiter and the Fates in the *Aeneid*', *CQ* 29 (1979) 361–71.

> tam ficti prauique tenax quam nuntia ueri.
>
> *Messenger alike of wicked lies and truth.*

> dat somnos adimitque et lumina morte resignat.
>
> *Bringer of sleep and awakening, unsealing the eyes at death.*

The flight of Mercury is one of the greatest passages in the *Aeneid* (R. D. Williams rightly calls it baroque,[16] and sensitively points out the ambiguities of diction by which Virgil maintains a description of the mythological cosmic giant Atlas in terms of a vast landscape). The god passes through the firmament, past the mighty shape of Atlas, astronomical, geographical and anthropomorphic, turning the world on his shoulders, his head a forest of vine-trees in a cloud of wind and rain, snow on his shoulders, ice on his beard: an extraordinary passage unsurpassed by Milton in his description of Satan's flight to earth in *Paradise Lost* II,[17] it yet does not hinder the larger movement of the epic narrative, for Mercury lands like a bird (cf. Satan again) and sees Aeneas founding and building in Carthage. Since in Latin the accusative object can precede the verb, Virgil can compose his change of scene and character like a film director moving the camera:

> Aenean fundantem acres et tecta nouantem conspicit.
>
> *Aeneas founding a citadel and building houses He sees.*

We have moved from the seeing Mercury to the seen hero; the reader's 'mind's eye' moves with the narrative. In VII the transition from Latinus to that foreign, yet soon to be

[16] R. D. Williams on 4.238ff. Cf. Viktor Pöschl, *The Art of Virgil* (Ann Arbor 1962) 144–5.
[17] 2.910–67 (note the appearance of Rumour at 925), 1010–55.

naturalised, son-in-law who, unknown to the king, is already on Italian soil, is effected by a briefer bridge-passage which is also a camera-tracking flight: this time of Rumour, flying through the cities of Italy with news of the prophecy,

> when the flower of Trojan manhood
> Were making fast their ships by a grassy riverside.

(I have translated *Laomedontia pubes*,[18] an archaic periphrasis, in a deliberately 'flowery' style: the poet clearly intends to emphasise the maleness and ripeness of the Trojans in the context of the prophecy, the coming intermarriage not, presumably, only of Aeneas to Lavinia but of his peers to other Italian girls, in a typical dynastic legend which parallels the 'rape of the Sabine women'.)

The transition is assisted further by associating Aeneas too with a divine portent carrying the same kind of dynastic meaning. At their first ritual meal on landing in Italy, a kind of 'thanksgiving', the Trojans eat the wheat cakes (chapatis) which have served them as plates. Aeneas's son (in one of Virgil's most felicitous touches) greets the portent, but as a joke, not realising its significance:

> 'heus, etiam mensas consumimus?' inquit Iulus,
> nec plura, adludens. ea uox audita laborum
> prima tulit finem . . .
>
> 'Hey, are we eating the dinner plates too?' says Iulus,
> Just joking, nothing more. But the words he spoke
>   brought
> The first sign of an end of their labours . . .

Again the key word *finem* is associated with the equally significant *laborum*. An end of their labours – or 'the end'? On the archetype of the labouring hero fighting for civilisation, the figure of Hercules who will enter the narrative in VIII, Virgil constructs a typology in which Aeneas too becomes a

---

[18] Fordyce, *Aen. VII–VIII* on 7.105.

labourer for civilisation, to whose sufferings an 'end' is to be granted, although in a larger sense, that of *imperium sine fine*, the nation (*nepotes*) descended from Aeneas will labour on unceasingly from generation to generation.

The portent of the plates, foretold as a foundation-myth in *Aeneid* III, here comes true. It is greeted by the hero's son in a clear parallelism with what we have just been reading: so Faunus's descendant Latinus (*o mea progenies*) greeted and accepted the message of the *incubatio*. The *uox audita* of Iulus's joke corresponds to the *subita ex alto uox reddita luco est* of the previous scene. The prophecies are drawn together in the reader's mind as the two sides in the coming conflict, indigenous Latins and immigrant Trojans, are drawn together in the war which must disturb, before renewing and strengthening, the ancient peace of Saturn in pastoral Italy.

The passage following this oracular *bon mot* offers the reader another structural correspondence with VIII. He will not at a first reading-through of the narrative be ready to assimilate it, but when he reaches VIII it will echo in his mind with reverberations from VII and bind the experience of reading the two books closer together in his mind. Aeneas speaks solemn ritual words linking the sacred land of Italy with the *penates* the faithful Trojans have brought from Troy.

> 'salue, fatis mihi debita tellus
> uosque' ait 'o fidi Troiae saluete penates:
> hic domus, haec patria est.'

Aeneas is already *indiges*, naturalised. The collation of *domus, penates, tellus, patria,* is powerful and evocative.

> *All hail, land promised me by fate, and you,*
> *My faithful Trojans, all hail your household gods.*
> *This is our home, this is our native land.*

So in VIII, another *uates*, the river god Tiberinus, explains to Aeneas that another foundation legend like that of the miracle of the plates is to occur, the symbolic sow with her thirty piglets.

> O son of heaven, who now brings back to us
> Safe from its foes for ever the town of Troy,
> Long awaited in Latium, here is your abiding
> Home, here rest your household gods.

The 'invasion' is over, the process of assimilation is about to begin.

Ritual words are followed or accompanied by ritual action, libations, prayers, the drinking of wine. They resume the feasting with a new sense of its significance.[19] What began in VII as a formal thanksgiving for safe landfall has become a celebration of true homecoming; what began in VIII as a ritual Aeneas did not understand becomes (after Aeneas and the reader have gone through the experience of the story of Hercules and Cacus) a celebration of salvation and deliverance typologically central to the entire *Aeneid*. As in VIII, Aeneas prays to local deities, for the omen of the plates has confirmed the hallowedness of the locality: to the *genius loci*, to Earth, oldest of the gods, to Nymphs in rivers as yet unnamed.

So ends the Trojans' first full day in Latium. They had previously passed a day in Cumae, near Naples, whence Aeneas had made his descent into the underworld and the Sibyl had moved him through his timeless yet diurnal progress with the words *nox ruit, Aenea, nos flendo ducimus horas*, 'the night is fast coming, Aeneas, yet we spend the hours in weeping'. Now for the second time in less than 150 lines there is a daybreak formula. These formulas are important in the *Aeneid*. They are not, of course, formulaic in the technical Homeric sense, but they function in the same way: they bind the long, often digressive narrative together, so that the reader retains a sense of forward movement despite the many long passages in which narrative time is suspended and a different temporality, that of the implied reader's 'now', comes into effect.

The new day that dawns at 7.148 is a momentous one. The Trojans explore the coastline of Latium near the mouth of the

[19] See Eden, *Aen. VII* on 7.158 and 601.

Tiber. Only a few lines after Aeneas has invoked in prayer the spirits of rivers yet unnamed the explorers are said to note 'the waters of Numicus and river Tiber'. The poet himself has named the rivers now. By their act of lustration the Trojans are taking possession of Virgil's Italy. There is no question of 'anachronism' in the use of Italian names in the supposed heroic age of the twelfth century B.C. For Virgil history is a series of cyclical paradigms, events and figures moving in and out of different time-scales. The structure of the *Aeneid* is synchronic, not diachronic. One attraction for the poet, and for his Augustan readers, of Greek (Homeric and post-Homeric) myth is that it made possible an apparently retrospective extension of the continuity of cultural awareness, stretching back behind Romulus and the traditional founding of the city into a glorified tribal prehistory. The rivers already have Italian names and the Trojans learn them. One of the promises which Juno proleptically exacts from Jupiter in the final scene of the *Aeneid* is that Troy and its language should vanish without trace and the Latins keep their ancient tongue:

> ne uetus indigenas nomen mutare Latinos
> neu Troas fieri iubeas Teucrosque uocari
> ant uocem mutare uiros aut uertere uestem.

indigenas is related to *indiges* (*indigetem Aenean*: Jupiter has so described Aeneas in his first words to Juno at the start of their final scene, 12.794, referring to his destined immortality): it is the local, the native, which will survive and, like Aeneas himself, be immortalised.

> *Do not make the Italians, the old inhabitants, change their old name,*
> *Do not bid them call themselves Trojans or Teucri,*
> *Change their language, alter their dress.*

Having spied out the land Aeneas proceeds to another act wholly in accord with Roman practice, the seeking of allies. In a weightily spondaic Ennian line he sends a round hundred ambassadors to the sacred city of the king.

> centum oratores augusta ad moenia regis

The epic diction – the round number, the archaic word for envoys – conveys a ritual act and removes the narrative from the world of chance. There is a strong sense in this book of all things being done in due order, the laws of cause and effect being both historical and narrative *données*. The *uates* is in control. There is an analogy between the planned order and end of the fiction and the 'end' of the cycle foreseen by Jupiter, so that the intervention of Juno will strike the reader with double force; both Jupiter and the vatic author himself permit it, guarantee, so to say, the effects which must issue from it and carry the narrative further towards its end. Thus when Turnus seems to unleash, through the instrumentation of Allecto, the fury sent by Juno, the madness of war, control and ritual order are actually made by the reader to slip away from the narrative, he begins to sense a speeding up of the story, he shares the characters' experience of human helplessness, he is overwhelmed by the representations of chaos and war. But first, after Latinus's careful and deliberate *incubatio*, Aeneas in his turn behaves with due deliberation as befits a Roman leader *pietate grauem ac meritis*: those words, 'weighty with *pietas* and merit', come from the poem's celebrated first simile (1.151ff.) in which the calming of the storm by father Neptune is compared to the calming of a mob by a leader with moral authority and power to act. The man in the simile is carefully generalised – *si forte uirum quem*, 'if there should be some man possessed of these qualities'. That such a man exists, and is Aeneas, the poem shows: *pietas* indeed is a cliché for his character. All his actions in book VII are acts of *pietas*: the prayers, libations, *lustratio*, the despatching of envoys, and even that most Roman of acts, the building of a fortified camp, *in morem*, as Virgil says, 'in the traditional way'. The 'tradition', once more, is Roman, not Trojan: the shallow trench, the walls, the staked rampart. Again, the military traditions of the heroic age are assimilated to those of the Roman coloniser. A more famous instance of *mos* transposed from Roman into mythical times forms the conclusion of book VII.

Meanwhile, the correspondences between this book and VIII continue. The Trojans' envoys arrive at Latinus's citadel and are received by the king. In VIII, Aeneas himself arrives as a suppliant, also seeking military aid, at the settlement of the Arcadian king Evander thirty miles upstream on the site of Rome itself. Evander's settlement is described as modest and humble, a collection of huts on the Palatine: his own house is called *angustus*, confined, cramped. In contrast, Latinus's citadel, combined temple and *curia* ('senate-house') is grand, and grandly described: it ominously recalls the now fallen citadel of Priam.

> Tectum augustum, ingens, centum sublime
>   columnis
> urbe fuit summa . . .
> horrendum siluis et religione parentum.
>
> *An august house, mighty, lofty with a hundred columns,*
> *Stood on the citadel . . .*
> *A place of awe in the woods where the old faith*
>   *survives.*

The word *augustum* echoes *augusta ad moenia* 17 lines earlier. It contrasts with the *angustum* of Evander's house. Roman writers were fond of word-play, and the implied reader would have registered a significant assonance. The indigenous Italian ruler lived in a grand, hallowed settlement, yet one, like Priam's at Troy, doomed to be conquered by an army from over the sea. Conquered, but not destroyed: assimilated, in the Roman manner. The word *augustus* is a religious word meaning 'having received divine blessing' — as indeed Latinus has, being the destined ancestor of a new race. Its possible etymology from *augere*, 'increase',[20] is specially apposite to the

[20] Ovid, *Fasti* 1.609ff.

indigenous king whose local powers must at last be subsumed in Aeneas, nicknamed *indiges* precisely because this is not what he started off by being.

The poor immigrant Evander lived on the Palatine in an exiguous cottage, the prototype of Augustus's own house on the Palatine. Yet Augustus lived, as it were, next door to the famous and splendid temple of Apollo he himself had dedicated in honour of his victory at Actium over Antony and Cleopatra. Thus Latinus's citadel, standing in its numinous pastoral landscape, its hundred columns themselves images of the trees which surround it, reconciles the tension between city and land, grandeur and simplicity. Evander's house on the Palatine had been blessed by the presence of an earlier cult-figure also, like Aeneas, subsequently deified, for Evander had once entertained Hercules, the type of the labouring saviour-hero. Latinus's citadel contains figures of antique Italian rural deities – the cult of Hercules was a Greek import through Etruria, and many of the old Italian gods were themselves assimilated to various Greek counterparts. Latinus's citadel is a place of awe, supernaturally charged with the presence of divinities.[21] As Virgil had written in an early pastoral poem, *habitarunt di quoque siluas*, 'the gods also lived in the woods'.[22] Among the deities in Latinus's citadel is Saturn, who colonised Latium after being expelled from heaven, the first of a paradigmatic series of blessed outsiders who brought peace and culture to Italy, and whose descendants the Trojan envoys now face.

4. Dynastic

Exchanges of lineage are an epic convention. In *Iliad* VII Diomede and Glaucus exchange details of their ancestry when they meet in battle. But the long scene between Aeneas's envoy Ilioneus and King Latinus has a larger structural and

[21] On parallels between *Aen.* VII and VIII see Gransden, *Aen. VIII*, Introd. 22–31.
[22] *Eclogues* 2.60.

aitiological purpose. Following on Latinus's *incubatio*, and his dream-prophecy foretelling the arrival of a foreign son-in-law, it establishes the course of the rest of the poem: a pledge of peace which yet leads inevitably to war. Virgil's peaceful embassy leads us into his Iliad, but thematically it is different from anything in the *Iliad*: for it expounds Aeneas's divine right of succession and incorporates it into the narrative. Latinus must be led to the conviction that Aeneas is indeed the oft-foretold stranger from over the sea, and this conviction must in turn provide Turnus with a plausible *casus belli* and for the poet (which is the same thing) the plot of his Iliad.

Thematically, Virgil's embassy, and the whole of the two opening books of his Iliad, VII and VIII, have strong Odyssean affinities. First there is a *nostos*, a landfall by a returning hero (for we soon learn that an ancestor of the Trojan royal house actually originated from Italy), as in *Odyssey* XIII; this is followed by a theoxeny[23] in *Aeneid* VIII which is modelled on the scene between Odysseus and Eumaeus in *Odyssey* XIV. Thus two consecutive books of the *Aeneid* follow the pattern of two consecutive books of the *Odyssey*.

For the embassy of Ilioneus can have no counterpart in Homer's *Iliad*. The only embassy in that poem is the abortive one to Achilles in book IX. The plot of the *Iliad* requires such an embassy (the Achaians would naturally have tried to persuade their greatest champion to reconsider his refusal to fight) and also requires it to fail, for Achilles must return only to avenge the death of Patroclus, his wrath no longer directed against Agamemnon but now against the Trojans and Hector. The wrath theme, perhaps Homer's supreme psychological invention, could not be allowed merely to peter out with the return of Achilles. It had to run its full and terrible course. It had to lead naturally into the great *aristeia* culminating in Hector's death and the subsequent dishonouring of his corpse. Only if the wrath theme ran its full course could the subsidence of the wrath in book XXIV form the proper ending

[23] See Gransden, *Aen. VIII*, Introd. 26–9.

of the poem. Achilles started the wrath theme in book I; only he can end it in book XXIV. We are made aware that the gods themselves wish this end; but they only assent to the end as they assented to the beginning; they do not engineer it. Homer had invented, for the purpose of his narrative, a debt owed by Zeus to Thetis which she can use to persuade Zeus to allow Trojan victories. Achilles himself does not assume that his absence will by itself ensure those victories; it needs the intervention of Zeus which thus becomes essential to the story. It is this which turns the hero's absence into a military disaster. At the end of *Iliad* I Zeus knows that his Trojan sympathies have already displeased Hera even before Thetis's plea. He turns angrily on Hera for complaining at his partisanship and silences her, as usual, by proclaiming his superior force. Hera is afraid, the other gods troubled; the strife on earth reverberates in Olympus.

Virgil's chief task in undertaking his Iliad was nothing less than the removal of the wrath theme from his story. This does not mean the removal of *furor*; but Virgil's *furor* is the madness of war itself; there is no quarrel over a *geras*.[24] Even if we see in Turnus's anger over 'Lavinia disespoused' an echo of Achilles' anger over the loss of Briseis, Lavinia remains the cause of war, not a prize of war; she is Helen, not Briseis. Virgil removes from his epic – for he does not need it – the one indispensable invention of Homer's *Iliad*. He wants to dissociate his Italy – Turnus's Italy too – from the barbarities of Homer's world when, in Pope's words,

> a spirit of revenge and cruelty, joined with the practice of rapine and robbery, reigned throughout the world; when no mercy was shown but for the sake of lucre; when the greatest princes were put to the sword and their wives and daughters made slaves and concubines.[25]

In the *Aeneid*, Turnus is not modelled on Paris; in terms of

---

[24] On the theme of the *Aeneid* compared to the theme of the *Iliad*, see (e.g.) Kirk, *Homer* 92–4. *geras*: a prize of war.
[25] From the preface to his translation of the *Iliad* (World's Classics edn, xvii).

uirtus[26] he is a second Achilles, beautiful and nobly born, no unworthy suitor of Lavinia, never sneered at as was Homer's Paris, dispossessed not by an act of adultery but by providence itself, historical necessity. Yet Aeneas, like Homer's Menelaus, must cross the sea to claim his lawful bride. Moreover it is not Turnus but Aeneas who must carry out the Homeric revenge-element in the story by killing Turnus for Pallas's sake as Achilles had killed Hector for Patroclus's sake.

Virgil thus assimilated to an Iliadic plot from which the 'wrath theme' had been removed, an Odyssean *nostos*, casting Aeneas simultaneously as rescuer of Lavinia–Helen from an unlawful alliance and as homecomer to a land legitimately his. The prophets foretold his role not only as husband – a prophecy the hero himself first heard from his dead wife Creusa in Troy –

> For you there awaits long exile, miles of sea to cross,
> And you'll come to Italy, where Etruscan Tiber
> Through rich pastures of heroes slowly winds.
> Happiness there attends you, and a kingdom,
> And a royal marriage.

but also as *dux*: acclaimed by both Latins and Etruscans (though this he and the reader do not yet know) as their heaven-sent leader against a tyranny which existed before he came and in which he had no part. He came, then, to Italy with unblemished *pietas*; even the affair with Dido had been engineered against him, as an impediment to his destiny by Juno and out of misguided pity by Venus.

Structurally, the address of Latinus to the Trojan envoy Ilioneus offers one of many important correspondences between *Aeneid* I and VII. In book I, Ilioneus is the first Trojan to address Dido, again in Aeneas's absence (he at this time thinks Aeneas may have been drowned, a strange foreshadowing of his actual death by drowning, a death also prefigured,

---

[26] *uirtus*: the word is connected with *uir*. 'Manliness' has now a rather Victorian ring to it.

even more strangely, in the haunting Palinurus episode). Dido greets him cordially, says that the fame of the Trojans is widely known, and offers help. In VII Latinus speaks first, a formal address of welcome, again adducing the widespread fame of the Trojans: cf. Dido's words

> quis genus Aeneadum, quis Troiae nesciat urbem

and Latinus's

> ... neque enim nescimus et urbem
> et genus, auditique aduertitis aequore cursum.

The fame of Troy (who has not heard of it?) is a *donnée* of the legend of Aeneas. Virgil introduced it, indeed, in his first book, when Aeneas gazes at the scenes from the Trojan war already depicted on the walls of Juno's temple at Carthage, a passage to which we shall return. 'Where in the world', Aeneas asked Achates, deeply moved, 'is there a place which is not full of our labour?'

But in the Italian seventh book it is not the splendours and miseries of the Troy story which strike Latinus. Virgil's insight into human behaviour told him that what most matters to Latinus must be that this is the son-in-law from abroad prophesied by his ancestral oracle. It is one of the poet's finest and subtlest strokes. After Ilioneus's speech of greeting Latinus sits lost in thought.

> But what most affected the king
> Was not purple robes or the sceptre of Priam.
> No. His mind dwelt far more on his daughter's marriage,
> And he thought again of old Faunus's prophecy:
> Here was that son-in-law from a foreign land, by fate foretold,
> Who'd share his kingdom and whose descendants, for virtue renowned,
> Would take over the world.

The answer Ilioneus gives to Latinus's speech of welcome is

set out in conventional rhetoric. Each point is taken up, answered and developed. Latinus's points were, briefly: we know who you are, the Trojan fame is widespread, but what do you want and why are you here? Have you been driven on to our shores by bad weather, or some error of navigation? But however you got here, be assured of hospitality from the Latins, descendants of Saturn, from whose shores, they say, Dardanus himself, your own royal ancestor, long ago set out for Asia. Ilioneus's answer is: neither bad weather nor any error in navigation has brought us here; we planned to come here and we wanted to come here (*consilio* . . . *animisque uolentibus*), to this city of yours, driven out of a kingdom once the greatest under the sun. We could have gone elsewhere, many people wanted us to join them (a covert allusion to Carthage),

> sed nos fata deum uestras exquirere terras
> imperiis egere suis.
>
> *but our fate was, to seek out your land.*
> *The gods so willed it.*

This formal diplomatic exchange emphasises both the greatness of the fallen civilisation, Troy, and the moral quality of the flourishing Italian culture established by Saturn; from the union of these two worthy partners the forthcoming new nation will be born. Latinus's speech proudly proclaims his people's origin:

> know that the Latins
> Are Saturn's people. No force or law compels us to
>   be just,
> But our own will, and the tradition of the old
>   religion.

The age of Saturn, the mythological 'golden age', is described again in *Aeneid* VIII, in the parallel embassy undertaken by Aeneas in person to the Arcadian immigrant king Evander, who expounds to him the ancient traditions of

Latium, beginning with the coming of Saturn. Before his time the indigenous population lived without tradition (*mos*) or civilisation (*cultus*). They had no knowledge of agriculture or of the harvesting and storing of food, but lived on berries or by hunting. Virgil, in his characteristically syncretistic and assimilative style, conflated two accounts of primitive man: an evolutionary one, found in Lucretius, in which early man was nomadic, living off the land, ignorant of fire, in conflict with the wild beasts, without laws; later man developed into a social being, able to make fire and shelter; and a Hesiodic account, in which a 'golden' race lived in peace under Saturn: for them 'the fruitful earth brought forth in abundance of its own accord'. In Hesiod's anti-evolutionary myth, the races which followed this first one showed a steady deterioration. For Virgil the fruitful abundance of nature provided a figure for the old rural Italy, which he celebrated in his second *Georgic* with a picture of the blessed life of the farmer, for whom trees fruited *sponte sua*. Hesiod's golden race were free from toil, as were Adam and Eve in Milton's Eden, yet it was far from Virgil's moral purpose (and conflicted uneasily with Milton's work-ethic) to say in the *Georgics*, a poem about farming, that men did not have to work the Italian land, for all its natural fruitfulness. The earth indeed is *iustissima*, a significant adjective since in Virgil's myth Astraea, goddess of Justice, left Italy last of all the lands of the earth when she finally quitted the human scene; there is enough to sustain all, but only if men cultivate a return to the old simple ways and eschew high office and metropolitan splendours. But to the cycle of work there is for the farmer no end, and this is in clear antithesis to Hesiod's golden race whose life of endless feasting without toil clearly derives from Homer's account of the Olympian deities.[27]

The relation between agricultural and political order is clearly stated in the description of Latinus's kingdom. The statues of the old rural deities in his citadel denote an agrarian

---

[27] On the relation between the Hesiodic and 'agricultural' golden ages see P. A. Johnston, *Virgil's Agricultural Golden Age* (Leiden 1980).

economy appropriate to the early settlements, for which the sophisticated Augustan poets had such nostalgic hankerings. Virgil refers in the second *Georgic* to *res Romanae perituraque regna*, 'the power of Rome, transitory régimes', as things to which the countryman is indifferent.

> Only thin smoke without flame
> From the heaps of couch grass;
> Yet this will go onward the same
> Though Dynasties pass.[28]

It is sometimes suggested that Virgil did not really have his heart in the concept of *imperium sine fine*, 'empire without end', so grandly proclaimed by Jupiter in the first book of the *Aeneid*. But we must distinguish the kinds of decorum proper to heroic and didactic epic, and the kinds of statement which can be made in each genre. In the *Georgics* Virgil contrasts the transitory upheavals of power politics with the eternal rural cycle. Hesiod, the first poet of didactic epic, had written of the need to work hard and live a life pleasing to the gods. For the reader of the *Aeneid*, the legend of Saturn's reign in Italy may be said to provide an ambiguous and nostalgic element in the heroic story of how a band of war-weary Trojan exiles, with help from a poor Greek émigré colony huddled in hut-settlements on the Palatine, turned Italians into Romans.

The coming of Aeneas disrupts the static régime of Latinus. Things start happening. The machinery of heroic epic invades a simpler tribal world. If the war in Italy has a cause, it lies in the *fata deum*, the articulation in epic of historical necessity. The grand catalogue of the Italian chiefs which ends *Aeneid* VII does not, in any case, suggest a people ignorant of warfare.

Although they do not need laws to make them just, the Italians have laws. Evander in *Aeneid* VIII tells us how Saturn introduced simultaneously the laws of agriculture and political science. Saturn's rule in Italy was the creation of an exile in the first era of Olympian power politics, the world of things as

---

[28] Hardy, 'In Time of "The Breaking of Nations" ', in *Moments of Vision* (London 1917).

they are, presided over by Jupiter. But the just and fruitful earth which gave forth *sponte sua* (Hesiod's *automate*) did not mean that men lived only for the day. They worked, planned, husbanded, stored; laws and traditions bound them willingly to nature and to each other. In Milton's Eden, Eve answers Adam's proposal that she should stock the larder with the words

> ... small store will serve, where store,
> All seasons, ripe for use, hangs on the stalk,
> Save what, by frugal storing, firmness gains.

It is clear that Milton too responded to an ambiguity in the prelapsarian myth: could there really have been a time without the need to work, even before the curse of the fall ('by the sweat of thy face shalt thou eat bread')? Milton emphasised, as Virgil had done in the second *Georgic*, the moral value of labour:

> Man hath his daily work of body or mind
> Appointed, which declares his dignity.

The nature of this 'work' in Milton's epic is pastoral not agricultural; epic heroes are not farmers. The labour of Adam and Eve before the fall is 'pleasant'; yet at nightfall, when Eve's thoughts turn to love, Adam is already planning the next day's pruning and lopping:

> Tomorrow ere fresh morning streak the East
> With first approach of light, we must be risen,
> And at our pleasant labour, to reform
> Yon flowery arbours, yonder alleys green,
> Our walk at noon, with branches overgrown.[29]

Milton here introduces into his prelapsarian world a familiar poetic topos: the need for man to rise at dawn and work, despite the pleasures of love.[30] Skilfully Milton removes from

---

[29] *Paradise Lost* 5.321–5, 4.618–19, 4.623–7.
[30] On this topos see further Gransden in West and Woodman, *Creative Imitation and Latin Literature* (Cambridge 1979) 159–62.

the topos the note of postlapsarian sadness which we associate with it:

> Aurora interea miseris mortalibus almam
> extulerat lucem referens opera atque labores
>
> *Morning meanwhile to wretched mortals brought forth*
> *Her blessed light, bringing back work and labours.*

This is the world of heroic conflict and endeavour; those lines from *Aeneid* XI refer to the desolation of a battlefield. Into this world of war the Latins are now to be dragged; elsewhere in Latium there are chiefs and heroes ready and matched for the Iliadic struggle with the battle-seasoned and defeated Trojans.

The modern reader will probably skip the dynastic details of the embassy. Latinus refers to a dim memory of old men saying that Dardanus, founder of the royal house of Troy, had been born in Etruria, in Corythus (perhaps the modern Cortona). What value, then, did Virgil's own implied reader, his Augustan contemporary, place on all this legendary material? Was the story of Aeneas more significant, say, to the Augustans than the story in Geoffrey of Monmouth of Brutus the Trojan as the eponymous founder of the British people was to the Tudors? Or what of the farrago of pseudo-chronicle with which Spenser in *The Faerie Queene* tried, or seemed to be trying, to guarantee the dynastic legitimacy of the ruling house?[31] Both these writers were imitating Virgil, and clearly supposed that such material was appropriate to national epic.

But in terms of narrative, and this is the only aspect of the material relevant to the modern reader of the *Aeneid*, the dynastic argument is important since it enabled the poet to assimilate his Iliadic story to an Odyssèan one and thus to combine both the Homeric epics into a single narrative. The argument established that the *dux externus* came not as an invader but as a hero returning to the land of his fathers. With this Odyssean *nostos* a vast cycle came round and completed

---

[31] See book II canto x.

itself: the going forth of Dardanus, a son of Jupiter, from Etruria to Troy, the eventual fall of Troy to the Greeks, the return to lead the Etruscans to victory of the Trojan hero marked out by Homer himself for survival 'that the race of Dardanus should not perish', the leader most renowned for *pietas*, son of Venus and thus himself a descendant of Jupiter. The dynastic exercise legitimises the war in Italy, and while retaining the Iliadic motif of a quarrel over a woman, subordinates this to a larger concept of world-history; a concept which itself transforms the narrower patriotism of Homer's *Iliad*. The Greeks could take a pride in the tale of how their ancestors sacked the greatest city of Asia, as later they defeated the Persians. But the theme of the *Aeneid* is the actual disappearance of the Trojans from the world-stage altogether. In the words of Juno in her last prayer to Jupiter, in *Aeneid* XII,

> sit Romana potens Itala uirtute propago
>
> *Let the might of Rome be the child of Italian virtue.*

But before Juno can make that plea to Jupiter, she has still a spectacular role to play as the traditional enemy of the Trojans.

5. Juno

The Trojan embassy to Latinus in book VII, like its counterpart in the next book, the embassy of Aeneas himself to Evander, is successful. Latinus's second speech to Ilioneus, a cry of joyful welcome, bursts upon the reader in mid-line:

> tandem laetus ait 'di nostra incepta secundent . . .'
>
> *At last in joy he speaks: 'May the gods prosper*
> *What we have here begun . . .'*

He offers gifts, alliance and peace. The whole exchange follows a series of traditional verbal gestures, but the reader will recall the last time the Trojans were so received: by Dido, who also offered gifts and alliance. That offer history could not fulfil; the new alliance, in contrast, will constitute the foundation of the Roman nation. Latinus quotes the words of Faunus's prophecy about Lavinia's future husband, referring again to the people who 'coming from over the sea shall with their blood our name glorify to the stars'. *Our* name: for the prophecies are to be exactly fulfilled in the *fait accompli* of history which will be confirmed in book XII. The Trojans disappear into legend, the Italians and the Romans live. So the envoys return to camp with good news. *pacemque reportant*: 'they bring back peace'. The words end a paragraph and conclude the first section of the book. The transition from that apparently secured peace to the eruption of Juno and the fury of war into the epic, and into the reader's shaping of the narrative, is one of the most effective 'leaps' in the *Aeneid*. With a dramatic *ecce autem* the next paragraph shatters the mood of joy and peace.

> But look, now, there came from her haunt in
>   Argos
> Jupiter's cruel consort riding the air,
> And there was Aeneas, joyful, and the Trojan fleet,
>   and from a far
> Promontory in Sicily she looked out and saw them
> Making camp, high and dry,
> No more sailing for them, and her heart was bitter.

Critics are now beginning to pay more attention to the importance, in reading any long fictional narrative, of such features as gaps, transitions, juxtaposition of sections, variations of pace, parallels, correspondences, chiastic arrangements. All these 'complement the verbal by a wider structural approach',[32] and help to explain the effect on the reader of such phenomena as the triadic division of so many books of the *Aeneid*. It may be helpful here to illustrate what I mean with an example drawn not from epic but from a novel:

---

[32] See Ruthrof, *Reader's Construction* 40.

the transition from the end of part II to the beginning of part III of Forster's *A Passage to India*. Fielding has sailed home from India through the Mediterranean to Venice, and the implied reader follows him home and constructs a significance in this stage of the narrative out of his own (probably European-based) experience. Part II ends as follows:

> The Mediterranean is the human norm. When men leave that exquisite lake, whether through the Bosphorus or the Pillars of Hercules, they approach the monstrous and extraordinary; and the southern exit leads to the strangest experience of all. Turning his back on it yet again, he took the train northward, and tender romantic fancies he thought were dead for ever, flowered when he saw the buttercups and daisies of June.

'Extraordinary' is a key word of the novel, occurring in the very first chapter ('the extraordinary caves'). It is Forster's word, and here we identify with the narrator, yet perhaps, after more than fifty years, the Mediterranean is no longer quite the cosily assumed norm it was in the days of the classical enlightenment. To many people today, one suspects, Indian strangeness seems less strange and Mediterranean normality less central than once it was. The last sentence, with its echo of Browning, perhaps deliberately sentimentalises. Let us assume that the reader chooses not to stop, though he has reached a major articulation of the narrative. He sees next:

> PART III: TEMPLE
> Chapter XXXIII
>
> Some hundreds of miles westward of the Marabar hills, and two years later in time, Professor Narayan Godbole stands in the presence of God. God is not born yet – that will occur at midnight – but he has also been born centuries ago, nor can he ever be born, because He is Lord of the Universe, who transcends human processes. He is, was not, is not, was.

The reader's construction of the novel's significance as a narrative depends on his apprehension of this abrupt, crucial and dramatic transition, from the romantic fantasies of an Englishman on his way home from India (apparently confirmed by the narrator in his role as moral commentator, a role Forster continually slips into) to the celebration by a Brahmin of a Hindu festival. The exalted diction here is itself in marked contrast to the more familiar tone of the paragraph which ended part II, and although the passage begins as narrative it too slips into moral comment: but now the comment is expressed not in the form of opinion, to which the implied reader is presumed to subscribe (how strange India is, what a relief to get back to Europe) but in the form of religious paradoxes, stated as grammatical facts. The juxtaposition of opposites is itself part of our apperception, and the meaning of the novel does not merely reside in the verbal changes between the two passages but in the space between them, where the articulation of the novel's tripartite structure turns upon a change of time, place, scene, character, and the disappearance of the 'voice' of European rationality; and even though that voice will return, it can never, after this transition, sound the same. The modifications which the reader will find himself making will be dependent on his recollections of such transitions.

In *Aeneid* VII, the joy and peace established for the reader in the key words *laetum* and *pacem* in the first section of the book must at once be modified as he proceeds to encounter the dark, brooding figure of Juno, watching, hating. Her monologue is just thirty lines long, the same length as Jupiter's prophecy of the destiny of Rome unfolded to Venus and the reader in book I. For this is the anti-prophecy, standing in structural and thematic antithesis to Jupiter's vision of peace: *claudentur belli portae*, Jupiter had said, 'the gates of war shall be shut', words the reader will recall when at the end of the long central section of book VII Juno breaks those gates open.

Juno's entry into the second half of the *Aeneid* takes the reader back to her entry into book I. That first appearance had been menacingly signalled by the poet, for he gives her (1.36) the epic's first spondaic line: throughout the poem spondaic lines carry special weight and emphasis:

> cum Iuno aeternum seruans sub pectore uulnus

The contrast in that first book between the joy of the Trojans, hoisting full sail for the open sea, and Juno, 'nursing in her heart eternal pain', her brooding hatred about to shatter their new-found optimism, is precisely paralleled in VII when the joy and peace which followed the embassy to Latinus are shattered by the epiphany of Juno. In book I, the motif of her pain (*uulnus*, 'wound') is again established immediately; later, only two other characters, both Junonian in their *furor*, are associated with that same figure of the *uulnus*, and they are Dido, Aeneas's chief impediment to success in his Odyssey, and Turnus, his chief impediment to success in his Iliad.[33]

Juno's monologue in *Aeneid* I also corresponds thematically to Poseidon's monologue in *Odyssey* V, in which he determines to send a storm to delay Odysseus's fated return to Ithaca. Juno's monologue, however, is much more intense and full of anger than Poseidon's: she expresses bitterly her frustration at not being able to stop the Trojans from reaching their destined goal, and her determination nevertheless not to admit defeat: in these respects she is the model for Milton's Satan, with his 'sense of injured merit' and his determination to hinder, though he cannot ultimately alter, God's plan for the salvation of mankind. The two processes of Virgil's epic with which Juno can interfere are, precisely, its two 'halves', the two movements of Aeneas's mission, his Odyssey and his Iliad.

But Juno's first monologue and her scene with Aeolus, god of the winds, have also important affinities with the *Iliad*. In *Iliad* XIV Hera/Juno has watched Poseidon helping the Greeks and determines to beguile Zeus into sleeping with her so that the Greeks may continue to win victories. (She knows that Zeus is in his heart pro-Trojan and that he made his promise to Thetis in defiance of her:

> Even now she [Hera] forever among the immortal gods
> Upbraids me and says I help the Trojans in battle.)

[33] See Pöschl, *The Art* 109–12.

In *Iliad* XIV Hera bribes and cajoles other deities, including the pro-Trojan Aphrodite, into helping her plot against Zeus. Sleep himself she persuades to visit Zeus by promising him marriage to one of the Graces, Pasithea. In *Aeneid* 1 Juno similarly promises Aeolus Deiopeia, the fairest of the fourteen nymphs who attend her, if he will unloose the winds against the Trojan fleet. This is to be done without the knowledge of Neptune/Poseidon, whose prerogative storms are: a variant of the plot of Homer's Hera to allow Poseidon to help the Greeks while Zeus sleeps with her. When in *Iliad* XV Zeus wakes up there is an interesting glimpse of a power-struggle among the gods. Poseidon objects to being ordered to stop helping the Greeks: he claims that when the universe was divided Zeus won the sky, he himself the sea, Hades the underworld, 'but earth and high Olympus are common to all'. Zeus also refers angrily to another occasion when Hera tried to exercise her influence in his despite, against his own son Heracles, after his legendary attack on Troy:

> You with the north wind's help winning over the storm blasts drove him
> with evil intent across the desolate sea.

I think Virgil recalls this allusion too in *Aeneid* 1. Juno drives Aeneas across the desolate sea with evil intent, just as, long before, after a previous sack of Troy, she had driven Zeus's own son, himself the type of the labouring and suffering hero.

Thus in the opening of *Aeneid* 1 Virgil assimilates elements from both the Homeric epics. Zeus in *Iliad* XV, awakening in anger, orders the reluctant Poseidon out of the battle, allowing Hector to rally the Trojans and counter-attack. In *Aeneid* 1 Neptune emerges from the waves, *grauiter commotus*, 'greatly disturbed'; rebukes the winds, reaffirms, as in the *Iliad*, his hegemony over the sea (but here his adversary is not the king of the gods, merely the subordinate Aeolus); and allows Aeneas to rally the Trojans. In *Odyssey* V Athene checks the course of the conflicting winds sent, this time, by Poseidon himself, and allows Odysseus safe landfall in Scheria.

Odyssean and Iliadic patterns of check and countercheck are thus blended into the narrative sequence storm – survival – landfall. Moreover, the storm Juno wheedles out of Aeolus corresponds structurally to the plague of arrows which breaks against the Achaians at the start of the *Iliad*, leading to the quarrel between Agamemnon and Achilles and to Hera's complaint that Zeus appears to be helping the Trojans, even though not now out of general sympathy and partisanship but in fulfilment of his promise to Thetis on behalf of her son Achilles. This last motif reappears in *Aeneid* I when Venus reproaches Jupiter for his apparent hostility to the Trojans, a reproach which elicits the prophecy of the future greatness of the Trojans as founders of Rome.

Juno's insatiable anger against the Trojans is first mentioned in the fourth line of the *Aeneid*, *saeuae memorem Iunonis ob iram*. In Venus's sad and reproachful speech to Jupiter after the storm, the speech which elicits in reply Jupiter's revelation of the future, Venus mentions Juno only once, almost at the end of her complaint, and then not by name: *unius ob iram*, she says, 'on account of the anger of *one being*', a clear verbal signal to the reader.

Again in book V Venus complains to Neptune of Juno's

. . .

. . . *grauis ira neque exsaturabile pectus*
quam nec longa dies pietas nec mitigat ulla,
nec Iouis imperio fatisque infracta quiescit.

. . .

. . . *heavy anger and insatiable heart:*
Time does not soften it, nor any pity at all,
Even Jupiter and fate cannot break nor calm it.

Venus proceeds bitterly to complain that, not content with destroying Troy *nefandis odiis*, 'with an accursed hate', Juno pursues its very ashes beyond the grave, *causas sciat illa furoris*, 'I suppose she knows why she is so angry.' Venus's words echo the poet's own thought, from the opening of the poem;

do divine spirits really feel such wrath? The wrath of Achilles, Homer's wrath-motif, becomes in the *Aeneid* cosmically transformed into something dark, perpetual and inhuman, no psychologically motivated flare-up of *Ate* by a soldier under the stress of an extreme situation but a superhuman force of resistance to the historical process itself. Philosophically, Virgil's rhetorical question at the beginning of his poem is deeply felt and ambiguous: the words echo through the whole subsequent narrative, expressing a sense of doubt in the sensitive mind of the implied author: can the divine motivation of this story of suffering and death be accepted? But above this speculative and unanswered question, the great narrative of Juno, sweeping like the angel of death over the fields of Latium, continues to unroll with something of her own daemonic force.

There is no 'villain' in the *Iliad*. Poseidon's opposition to Odysseus in the *Odyssey* is nothing like so full of bitterness and hatred as Juno's for Aeneas. It may at first seem strange that Virgil, a sophisticated writer of (in the misleading phrase of Brooks Otis) 'civilised poetry' with access to nearly seven centuries of post-Homeric Greek culture including minds as psychologically and morally subtle as Plato's and Euripides', should have constructed a narrative in which evil is embodied in one of the most revered of Roman deities, a member of the 'Capitoline triad', the goddess of wedlock. The point is central to the *Aeneid*, and the sending of Allecto in book VII forces it on us with astonishing and dramatic violence.

We may now return to Juno's second monologue in *Aeneid* VII. She is angry, now, that the Trojans have survived all her opposition. Why couldn't they have stayed captive or dead? Or been consumed in the city's ashes? And then, in words which grandly confirm and recall for the reader Venus's complaint to Neptune in book v,

>   medias acies mediosque per ignis
> inuenere uiam. at credo, mea numina tandem
> fessa iacent, odiis aut exsaturata quieui;

JUNO

quin etiam patria excussos infesta per undas
ausa sequi . . .
. . .
ast ego, magna Iouis coniunx, nil linquere inausum
quae potui infelix, quae memet in omnia uerti,
uincor ab Aenea. quod si mea numina non sunt
magna satis, dubitem haud equidem implorare
    quod usquam est.
flectere si nequeo superos, Acheronta mouebo.
non dabitur regnis, esto, prohibere Latinis,
atque inmota manet fatis Lauinia coniunx:
at trahere atque moras tantis licet addere rebus:
at licet amborum populos exscindere regum.
hac gener atque socer coeant mercede suorum.
sanguine Troiano et Rutulo dotabere, uirgo,
et Bellona manet te pronuba.

Through steel and through fire
They have found a way. Then my godhead
Must have lost its power, or, my hatred exhausted, I
    slept.
No . . . I have pursued them across the sea,
. . .
I, Jupiter's great consort, have tried all I could, have
    gone here and there,
And I'm being beaten – by Aeneas. So if my great
    powers
Are not enough, shall I hesitate to invoke others,
    wherever, whatever they be?
If I can't move heaven then I'll move hell.
I can't stop them – so be it – from settling in Latium,
The marriage to Lavinia is fixed by fate,
But I can drag it out, I can tear these royal nations apart,
Let the son-in-law meet the father-in-law, it shall cost
    them dear,
Virgin, the blood of Troy and Italy shall be your dowry,
Bellona lead you to the altar.

Bellona is shown on Aeneas's shield in book VIII as companion to Discordia, civil strife. The Latin word I have translated by the phrase 'lead you to the altar' is *pronuba*. This has already occurred in book IV, where Juno herself acts as *pronuba* in the doomed mock-marriage of Dido and Aeneas. Juno is the bringer-together of opposing forces, not in order to produce harmony out of discord but to engender further bloodshed. Aeneas's disastrous liaison with Dido in the first half of the poem is in structural and thematic antithesis to his divinely ordained liaison with Lavinia in the second half. Dido's love-sick restlessness, her Bacchic frenzy of passion, is recalled in VII in the Bacchic frenzy of Lavinia's mother, Latinus's queen Amata, who abducts her daughter to the woods and hills, followed by other matrons, for the madness which the Fury Allecto, sent by Juno, spreads through the land is contagious. Amata enacts a kind of spontaneous Bacchic rite. Virgil had used the language of Bacchic orgy (associated for the implied Augustan reader with Asiatic rites) in book IV; now, in a more extended description, the domestic peace and harmony of Latinus's city are disrupted and destroyed. *noua quaerere tecta . . . deseruere domos* ('seeking new homes, they left their dwellings') suggests women leaving a doomed city, and recalls for the reader how the Trojans in *Aeneid* II fled to the woods of Mount Ida from the ruins of Troy.

The speed and sweep of Virgil's narrative of the sending of the fury Allecto are dramatically heightened by the use of the Latin historical present, a tense often metrically convenient in hexameter verse, found in English narrative but not used in the epic narratives of Spenser and Milton and perhaps retaining in the vernacular a popular anecdotal flavour. But in the high style of Latin epic poetry it is very common. Virgil switches from past tenses to present and back again indifferently, often in the same paragraph.[34]

In a few hundred lines we see Latinus's plans and his

[34] Very little interest has been shown in the standard commentaries in this usage. The tense often has a 'detemporalising' effect on the reader. 'When' things happened becomes less important than 'that' they happened and 'how' they happened.

domestic life overturned. Allecto is the symbol of how wars start. Amata's first words, before Allecto's *furor* begins to work in her blood, are mild and sad. She has set her heart on her daughter marrying Turnus and she expostulates with her husband in a very touching and reasonable manner, even suggesting that the prophecy about the foreign son-in-law might apply to Turnus if one regarded the Rutuli, as 'outside' the rule of Latinus, and if one remembered that Turnus had Greek blood. Here the narrator has indicated a strong objection to Turnus's eligibility, for the blood of Greece is as accursed and tainted as that of Troy is pure and blessed. But soon the madness begins to work and the Bacchic passage follows. With things now already out of control Allecto passes on to Turnus.

Her visitation of Turnus while he sleeps in his citadel at Ardea is told in the same rapid powerful narrative technique, with repeated use of the historic present. The Fury insinuates itself into the hero's unconscious mind in the form of an elderly priestess of Juno, bidding him declare war on the Latins and Trojans and so avenge his honour. Knauer has pointed out that the passage corresponds to that in *Iliad* II in which Agamemnon is visited by a delusive dream offering him immediate but unachievable victory.[35] Turnus's first reaction, like Amata's, is a controlled one – he speaks from the world of sleep and dreams – but he cannot resist a sneer at the old woman: 'you look after your temple, mother, and leave war and peace to men'. Those last words form a resoundingly epigrammatic epiphonema deriving from Homer: *bella uiri pacemque gerent quis bella gerenda*.

Allecto's response is one of the most startling passages in the *Aeneid*. Stung by Turnus's sneer, she becomes what she really is – no elderly priestess but the Fury herself, a vision of horror insinuating itself into the very soul of the sleeping hero. She hurls back the sneer –

So I'm too old . . .

---

[35] See Knauer, *Die Aeneis* 234–7. Both dreams are followed by a catalogue of troops.

> Look! I am one of the sisters of hell,
> I make war and death.

Her last words, *bella manu letumque gero*, echo Turnus's epiphonema and form one of the most powerful unfinished lines in the *Aeneid*.

Turnus wakes up, literally war-crazy, sweating with terror, crying for arms:

> arma amens fremit, arma toro tectisque requirit,
> saeuit amor ferri et scelerata insania belli,
> ira super.
>
> *Crazy he cries war, gets up for war, dresses for war,*
> *Maddened by love of battle and the wicked madness of*
>   *war,*
> *And wrath too.*

The word-play *arma amens* is echoed from Aeneas's own words when he speaks to Dido about his last vain fight to save Troy, *nec sat rationis in armis*: nor could there be any rational purpose in fighting, said Aeneas, recalling a lost cause. This time it is Turnus who calls for arms without enough justification, but as in Troy, *furor iraque mentem praecipitat* (2.316–17); wrath and madness are a constant element in war.

In accordance with Virgil's normal triadic structure, the episode of Allecto, the central section of the seventh book (flanked by the embassy of Ilioneus and the Catalogue of the Italian leaders), is itself divided into three sections. Having visited Amata and Turnus, having destroyed the domestic harmony of Latinus's city by turning respectable women into maenads, deserters of the home and hence in moral antithesis to the Augustan ideal of the wife and mother as portrayed by Virgil in the second *Georgic* – *casta pudicitiam seruat domus* (and cf. 8.408–9) – Allecto now visits the Trojans and turns a hunting party into a *casus belli*. The shooting by Ascanius of a pet deer belonging to the daughter of Latinus's chief herdsman, was says the poet,

> prima laborum
> causa . . . belloque animos accendit agrestis.

Thus a rural tribe long at peace are suddenly clamouring for war and vengeance. The injured Amata, the supplanted Turnus, the local farmers, unite against the newcomers. Virgil understands so well how the immigrant can always be made a scapegoat.

Here is another correspondence with the story of Dido. Just as her Bacchic ranging finds a dramatic counterpart in the scene with Amata, so too a hunt plays a significant part in both books IV and VII. In IV, Ascanius enjoys himself hunting and hopes for a kill – then, abruptly, the storm drives the lovers into the cave, the hunt is forgotten, Juno's engineered mock-marriage draws Dido into the counterplot in which her role is that of sacrificial victim. Now in VII, again newly arrived on land, the Trojans enjoy a hunt, and again it ends in disaster. Ascanius gets his kill this time: but as in IV Dido is likened to a deer slain by accident, so now the actual slaying of a pet deer takes on a symbolic force. The description of the creature, wild yet tame, wandering freely by day in the forest yet at night returning to take food from its mistress's hand, is in Virgil's most delicate pastoral vein. The key word *errare* is used twice of the animal, once of the bowman's arm (*nec dextrae erranti deus afuit* underlines the sense, so strong through the poem, that what may seem pure randomness or coincidence can also be seen as divinely planned): Virgil carefully builds up a picture of apparently digressive and decorative pastoral, the animal roaming at random, Ascanius's hounds picking up the unexpected scent, the cooling stream in the midday heat, the young hero's excitement, and the arrow going home, like the huntsman's arrow in that famous simile in book IV, without the bowman realising the significance of the hit. Nor did Aeneas know how he had struck home to Dido's heart. The finality expressed by the enclosing word order in the account of the deer's slaying

> actaque multo
> perque uterum sonitu perque ilia uenit harundo

> *shot with a rushing*
> *Sound through womb and loins came the arrow.*

is reinforced by the rhyme with *secundo* five lines earlier. It is the prelude to the many deaths of heroes which will occupy the last four books of the poem.

These deaths begin at once. A disorganised preliminary skirmish takes place, the herdsman's eldest son is slain, together with one of the Latin elders. Events move quickly, the narrative quickens with them. Allecto reports to Juno

> en perfecta tibi bello discordia tristi

> *See, I have done it for you, discord, war's desolation.*

Juno banishes the fury to hell and herself puts the final touch to war's masterpiece. The narrator brings the threads together. The farmers hurry to Latinus with the tale of the hunt that turned to bloodshed. Turnus emphasises his rejection and the Trojan usurpation, Amata and her women return from the wooded hillside. Against all this the aged and pacifist king is powerless.

> So it was. Everyone was for accursed war, against
> The omens and oracles of the gods, against divine
>   will . . .
> And cruel Juno had her way with things.
> Helpless, Latinus cried in vain to heaven,
> 'We are shipwrecked by destiny,' he said, 'borne
>   away on the storm blast.
> You'll pay for this sacrilege in blood,
> Oh my poor people, and as for you, Turnus, you'll
>   pay too,
> Grim punishment for sin, and you'll pay to heaven,
>   when it's too late.'

6. Catalogue

Book VII ends in grandly formal style with the ceremony of the opening of the gates of war by Juno and the procession of the Italian chieftains. The ceremony, which Virgil calls by that 'great Roman word' *mos* ('tradition'),[36] is supposed to have grown up in Rome under the kings, but is here 'telescoped' back in time, behind Rome, behind Alba Longa, to the legendary heroic age. By proposing an imaginative continuity of culture and tradition in Italy stretching back to the remotest past, Virgil emphasises the native contribution to Rome's dual descent. The civilisation of Troy, its wealth and *pietas* (to which Zeus himself had paid tribute in the *Iliad*) had been attested by Homer;[37] it is more important, therefore, for Virgil to include in his poem that element of Roman culture which is independent of Greek tradition and had throughout the republic been preserved alongside the process of assimilating the Greek heritage.

In the first book of his Iliad, Virgil has constructed a *casus belli* out of the Homeric theme (almost a trademark) of quarrels over a woman. But his real interest is in analysing the way a war starts: the shooting of a pet animal is as important as the slighting of a hero. There is no confrontation between Turnus and Aeneas corresponding to that between Agamemnon and Achilles in *Iliad* I; and the abortive duel between Paris and Menelaus over Helen in *Iliad* III becomes the effective climax and conclusion of *Aeneid* XII. In the *Iliad*, those fruitless and frustrated confrontations take their place in the general story of the war and also in the wrath theme which was Homer's special contribution to the Troy-cycle. From the Homeric *Iliad* Virgil has removed not only the wrath theme, in its Homeric form at least, but the general pervading sense in Homer of war being a proper occupation for a hero. It is not

[36] See Conway on 1.264.
[37] *Iliad* 4.31-49.

just that the Greeks have already besieged Troy for nearly ten years. Before that they were engaged in besieging and sacking Eteion. Raids for plunder were imagined by Homer as a way of life for the magnificent chieftains of the bronze age. Throughout the *Aeneid* Virgil, in contrast, harps on the insanity of war: phrases like *amor ferri et scelerata insania belli*, *insani Martis amore*, condemn war as the worst manifestation of *furor* and civil war, *discordia*, as the worst form of war.

In this larger sense only does the Roman poet retain and indeed intensify the wrath theme; it is no longer the anger of one impetuous and arguably paranoid hero but a psychological thesis on mass hysteria (the Bacchic behaviour of the Latin matrons in VII might be thus classified).[38] Only very recently in Virgil's own lifetime had the horror of *discordia* yielded to the peace of the Augustan settlement. Augustus recorded the fact that under his administration the gates of war were shut three times, after having been open for two centuries. In their ceremonial opening by Juno, Virgil offers a paradigm of pre-Augustan *discordia*. The *mos* of the opening of the gates can have no Homeric counterpart; but with great skill Virgil has assimilated it to a Homeric 'Catalogue'.

The opening of the gates is recorded in a grandly spondaic line appropriately echoing Ennius, father of Roman epic poetry:

> Belli ferratos rumpit Saturnia postis
>
> *Juno breaks open the iron gates of war*

and this is the signal for general mobilisation:

> ardet inexcita Ausonia atque immobilis ante;
> pars pedes ire parat campis, pars arduus altis
> puluerulentus equis furit; omnes arma requirunt.

These lines defy translation, with their rapid movement (the first of the three is virtually without any caesura) and their

---

[38] Cf. the Messenger's speech in Euripides, *Bacchae* 689ff., Catullus 64.255–64.

astonishing use of alliteration ('a' and 'p'). The sense is that Latium, till now static and uneventful, is suddenly swept by war-fever: infantry, cavalry, all rush to answer the call to arms. These are the heroes who, though on the side doomed to defeat, will none the less, in Dante's words, die for Italy, with no lesser patriotism than the Trojans Nisus and Euryalus or the Arcadian Pallas.[39]

The Catalogue is one of a sequence of episodes from Homer's *Iliad* which are distributed through the second half of the *Aeneid*, in an order quite different from Homer's. The funeral games in *Aeneid* V are wholly transposed from their Iliadic context as games in honour of the fallen Patroclus and put into the story of Aeneas's Odyssean wanderings. Then follow:

Aeneid VII: Catalogue (*Iliad* II)
Aeneid VIII: Shield (*Iliad* XVIIII)
Aeneid IX: Doloneia with embassy (*Iliad* IX, X)
Aeneid X: council of gods and 'Patrocleia' (*Iliad* XX, XVI)
Aeneid XI: truce, funeral, council of war (*Iliad* VII, II, XVIII, XXIII)
Aeneid XII: death of Turnus (*Iliad* XXII)

A close study of the 'intertextuality' of the *Aeneid* and its Homeric paradigms can throw much light on structure and narrative technique. The placing of the funeral games, for instance, in *Aeneid* V serves the same structural and narrative purpose as the placing of the original games in *Iliad* XXIII: both passages act as transitions leading down from one climactic episode and up towards the next. In Homer, the games separate two acts by Achilles: his killing of Hector, the conclusion of his *aristeia*, and his ransoming of the body of his dead foe. In between, we see Achilles more relaxed, perhaps, than anywhere else in the poem, his *furor* appeased by the grim pyre and its attendant sacrifices in honour of his fallen

---

[39] Dante, *Inferno* 1.1.107–8.

comrade. Virgil too uses games to lead away from one climactic episode, Dido's death, and towards another, the descent into the underworld: both episodes 'star' Aeneas, as the episodes in *Iliad* XXII and XXIII had 'starred' Achilles, and in Virgil's games, too, we see Aeneas in more relaxed mood. Virgil transposes the games from their Homeric association with the battlefield and with the hero's friend and places them in the Greek world of Aeneas's Odyssey, associating them with the death of Aeneas's father. He thus retains their Greek flavour, despite the very Roman exercise of the *lusus Troiae*, and makes a further point by their excision from his Italian Iliad. Their absence from book XI (say) gives to the last two books of the *Aeneid* an unrelieved tragic grandeur.

It is worth remarking that Virgil's games in *Aeneid* V are followed by the episode of the burning of the ships, an Iliadic incident which nearly recurs, as we shall see, in book IX, when Turnus's attempt to fire the Trojan fleet is foiled by their miraculous, 'Odyssean', metamorphosis. In book V, the disaster is partially averted by Jupiter Pluvius. In both V and IX, the firing is initiated by Juno through the agency of Iris, the same grand spondaic line

> Irim de caelo misit Saturnia Iuno
>
> *Iris heaven-sent by Juno Saturn's daughter*

being repeated from V.606 at IX.2. Thus an Odyssean book of the *Aeneid*, containing an Iliadic funeral games, in a non-Iliadic context, is thematically linked forward to the Iliadic ninth book.

Nor indeed could it have been appropriate for Aeneas to stage games for Pallas, whom he had known for so short a time and whose death while under his *contubernium* was a source of grief only to be assuaged by ending as quickly as possible the campaign which had claimed him as its victim.

The Catalogue in *Aeneid* VII is perhaps more than anything else in the *Aeneid* a total transformation of its Homeric model.[40] The Catalogue in *Iliad* II consists of a long parade of the Achaian contingents, which is generally agreed to have existed as a separate piece prior to the composition of the monumental *Iliad*, to which it has been in part assimilated, followed by a shorter catalogue of the Trojan leaders, which may have been composed specifically for the *Iliad* and added to round off the book. In any case, the Catalogue obviously belongs to an earlier phase of the war than that being chronicled by Homer, though the contents have been adapted somewhat to fit the Iliadic situation. There is also the much more moving (because seen through the eyes of Helen herself) 'Teichoskopia' in *Iliad* III.[41] Helen is portrayed as deeply divided between love for her native land and an acceptance, albeit sometimes a self-reproachful one, of the trouble caused by her own sexuality. The poignancy of the passage reaches its climax in the reference to Helen's two brothers, whom she cannot point out for they are not in the army, she does not know why: perhaps they never enlisted, or perhaps they are ashamed to show themselves because of their sister; but Homer tells us that they are dead.

Virgil makes little use of the Teichoskopia in his Catalogue. If he borrows from its technique anywhere in the *Aeneid* it is in the *Heldenschau* in book VI, where two people gaze on a procession of heroes, one identifying them for the other; Virgil even adds an analogous 'pendant' figure of pathos to correspond to the dead brothers of Helen, the young Marcellus, unborn yet also dead before he could assume his rightful role. The catalogue in VII shows affinities with the Shield in VIII as well as the *Heldenschau*: three successive books of the poem, VI, VII, VIII, end with patriotic parades of characters from Italy's past.

The Catalogue in book VII also transforms its Iliadic model in that it occupies the proper chronological place of a muster of troops, that is, before the war, not near its end: perhaps such a

---

[40] On the Homeric catalogues see M. M. Willcock, *Companion* 22–38, and (ed.) *The Iliad of Homer: Books I–XII* (London 1978) 204–15.
[41] See above, Prologue.

catalogue would have figured also in one of the earlier Greek primary epics, at the point where the Greek fleet is becalmed on the way to Troy and Agamemnon is directed to sacrifice Iphigeneia. No such difficulty beset Virgil, who is chronicling a whole brief campaign from its origins in resentment, hysteria and xenophobia down to its destined end.

Virgil's literary technique in the Catalogue owes something to Hellenistic aitiological poetry, especially in his treatment of Virbius. But more important from the narrative point of view is the close linking of the Catalogue to the second half of the poem. Virgil concentrates on the key figures of the coming campaign: Mezentius, despiser of the gods, and his beautiful young son Lausus, who lead the procession, are central figures in the war. Mezentius is an Etruscan king expelled by his own people for tyranny and allied now to Turnus, a partnership of which Aeneas and the reader will learn in book VIII. Aeneas himself kills them both in book X. Camilla, who ends the procession and whose portrait closes book VII, dies in book XI; along with Turnus and Mezentius she is one of Aeneas's three greatest foes. She is an attractive, half magical figure, whose name would suggest to the Romans the ideal warrior of the republic, Camillus, servant of the gods.[42] The touchingly beautiful lines in which the poet tells us how she looked 'as if she could glide over wheatfields without crushing the ripe ears and over the sea itself without wetting the soles of her feet', do indeed seem to idealise this warrior maid, prototype of Spenser's Britomart,[43] the Penthesilea of the continuation of the *Iliad*. But the reader, with a sense of hindsight from a point beyond that which the narrative has so far attained, the product perhaps of a memory of an earlier reading or some assimilated awareness of tragic irony, knows that this exotic and idealised creature will die. What is more, it will be her love of finery and gorgeous apparel which will undo her. Here in VII, after the 'magical' passage just quoted, Virgil ends by telling us (in perhaps the only passage in the Catalogue which

---

[42] On Camillus see Fordyce, *Aen. VII–VIII* on 7.803ff.
[43] See *Faerie Queene* III.2.6.

recalls the Teichoskopia) how she seemed to the matrons who accompanied Amata. They saw no miracle-girl gliding through the air; what fascinated them were her royal costume and accessories. So our last glimpse of her until book XI, her *aristeia* and death, is not through the eyes of the author but through the eyes of the matrons, as they gape at her hubristic splendours of purple and gold and – the final touch – at her pastoral myrtle-staff converted into an iron-pointed lance. She is a very Italian figure (myrtle is a common seaside plant in Italy) and takes us back to the cedar-wood statues of the old Italian deities in Latinus's palace. She provides a strange, ambiguous link between the pastoral and the heroic world. The matrons gaze at her just as, towards the end of book VIII, the women of Pallanteum gaze in wonder upon Aeneas as he rides out to Caere. Here, perhaps, in the close of the Catalogue in VII, we catch something of the impression the heroes of Greece made on Helen and Priam as they looked down from the walls of Troy in *Iliad* III. But those heroes were ultimately victorious. Around Camilla there clings proleptically the sadness of defeat, for all her finery and show – indeed, perhaps because of them.

7. Diplomatic

At the end of the first section of *Aeneid* VII (line 285), before the irruption of Juno and Allecto into Latium, the Trojan embassy led by Ilioneus returned to Aeneas's camp with good news: *pacemque reportant*. Aeneas himself disappears from the narrative of book VII at line 159, when the embassy sets out, leaving him busy constructing the first Trojan camp on Italian soil. When we meet him again, at the beginning of VIII, he is deeply troubled. The war preparations at the end of VII have undermined Latinus's authority and his pledge of peace seems already weak. Meanwhile, another embassy has set out from the other side: the Latins are seeking help against Aeneas from his old enemy at Troy, Diomede, now also settled in Italy.

88   PEACE

Aeneas himself must now seek further allies: with Latinus powerless and Turnus assuming the hegemony over the chiefs of Latium, he must try for aid elsewhere, so he strikes north, first up the Tiber to Evander's settlement and then, further afield, to the Etruscan king Tarchon. The visit to Evander follows a night vision in which the river god Tiberinus appears and reassures him.

> Child of the gods, who hast taken Troy from its enemies
> And brought it here and saved it for ever and ever,
> You are the long awaited one. Here in the fields of Latium
> Is your sure home . . .

The reader recalls the words of Aeneas at the omen of the eating of the 'dinner-plates' in VII. The key words *domus*, *penates*, recur. But despite this grandly reassuring night vision (itself in conspicuous antithesis to the vision of horror which has insinuated itself into the sleeping Turnus in VII) Aeneas makes his visit to Evander as a suppliant, *in rebus egenis*, and the prophecy of the Sibyl in book VI now comes true. As she had foretold, Aeneas must seek salvation where he would least expect to find it, in a Greek city, for Evander had come from Arcadia before the Trojan war and had known Anchises. His settlement of Pallanteum stands on the site of the future Rome, especially the Palatine hill, home of Augustus himself, and Aeneas's visit allows Virgil a detailed and highly original excursus on the monuments of that first city. We see it all through the wondering eyes of the hero. So much of the poem's action is seen through mediating eyes. Aeneas looks at sites familiar to the implied reader but strange to him. When he looks at the Shield given him by Venus at the end of VIII he sees pictures but does not know the people and events which they depict: again, these are known to the implied reader. It is part of the loneliness of Aeneas's destiny that he must inaugurate the history of a people whose symbols he cannot interpret. He is almost like Wells's time-traveller, 'wandering between two worlds'. He must trust the future. This is a very hard thing for any of us to do, and to my mind amply accounts for the doubts and anxieties to which he is prone. The fact that the future is frequently and reassuringly revealed to Aeneas by accredited divinities and oracles does not wholly remove his anxieties. Again, Virgil speaks psychological truth. The destruction of Troy and the abrupt end of his past give Aeneas a massive sense of insecurity. Dido is the first person since his wife died who shows him any love. No wonder he wants to stay with her, and his necessary departure and her death merely add to his doubts. It is true of modern men and women as well as of heroes that, despite continual reassurances, they continue to doubt themselves and their future.

Moreover, the modern reader, unlike Virgil's implied Augustan reader, may well be nearly as ignorant as Aeneas of the historical significance of events, people and places displayed in book VIII. The modern reader, then, must make that implied Augustan reader's response a part of his own reading experience. To some extent, I suppose, this process forms part of the reading of any ancient text, but I think it belongs to readings of the *Aeneid* in a special way. The poet's manipulation of disparate temporalities (those of Aeneas and the implied reader) becomes for the modern reader a paradigm of his own temporal dislocation. In Aeneas Virgil has created a hero who is only partially able to relate to the things he sees and learns. He is thus a figure of every reader.

Aeneas's journey to Pallanteum and his first reception by Evander are modelled on passages in the *Odyssey*; *Aeneid* VIII becomes fully Iliadic only in its last triad, the great ecphrasis of the Shield. Again, the Homeric episode acquires a new meaning. Achilles had lost his own shield when Hector took it from the corpse of Patroclus. Aeneas has not yet fought in Italy, and the shield brought by his mother Venus (as Thetis had brought Achilles' shield) is a symbol carrying the history of that Rome which has not yet come into existence for Aeneas in the narrative time of the story; but which for the implied reader is already the eternal city of the Augustan writers. Livy says that the city's eternity depended on the perpetual renewal of its forms of government (*noua imperia*).[44] When Aeneas gazes on the cluster of legendary prehistoric ruins and 'contemporary' hut-settlements which make up bronze-age Pallanteum, the implied reader sees the splendid temples of Jupiter Capitolinus and Apollo Palatinus, images of both of which are projected on the Shield, while the modern reader sees beyond these, beyond the ironic vision of Gibbon, when he described the fallen ruins of the imperial city as observed by two Renaissance courtiers,[45] down to the archaeological preservations visible in our own time. The reader's perspective lengthens and draws out continually, the poem's temporalities are in his control, its narrative time unfolding as a constant 'present' within an unstable 'past'. The historic present allows the reader to control and stabilise these syntactical instabilities within a single 'interpreting' now, which is nothing else than his own act of reading. What emerges is a kind of vertically stacked structure of temporalities.

Aeneas's embassy to Evander closely parallels in form and structure the embassy of Ilioneus to Latinus: the common technique of 'doubling' (thus Evander's offer of his son Pallas parallels and doubles Latinus's offer of Lavinia). Both embassies start with the same question from hosts to envoys: *quae causa* (7.197, 8.111), 'What reason brought you here?': both offer dynastic arguments to support their case. Latinus says Dardanus came from Italy; Aeneas reminds Evander that Trojans and Arcadians also share a blood-relationship. But the second embassy is more urgent. When Ilioneus was despatched it was a kind of courtesy visit: there was no reason to fear aggression; now, says Aeneas, his Trojans alone stand between the Rutuli and the subjection of all Italy: *omnem Hesperiam* recalls *totam Hesperiam* in the prelude to VII, 'all Italy compelled to arms'.[46]

[44] Livy 4.4.
[45] This passage is reprinted in Gransden, *Aen. VIII*, Introd. 34–5.
[46] 7.434, 8.148.

The day on which Aeneas came to Pallanteum was itself a significant one. *forte die*, says the narrator: it so happened that on this very day the rites in honour of Hercules were being celebrated at the deified hero's Great Altar to mark the anniversary of his killing of the fire-breathing monster Cacus who had once haunted the Aventine hill. This annual rite at the Great Altar took place in historical times on 12 August, and this, therefore, is the day on which Virgil supposes Aeneas to have arrived. In the year 29 B.C., on 13 August, Augustus began his triple triumph in celebration of his victory at Actium over Antony and Cleopatra, as depicted at the end of VIII on the Shield. Thus Aeneas's arrival at Pallanteum on 12 August and his overnight sojourn both follow the arrival of Hercules and his victory over Cacus and prefigure the arrival of Augustus from his triumphs overseas: Hercules, too, had come from a previous victory elsewhere over another monster – another instance of epic 'doubling', but here the parallel between the three heroes is carefully worked out. The *furor* with which Hercules hunts down and kills Cacus perhaps underwrites the *furor* with which Aeneas finally kills Turnus. The story of Hercules, narrated to Aeneas and the reader by Evander, is thus an aitiological allegory: it pretends that the rite of the Great Altar was traditional and not a late Greco-Etruscan import; it presents a cyclic view of history and links two deified heroes in the cults of Rome, both in fact of Greek origin: Hercules, naturalised in Etruria and Aeneas, naturalised in Latium. The story also has a topographical function appropriate in a book centring on the sites of Rome: Cacus was a cattle-rustler, and the theft of a god's cattle is a mythical motif of common occurrence, e.g. the oxen of the Sun in *Odyssey* XII. It is here localised and appropriated to Roman legend, as were other stories depicted on the Shield, some probably assimilated from Greek counterparts, others, like the story of the geese which were said to have given warning of the imminent threat to the Capitol by the Gauls, perhaps native. All are stories of salvation from danger, of rescue, of heroism in extreme peril: all emphasise the *facta* of heroes. We *keep* this day holy, says Evander, because on it we were *saved* from great danger: the Latin word for keep and save is the same, *seruare*.

The pastoral invitation of Evander to Aeneas to stay the night in his simple hut constitutes an Odyssean theoxeny following an Odyssean *nostos* modelled on *Odyssey* XIV. Virgil's problem at this stage of his narrative is not to lose sight of the Iliadic theme inaugurated in VII, and to relate the Odyssean theme of homecoming to the 'greater matter' of the *Iliad*. It is at this point that he introduces a new character, Pallas, Evander's son. He greets the Trojans on their arrival at the Forum Boarium (where the Great Altar stood). It is one of Virgil's most imaginative strokes of dramatic irony. In stunned amazement and fear the celebrants at the altar rise from the communion table as the tall ships glide silently under the trees. It is Pallas who, with 'ill-starred gallantry',[47] orders the celebrants not to break their ritual but himself picks up a weapon, *audax . . . obuius ipse*: daringly confronting the Trojans (who bear the olive branch of peace) he offers in his gesture a prefiguration of his doomed courage in book X when he chides the Arcadians for their fear and launches himself into the *aristeia* which ends with his death at the hand of Turnus. He is the Patroclus of Virgil's Iliad. He is entrusted to Aeneas by his father, and this relationship with its specific range of obligation, though deeply and characteristically Roman, also finds its Homeric counterpart in the *Iliad*, where, we are told, Patroclus, though older than Achilles, was taken in by Achilles' father when still a child (he had killed another child in a temper over a game of dice).[48] The relationship of the two friends is sketched in typical Homeric gossipy detail: we learn something about the characters' past which is fresh and surprising. The sense of human reality is one of Homer's greatest qualities. Virgil transforms this relationship into the embodiment of an abstraction, deeply felt, morally serious, and with no touch of Homer's sense of familiarity and

[47] See Fordyce, *Aen. VII–VIII* on Servius *ad loc.*
[48] *Iliad* 23.85–92.

background. Compared with the characters in the *Iliad*, Aeneas and Pallas have no past, they share nothing, their lives together begin in book VIII and end in book XI.

Thus Aeneas–Achilles meets his Patroclus, and, it may be said, by meeting him, dooms him. Pallas is drawn in to the fatal recension of the *Iliad*; he is predestined by the author and by the model of which he is a fixed part. The Odyssean parallel to the sending of Pallas cannot be regarded as crucial. Nestor hands over Peisistratus to be Telemachus's companion on his search for his father; but although, as we have seen, Aeneas's sojourn with Evander does have Odyssean parallels, especially from book XIV (the theoxeny of Eumaeus) the parallel from the Telemachia, though structurally plausible, has no relevance to the tragic irony already implicit in the entry of Pallas into the narrative and his departure with Aeneas to Caere in search of the military alliance with Tarchon in preparation for the war which starts in earnest in book IX and claims Pallas as its victim in book X.

It seems clear from the narrative that Latinus and his people would not have been drawn into the power-struggle between Tarchon and the exiled Etruscan chieftain Mezentius, were it not that Mezentius had been taken in by Turnus the *soi-disant* son-in-law of Latinus. Evander tells Latinus that there is a prophecy that no local chieftain will be able to defeat Mezentius, the Etruscans must choose a foreign leader, *externos optate duces*. Thus Virgil, by the use of the device of 'doubling', reinforces the marital prophecy with a military one and sets in motion an Iliadic conflict with a difference (but retaining the revenge pattern of the Homeric Patrocleia) centring on the overthrow of a tyrant and a marriage of momentous national significance in which patriotic motifs from Rome's actual history (the defeat of the Etruscans) are interwoven.

All this Evander tells Aeneas in the speech which he makes after their night's rest in his simple house on the Palatine (the Odyssean theoxeny). The story of how Mezentius was received by Turnus is itself 'doubled' from one of the scenes from Rome's early history depicted on Aeneas's Shield at the end of VIII, in which the exiled last king of Rome, Tarquinius, is taken in by Lars Porsenna. The reader may also recall a further parallel from Livy[49] (and Shakespeare), the story of the exiled Coriolanus who was received by the Volscian leader Aufidius. Mezentius's story explains his pre-eminence in the Catalogue in VII; his defection increases the military threat to the Trojans; the need for allies becomes greater; the Etruscans await the *dux externus* who shall rescue Italy from tyranny.

In the Catalogue, Mezentius's son Lausus is described as leading a large contingent from Caere (Agylla), the Etruscan city to which Aeneas goes in VIII to receive the Shield from Venus, the city which had expelled Mezentius. It seems feasible that some Etruscans remained loyal to Mezentius and followed him and Lausus over to the Rutuli; but in any case Virgil has modified the received Italian version of the story to suit his own narrative,[50] which primarily requires that wherever he goes Aeneas must be welcomed as ally and saviour – by Latinus, Evander, Tarchon. His progress as he reluctantly accepts supreme *imperium* is a figure of Augustus's own triple triumph depicted on the Shield. Aeneas's *imperium* is defined and confirmed *after* the threat of war in VII makes it impossible that the Trojan assimilation in Italy can be a peaceful process.

Just as the Catalogue has ended with the figure of Camilla, watched with awed admiration by the women of Italy.

turbaque miratur matrum et prospectat euntem,

so, now, in a further parallel between the endings of VII and VIII, the matrons of Pallanteum watch from within the walls the riding forth of Aeneas, Achates, Pallas and the other Trojans in a cloud of dust and a gleam of Homeric bronze.

---

[49] Livy 2.33–40.
[50] See Fordyce, *Aen. VII–VIII* on 7.653: the reference to a large Etruscan contingent on the Italian side may be a survival of the standard version of the story in which Mezentius and the Etruscans are called in by the Rutuli. But we must remember that VII and VIII doubtless contain some unrevised matter.

stant pauidae in muris matres oculisque sequuntur
puluheream nubem et fulgentis aere cateruas.

That same gleam of heroic bronze had first glanced across the waters of the Tiber when Aeneas's ships arrived at Pallanteum earlier in VIII. Thus the end of VIII provides both an inner symmetry for the book itself and a larger chiastic symmetry for the two books VII and VIII, so that there is a complex movement within the pair: each begins with a parallel embassy, each ends with a riding forth and a long ecphrasis depicting heroes. Aeneas moves through the books in a triumphal progress, despite an anxious period of need, from the fields of Latium up Tiber to the site of Rome and across country to Etruria; from there he will make one more triumphal re-entry into the narrative, in book X.

The ecphrasis of the Shield which concludes book VIII holds up the narrative and sums up the meaning of the poem. The narrative time of the epic, the time of the Trojan landfall and the coming war, is suspended while the reader enters a new time-scale, which is that of Virgil's annalistic record of the Roman past from earliest times down to his own yesterday. That time-scale itself immediately changes when the contemporary reader starts reading the poem. Now, the climactic 'yesterday' of the triumph of Augustus, planned by Vulcan the artificer of the Shield and surrogate figure of the artificer-*uates* to be the centrepiece in plastic terms and the culmination in linear ones of the entire ecphrasis, becomes itself merely one more historical memory, as remote and glittering to us as the gleam of Homeric bronze. The narrative climax, which the poem's implied reader would have endowed with all the splendour of yesterday, has vanished into the most distant perspective of time. For the modern reader, gazing on the Shield with Aeneas's eyes, the scenes depicted indeed proclaim no political significance.

The last scene on the Shield (or rather, the scene at its centre, the last to be chronicled, the last in time), depicts the *princeps* receiving offerings and reviewing the triumphal parade from the temple of Apollo Palatinus. The crowd (among them, again, the matrons of the city) watch with delight, as the long procession of victors and vanquished winds its way through the streets. Once more, Virgil has interposed a seeing eye, or many eyes (for Aeneas looks at scenes which are shown as themselves being looked at): as though the reader would need those other eyes. For the implied Augustan reader, Aeneas's naive and ignorant view is balanced by the eye of understanding, of recent memory, of delight in recognition. But if the modern reader cannot reconstruct the historical life of the poem, then he cannot assent to the rhetorical stratagems by which Virgil sought to influence the implied reader. They remain now only as technical hypotheses, experiments in temporality, pleasures of narrative.

PART II: WAR

1. Absence

The withdrawal of Achilles in anger from the fighting at Troy, after his quarrel with Agamemnon, and the run of Trojan victories which follow and continue until the death of Patroclus, constitute the narrative core of the *Iliad*. The Trojans saw their good luck as the result simply of the loss to the Greeks of their greatest warrior: so Polydamas in *Iliad* XVIII:

> So long as this man was angry with noble Agamemnon,
> For so long were the Achaians easier to fight against . . .

But a Trojan counter-attack was also the will of Zeus, and Homer invents an Olympian story to show this. Achilles' mother Thetis appeals to Zeus on her son's behalf, reminding him of an obligation she put him under (another Homeric invention, apparently) when she helped him put down a rebellion. Zeus acknowledges the obligation although he is aware that his consort Hera/Juno already thinks he is too pro-Trojan, and agrees to Thetis's request to allow Trojan victories 'until the Achaians do my son honour and exalt him from recompense'. Zeus does not do much about his promise until *Iliad* VIII, when there begin two days of fighting dominated (despite some Greek counter-attacks) by the Trojans. After book XVIII, when Patroclus is dead, Achilles and Agamemnon are reconciled and the Trojans' cruel, delusory run of victories peters out with Hector's death. In the returning symmetry of book XXIV it is Zeus who summons Thetis, and warns her that the gods have lost patience with Achilles. His honour has been sufficiently redeemed; he must ransom Hector's body. The wrath is over, and Zeus's promise fulfilled. Troy survives, but not for much longer.

The *Aeneid*, too, starts with a promise by the supreme deity to the mother of the poem's hero. In book I, Jupiter reassured Venus that his promise to give the Trojans empire without end still stood, despite apparent set-backs to Aeneas engineered by Juno. Now in IX fighting breaks out during Aeneas's absence, and there are some Italian victories. But Aeneas is not absent out of wrath or pique, and the war starts against, not in fulfilment of, the will of Jupiter: *quae contra uetitum discordia?*[1]

Book IX begins with a transitional verse linking the narrative to VIII, which ended with Aeneas receiving the magic Shield from Venus to Caere on his way north to seek Etruscan reinforcements. He forms an alliance with the Etruscan king Tarchon, though we do not see this in VIII, nor do we see Aeneas again until he returns to the war in X at the head of his new contingent of Etruscan allies.

There follow three successive spondaic lines charged with a sense of foreboding:

> Irim de caelo misit Saturnia Iuno
> audacem ad Turnum. luco tum forte parentis
> Pilumni Turnus sacrata ualle sedebat.
>
> *Iris was sent from heaven by Juno Saturn's daughter*
> *To Turnus the bold. By chance in the ancestral grove*
> *Of Pilumnus in a holy valley Turnus rested.*

Turnus now moves to the centre of the narrative. Again, the syntax controls and directs the reader's shaping of the narrative. Turnus's name is repeated, first in the accusative, then in the nominative. The effect is like that of a cinema camera tracking forward. The sequence is: Juno–Iris–Turnus. The verse depicting the sending of Iris by Juno is repeated from 5.606, where it inaugurates the episode in

---

[1] See ch. 4 below. Jupiter speaks these words at the council of the gods at the beginning of X (line 8). *Discordia* means for the implied reader nothing less than civil war, not 'the quarrels of gods as well as men' (Conington *ad loc.*).

which the Trojan women, weary of travel, set fire to the ships. Now another attempt is made to burn the ships, this time by Turnus. This attempt is foiled by their miraculous transformation into nymphs. The model for this miracle is the transformation of a ship into a stone cliff in *Odyssey* XIII.[2] Such an Odyssean marvel may seem strangely placed at the beginning of Virgil's Iliad, though paranormal manifestations and phenomena in which natural laws are suspended occur also in the *Iliad*. Here we find yet another of Jupiter's promises fulfilled: he had promised the goddess Cybele that the ships, made from pine trees sacred to her, will be turned into sea nymphs when their mission is completed.

What Virgil has done in this episode is to modify passages in the *Iliad* in which Hector does succeed (after one foiled attempt) in setting fire to the Greek ships, as part of the damage inflicted on the Greeks during Achilles' absence.[3] The motif of Aeneas's absence is stated at the opening of IX by Iris, when she calls Turnus to arms: *nunc tempus equos, nunc poscere currus*, 'time now to call up horses and chariots'. The fighting in this book goes the Rutulians' way in Aeneas's absence, just as the fighting in *Iliad* VIII–XVI goes largely the Trojans' way in Achilles' absence. Structurally, the metamorphosis of the ships is complex and ambivalent. Turnus's attempt to fire them is thwarted by a piece of predetermined mythological invention, but the ships vanish none the less. Yet another bit of Troy is removed from the tale. Aeneas no longer needs the ships. They have brought him home, and he will return to the fight triumphantly in book X at the head of a new Etruscan navy.

But Turnus sees the miracle as an omen in support of his cause. 'The Trojans', he cries exultantly, 'are now trapped. The seas are closed to them. And this land is in my power. Nor do I fear the promises of fate; it is enough, the Trojans have

---

[2] In the *Odyssey* Poseidon, with Zeus's consent, turns to stone the Phaeacian ship which has conveyed Odysseus to Ithaca, when it is heading back for the harbour at Scheria. Again, the ship is metamorphosed after its mission is accomplished: it is really a piece of spite by Poseidon.

[3] *Iliad* 8.215–20; end of 15; 16.122–9.

touched our shore. Now it is my turn to play my role, to destroy this hated people who have taken my bride, to take arms as once the sons of Atreus did. I do not need Vulcan to make me armour, as Achilles did, nor a thousand ships, nor a wooden horse to hide in. I shall fight in the light and burn down their camp, as once they say the walls of Troy, built by the hand of Neptune, subsided in flames.'

The grandeur, the vaunting and the challenge of this speech recall many heroic orations in the *Iliad*. The reader will also note the deliberate reference to the Iliadic quarrel over Helen. Turnus is made to project himself into an Iliadic role. The Sibyl in VI prophesied that Aeneas would find a new Achilles in Latium, but it is characteristic of the Virgilian mode of secondary epic that the characters in the story assume various roles. As we read on into the Virgilian Iliad, the patterns and motifs of the Homeric *Iliad* can be continually detected under the surface, like the traces of an earlier text on a palimpsest. These allusions are not just decorative or rhetorical. We embark now on a carefully constructed recension of the *Iliad*, and particularly of its central block, books VIII–XVI.

Turnus finishes his speech and dismisses his troops for supper and sleep. This directs the reader to *Iliad* VIII (the 'unfinished battle' book in which Zeus's promise to Thetis begins to be fulfilled), when Hector dismisses his troops after the abortive attempt to fire the Greek ships.

Night falls on the Rutulian camp. Structurally and thematically, this is a re-enactment of the famous night-piece at the end of *Iliad* VIII. During this night, which lasts through *Iliad* IX and X, two missions are undertaken: the unsuccessful embassy to Achilles by Odysseus, Ajax and Phoenix, which ends in his refusal to return to the fighting; and an intelligence reconnaissance, by Odysseus and Diomede, during which they capture and kill the Greek spy Dolon and the Thracian king Rhesus and his chiefs and remove their horses. These two episodes, embassy or Presbeia, and reconnaissance or Doloneia, take place in the same night and occupy the ninth and tenth books of the *Iliad*.

ABSENCE

The famous ending of *Iliad* VIII depicts the Trojans' night watch after their first successful day's fighting since Zeus began to fulfil his promise to Thetis, left in abeyance in books II to VII, which are largely devoted to various introductory and recapitulatory episodes. After this night watch there is to be a run of Trojan victories, during the continued absence of Achilles, which will culminate in book XVI in the death of Patroclus. Virgil has compressed the narrative structure of these books (*Iliad* VIII–XVI) into two books (*Aeneid* IX, X). The night watch of the Rutuli in *Aeneid* IX also marks the start of a run of Italian victories which will culminate in the death of Pallas. Virgil begins this sequence at 9.161. He incorporates a reminiscence of the start of *Iliad* IX, when Homer shifts the scene from the Trojan night watch to the camp of the Greeks, who in their turn set guards while they debate their next move. For in Homer, as we expect, the centre of the action is not the temporarily victorious, ultimately doomed Trojans, but the Greeks, temporarily on the defensive yet destined to triumph, both in the war itself and more immediately in the action of the *Iliad* after Achilles returns.

In *Iliad* IX and X Homer presents two Greek reactions to the Trojan offensive. In *Aeneid* IX, after a Rutulian night scene corresponding to Homer's Trojan night scene at the end of *Iliad* VIII –

> conlucent ignes, noctem custodia ducit
> insomnem ludo.
>
> *The watch fires gleam, in the guard-house they while away*
> *The unsleeping night with dice –*

Virgil takes the implied reader back to *Iliad* IX to show Aeneas's men (as Homer had shown Agamemnon's) wakeful also: not confident and carefree like the Rutuli, not drinking and dicing, but anxious at their leader's absence at a moment of peril.

2. Nisus and Euryalus

The story of Nisus and Euryalus which forms the central section of *Aeneid* IX, although structurally modelled on *Iliad* IX and X, is wholly unhomeric in tone and treatment. In Homer, the embassy and the Doloneia are unrelated save that both take place on the same night and both involve Odysseus. The two episodes are themselves different in tone. The embassy is an affair of bitterness and heart-searching. Achilles not only rejects Agamemnon's apology and refuses his gifts; he criticises the heroic code itself. 'The coward and the brave man, they have both died alike', he says, in the course of one of the most powerful speeches in the entire *Iliad*, and his refusal to return to the battlefield dominates the whole central section of the epic. The Doloneia, however, is on an altogether lower emotional plane. It takes no cognisance of the embassy just ended; the situation is that which obtained at the end of *Iliad* VIII. Agamemnon cannot sleep; worried about the Trojan offensive he summons a nocturnal war-council, as a result of which Odysseus (who has just returned from seeing Achilles, though there is no reference to this) is despatched with Diomede to try to spy out the enemy's intentions. On the Trojan side Hector makes a similar decision (a piece of rather obvious epic 'doubling') and Dolon is despatched to try to find out if the Achaians are still guarding their ships or have decided on retreat. The events of the Doloneia are never again referred to in the poem[4] and have no apparent effect on the narrative of book XI, where the arming of Agamemnon formally signals the resumption of hostilities.

Virgil combines the Homeric embassy and Doloneia into a single episode, the first conspicuous *aristeia* of his Iliad. The entire passage is suffused with the intense mutual affection of Nisus and Euryalus, and it is this which makes it so

[4] See M. M. Willcock, *The Iliad* 295.

characteristic of Virgil. The starting-point of the narrative is that the two are not sent out as spies: they volunteer for a mission of rescue, to inform Aeneas of the danger to the Trojans and to bring him back. Their feeling for each other has already been displayed for the reader of book v, where they play a prominent part in the foot-race. An accidental fall by Nisus, who slips in a pool of blood, offers a prefiguration of book ix:

> Unlucky Nisus stumbled
> In some slippery blood, and already confident of
>   victory
> Failed to keep his footing, overbalanced,
> Fell in the dirt and blood.

Nisus, still on the ground, trips the leading runner and enables Euryalus to win the race. Virgil has projected the love of a friend as obsessive and overriding. He has established the lengths these two will go to, the risks they are prepared to take for each other.

Nisus's love for Euryalus is mirrored in ix. The famous verse

> tantum infelicem nimium dilexit amicum
>
> *only he loved his unlucky friend too much*

brings back the epithet given to Nisus in v.[5] It also recalls a crucial passage in *Aeneid* I (474–5), where the poet first states a theme which dominates his epic in a way that it does not dominate the *Iliad*: the tragedy of those who die young in battle. Aeneas is in Carthage gazing at the murals in Juno's temple, where scenes from the Trojan war are depicted, among them the death at Achilles' hands of Troilus (not in Homer but from some later part of the cycle):

> parte alia fugiens amissis Troilus armis
> infelix puer atque impar congressus Achilli.

[5] *Aen.* 9.430, 5.328–38.

> *In another scene there's Troilus running away,
>   weaponless,*
> *Unlucky boy, no match for Achilles.*

The lines introduce two separate but related motifs: the deaths of young men, and unequal combat. They recur throughout the *Aeneid*. In x Pallas and Lausus, both young, both doomed, are not destined to fight each other: 'for each his destiny waits at the hand of a greater foe'.

In Homer the motif of those who die young is not a strong one. There is one famous formulaic epitaph, used of both Patroclus and Hector:

> The soul fluttering free of the limbs went down
>   into death's house
> mourning her destiny, leaving youth and manhood
>   behind.

But the idea of youth, *hebe*, is not seen as specially poignant. Most of Homer's heroes are in the prime of fighting manhood, seasoned warriors of nearly ten years' campaign experience, but in the *Aeneid* a significant distinction is made between chiefs like Aeneas, Turnus and Mezentius, and young, untried heroes like Pallas and Lausus, coming fresh into battle like so many on the western front in the First World War, protégés of older and more experienced soldiers. (We tend to forget that Patroclus, though less greatly born and a lesser warrior than Achilles, was actually older.)

Virgil finds a special pathos in the theme of the young soldier meeting a superior foe; Homer does not. 'Patroclus too is dead, and he was a better man than you', says Achilles fiercely to Lycaon just before he kills him (*Iliad* XXI). 'Do you not see what sort of man I am, how beautiful, how big, and I come of a good father and a goddess mother, but on me too death and strong destiny wait, some morning or evening or at high noon.' For Homer, the overriding pathos is simply awareness of mortality, from which none in the *Iliad* is exempt.

Virgil chronicles not a few weeks in a ten-year war but a complete war lasting a few weeks only. Death comes quickly to young men brought up to live in peace. Achilles' epic boast to Lycaon finds an odd echo in *Aeneid* x when Aeneas kills Mezentius's son Lausus. He alludes both to Lausus's youthfulness and to his inadequate prowess:

> Do you go crashing into your own death, taking risks you are too weak for?

Aeneas calls Lausus *infelix*, unlucky (cf. Troilus and Nisus) and *miserande puer*, 'pitiful boy', and says it should console him that 'you die at the hand of great Aeneas'.

The phrase *miserande puer* recalls another passage earlier in the *Aeneid* which throws light on the poet's deep sense of tragedy underlying the deaths of the untried. This passage is the description in book VI of Marcellus, Augustus's heir-designate, shown to Aeneas by Anchises in the pageant of heroes in the Elysian fields.

> Fate will let the world glimpse him for a little while only...

Marcellus too is called *miserande puer*:[6] that he would have triumphed had he lived links his early death with the untimely deaths of books IX and X. The story of Marcellus depends on the idea of rebirth, a doctrine which does not render the brevity of human life any less sad; indeed it perhaps renders it more so.

> stat sua cuique dies, breue et inreparabile tempus omnibus est uitae.[7]
>
> *Determined each man's day, brief and irrecoverable the time*
> *Of life for everyone.*

Those words are spoken in book X by Jupiter to Hercules, in a

[6] *Aen.* 6.882. [7] *Aen.* 10.467–8.

significant context which is also relevant here. Pallas has just sent up a prayer to Hercules, who, as we learnt in VIII, was his father Evander's guest at Pallanteum when he killed the monster Cacus. He has prayed to be allowed to kill Turnus. Hercules is powerless to grant such a prayer; it will take a greater warrior to kill Turnus. Jupiter then speaks the words just quoted, and goes on to refer to his own son Sarpedon, who fell at Troy and he could do nothing, and whose death, moreover, in *Iliad* XVI at the hands of Patroclus led to Patroclus's own death just as in *Aeneid* X the death of Halaesus at the hands of Pallas leads to Pallas's own death. *etiam sua fata uocant*, 'for Turnus too destiny calls', says Jupiter. Throughout Virgil's Iliad, starting with the first *aristeia* and self-sacrifice of Nisus and Euryalus who, like the Romans (called at 8.648, significantly, Aeneadae) on Aeneas's Shield, *pro libertate ruebant*, 'fell in the cause of freedom', the sense of *déjà vu*, already established in the Elysian fields, is overwhelming. For every rebirth there must be yet another death.

The narrative is highly dramatic. The friends are on watch, the fires burn through the night. Nisus speaks, and his opening words are striking in their impatience, as though he can no longer contain himself:

> Do the gods instil in us, Euryalus, this burning
>   desire for glory,
> Or is this dreadful longing a god inside us all?

This dreadful longing, *dira cupido*, has already figured in the underworld, in the context of reincarnation. Aeneas asked the shade of Anchises 'whence comes this dreadful longing for the light of life?'[8] The hero who has suffered so much cannot understand how those who have reached the larger air and ampler light of the Elysian fields should wish to be reborn, yet the life-force recurs and fights a regressive death-wish.

Nisus's question has also a larger significance, and one relevant to the entire psychology of heroic epic. Do our

---

[8] *Aen.* 6.721.

passions come from outside us – *Ate*, the disturber of men's rationality, referred to by Agamemnon – or from within ourselves? The question falls like a shadow across the whole poem, from its opening lines – 'Do heavenly beings really feel such wrath?' – down to the last book and the poet's last question about war-madness: 'Was this your will, Jupiter?'

Nisus's speech shows the same love for Euryalus which he displayed in the foot-race. Again, it is of his friend not of himself that he thinks.

> You can see how sure of things the Rutulians are:
> Hardly a light shines over there, relaxed with drink and sleep
> They've gone to bed. All's quiet. Now listen.
> I've been thinking, and this is my plan.
> Aeneas must be got back – all of us are saying it,
> Somebody's got to go and tell him what's happening.
> If they promise to give you what I shall ask them – as for me,
> The deed itself is glory enough – I think I can find
> A way through the lines by the foot of that hill to Pallanteum.

The Latin is simple and straightforward, the tone direct. But Euryalus insists on going too, and his words seem to pick up the concept of *dira cupido*: for this love of glory is death-bound:

> est hic, est animus lucis contemptor et istum
> qui uita bene credat emi, quo tendis, honorem.
>
> *Here's courage holds cheap the light and thinks that*
> *Glory you go to worth the price of life.*

'Here's courage holds cheap the light': this contempt for life is different from anything we find in the *Iliad*. In Sarpedon's speech to Glaucus, for instance,[9] it is made clear that risks have

---

[9] *Iliad* 12.310–28.

to be taken because men are mortal: if they were not, there would be no incentive, no point in taking the risks; yet the risks are not taken in order to court death, nor is there any inherent virtue in taking them. For Virgil, though he had access to spiritual consolations unknown to Homer, fate and death conspire to project a tragic sense of life as something to be endured. A pervasive *Weltschmerz* replaces the death-challenging vitality and zest of Homer. In the *Iliad*, the contrast between life and death is absolute. In the *Aeneid* the line between them is often faint and blurred.

The narrative style of *Aeneid* IX is direct and simple, yet quite unhomeric. Virgil had evolved for his early *Eclogues* a technique of supple and translucent elegance.[10] In his maturity he seems to have revived that style, but now it is deeper, plainer, less self-conscious, the pathos and sentiment stronger.

Various modifications of the Homeric narrative structure produce a tauter, more dramatic story. At Homer's war-council the volunteers are already present when the mission is discussed. In Virgil's narrative, the Trojans ponder how to get news of their vulnerable situation to Aeneas. Nisus and Euryalus burst into the tent, their plan ready, and put it across with all the force and enthusiasm of youth. The incentive is with them. The scene is structurally integrated into the Iliadic *Aeneid*, of which indeed it is a paradigm, determining the whole tone and treatment of the war narrative which comprises the poem's last four books.

In Homer, the embassy to Achilles is essential to the monumental *Iliad*, essential to the wrath theme, the Doloneia is not. The Doloneia, such as it is and for what it is worth, is a success, the embassy a failure, since Achilles does not return until much later in the narrative, yet it is the embassy we want to read now, with its long resonant speeches, its bitter insights. The story of Nisus and Euryalus is also a tale of

[10] Whatever terms we use to describe the *Eclogues*, 'they clearly imply a register far removed from that of epic' (see R. G. G. Coleman (ed.), *Vergil: Eclogues* (Cambridge 1977) 26). Not only are the modes of presentation different – the structure of the hexameters, uses and incidence of elision, lexical range, deployment of figures – but the presented worlds are different also.

failure, but not of bitterness or rejection, and the poet's and reader's involvement dramatises the narration and makes possible a transformation of Homer.

> Fortunate pair! If my poem has any power,
> No day shall ever take you from time's memory,
> So long as Aeneas's house by the immovable rock
>   of the Capitol
> Shall stand and the fathers of Rome have
>   dominion.

In the *Aeneid* the prophetic future occurs frequently in the first eight books. It virtually disappears from the narrative of IX–XII, the core of the Virgilian Iliad, to return at the end of the poem in the final scene between Jupiter and Juno, which stands in structural and thematic symmetry with the scene between Jupiter and Venus in I, where the promise of *imperium sine fine* is set out. Most of the passages in the future tense in the earlier books take the form of oracular or divine relevations; in VI the implied author speaks as a didactic or philosophical instructor in the Lucretian manner, using as his mouthpiece the character of Anchises: the signal for such passages is picked up by the reader in

> expediam dictis et te tua fata docebo
>
> *I shall disclose, teach you your destiny*

When the Trojan *penates* speak to Aeneas in his sleep and warn him that he must leave Crete and go to Italy (book III) the narrative voice is complicated by the fact that Aeneas is telling his story to Dido. (Students of book IV are apt to forget that Dido received a very early warning of Aeneas's destined goal.) What the *penates* tell Aeneas is couched in the form of an ecphrasis. Again, there is a clear signal for the reader:

> est locus, Hesperiam Graii cognomine dicunt . . .
> hae nobis propriae sedes.

> *There is a place the Greeks call Western Land:*
> *This is where we belong.*

The ancient and fruitful land of Italy, whence Dardanus himself, Troy's royal founder, had originated, enters the narrative. The *nobis* of the *penates* must be enlarged by the implied reader to include the speaker–narrator (Aeneas) and the whole Roman nation, for whom the words carry an emotive trigger, as though for the British the opening bars of 'Land of Hope and Glory' were played. Moreover, the *penates* themselves are only the mouthpiece of Apollo, and their speech to Aeneas begins with him: the signal is *canit*, he prophesies (so too of the Sibyl in VI), but it is also the signal-word for the function of the epic *uates*.

In the later books of the *Aeneid* there are only a few brief incursions into the future, and these are of a special kind, for they are the voice of Virgil himself, making a direct entry into the poem: not as the epic narrator, nor as the instructor or philosopher, nor as the empathising and experiencing 'I' of the poem's great emotive statements, but as the artist conscious of what he is doing. The story of Nisus and Euryalus is told with deep empathy, yet clearly it remains a story, with no independent existence outside the *Aeneid*. Here it must be distinguished from such historical passages as the account of Actium. Thus the poet's claim, 'if my poem has any influence', is a complex kind of statement. The poem's 'influence', its power, lies with the reader, and if there is a reader when the Capitol has fallen, as in fact there is, Virgil might seem actually to have underestimated his power. Horace, too, seems not to have thought about the possibility of Latin surviving Rome. The Augustans circumscribed their art within an apparently limitless order of temporality, the 'eternal' power of Rome, an image so powerful that the implied author did not, perhaps could not, see beyond it. The only image that is more powerful is that of time itself. We get a glimpse of this from Ovid, at the end of the *Metamorphoses*,

> perque omnia saecula fama
> . . . uiuam

but even Ovid does not envisage any poetic future for his work outside the context of Rome.

Thus the fact that, in the story of Nisus and Euryalus, a piece of epic *aristeia* in the Homeric mode has outlived the *imperium* of which it was supposed to be a preparation, changes the meaning of the passage and of the poem. It comes back into a purely fictional context, and what may seem a reductionist reading (Rome no longer matters, but it remains a good piece of narrative) has in fact set the poem free from its conditional historical context.

In the *Iliad* Helen says of herself and Paris

> We two, on whom Zeus set a vile destiny, so that hereafter
> We shall be made into song for men of the future.

This is a clear reference to the tradition of heroic song of which the monumental *Iliad* is itself the culmination. Helen's words are guaranteed by the fact that they appear in precisely that song for men of the future which they prophesy. The figure is surprisingly sophisticated, and recurs in Shakespeare's *Antony and Cleopatra* when Cleopatra, a character in a play, speaks as though she were the 'real' historical Cleopatra prophesying that one day she will be portrayed on the stage by a boy-actor. But Cleopatra's lines (act v, sc. ii, 213–20) differ from Helen's in that Helen foresees that her shame will be the immortal subject of heroic song; Cleopatra foresees that her real greatness will be, not immortalised but diminished and trivialised in art. What both passages share is an ironic self-awareness which is the voice, not just of an epic narrator but of an implied author who directs his readers towards an awareness of the metaphysics of fiction.

There is no instance in Homer of the poet himself claiming to have preserved an event by his song, and this is surely evidence of that oral tradition on which the song depends.

112 WAR

Homer is fascinated by the fact that the past can be remembered. The awareness his own heroes show of the recording process has been incorporated in the narrative by himself as monumental composer (though it may of course have been traditional). The pictures of the Trojan war embroidered by Helen, or Achilles' song of the deeds of heroes, are a kind of instant epic, or at least invite the reader to some such metaphorical reading. They show the beginning of a concept of history, of an exploration of the relation between events and their representation. But the motif of the artist, the conscious 'I', as the preserver and immortaliser of events is a topos of post-Homeric literature, from Pindar to the Renaissance. Virgil still pays lip service to the remembering Muses. Thus he twice has passages beginning

> Pandite nunc Helicona, deae, cantusque mouete
>
> *Open the gates of Helicon, Muses. Let my poem tell*

which are based on Homer. But he also has the more personal, Alexandrian form of invocation, in which the emphasis has changed from the song to its creator (9.525–8)

> Vos, O Calliope, precor, aspirate canenti
> quas ibi tum ferro strages, quae funera Turnus
> ediderit, quem quisque uirum demiserit Orco,
> et mecum ingentis oras euoluite belli.
>
> *You, O Calliope, I pray, inspire your poet singing*
> *What deaths by the sword and what demises Turnus*
> *Dealt out, what heroes each man sent to the underworld,*
> *And with me unroll the mighty documentary of war.*

In the epitaph for Nisus and Euryalus Virgil combines a pledge for the future – 'so long as . . . so shall' is a rhetorical formula familiar in various forms, in the protestations of lovers as well as in claims for the power of poetry to preserve the memory of past deeds – with another rhetorical figure, the direct address by the poet to his character:

Fortunate pair! If my poem has any power,
No day shall ever take you from time's memory . . .

He uses this figure again at the death of Lausus in x:

Here death's cruel accident and your most glorious deeds –
If the antique past may be credited with such work –
Yes, and yourself shall be my song . . .

Earlier in x, when Pallas, the principal character of the Virgilian Iliad, is killed, there is a more complex version of the figure:

Ignorant is man's mind of destiny and the future,
And can't control itself when fortune boosts it.
For Turnus the time shall come when he'll pray for Pallas
To be unharmed, give anything for that, loathe
This day, these spoils . . .
O you who return to your father, source of much sorrow and pride,
This was your first day of war, your last also.

Here, after a generalising comment on man's hubris and blindness to the future, the poet (not narrator but self-conscious author) considers Turnus in his moment of exultation, undercutting the narrative by jumping ahead to a point it has not yet reached, the point of Turnus's peripeteia. He emphasises Iliadic precedent and structure by echoing the warnings of the dying Patroclus to Hector and the dying Hector to Achilles. The poet then addresses the dead Pallas, intensifying further the emotional involvement the reader already shares. Homer, too, had employed the figure of apostrophe,[11] direct address to a character, most remarkably in

---

[11] On the tension between the narrative and the apostrophic modes see Culler, *Pursuit* 149–50. Apostrophe introduces a 'special temporality which is the set of all moments at which writing can say "now"'. The apostrophising author, himself a figure of the reader, 'substitutes a temporality of discourse for a referential temporality'. See also Prologue, 27–30.

XVI when he addresses Patroclus as his death approaches him: the reader is thus made to feel that that death, as a narrative climax, is approaching him in his act of reading.

> So in your fury you pounced, Patroclus . . .
> There, Patroclus, the end of your life was shown forth . . .
> And now dying you answered him, O rider Patroclus

The effect of these addresses is to create a new relationship between the singer and the song. For a moment the narrator, the impersonal epic bard, vanishes, to be replaced by another figure, who is not only controlling the narrative but is intensely and consciously aware (as the hearer/reader must now through this control become) of having reached a moment in the narrative in which feeling is too strong to be left to speak wholly inside the story. Our sense of grief for the doom of Patroclus cannot be wholly subsumed through narrative (however empathetic its presentation) nor through the grief of Achilles (although it is expressed in violent action).

Thus, although Virgil has not originated vatic empathy, he extends and intensifies its function. Our sense of grief for the fallen young heroes in the *Aeneid* is not wholly subsumed in the grief of those (chiefly Aeneas himself) who mourn them. The author interposes an intense emotional pressure, and not merely the emotional pressure which is generated by a crucial moment in the narrative, as Patroclus's fate prompted Homer to a bold use of the vocative, but an empathy so pervasive and sustained that the reader may find himself constructing out of an epic of traditional heroic prowess another, very different kind of epic, an epic of sensibility, in which reactions to events become as important as the narration of the events themselves, and perhaps more important.

Perhaps the most striking instances in the *Aeneid* of extended passages of vatic empathy are to be found in the two flower-similes which elaborate the death of Euryalus in IX and the funeral of Pallas in XI.

Homer has a flower-simile in *Iliad* VIII,[12] illustrating the death of Gorgythion, who is hit by an arrow intended for Hector. His head droops and is likened to the head of a poppy drooping under its own weight or that of rain. The simile works on the usual 'tangent' principle of primary epic: tenor and vehicle[13] meet at one point, even though divergent before and after. The tangent offers a verbal, not a visual parallel (which would often be absurd or grotesque), almost, indeed, a kind of pun. The delaying force of this simile, with its return to the tenor ('so his head bent slack . . .') keeps the vignette of this death of an unimportant character (the arrow was not even meant for him) a little longer in our minds and singles it out for pathos. The simile reminds us that in death all, even minor characters, become significant.

Another related simile in *Iliad* XVII,[14] illustrating the death of Euphorbos (an episode to which Virgil later makes an important structural allusion) is also relevant to the *Aeneid*. The falling hero, with his beautiful hair, is likened to an olive sapling raised and watered by a man in an exposed place, blossoming forth and then ripped out by a sudden violent storm-wind. Again, the tangent is not a visual detail – Euphorbos is not *like* a sapling – but the sapling was carefully nurtured by the husbandman as was Euphorbos by his father, and to no avail: both plant and hero were prematurely torn from life. The vulnerability of the sapling is seen by the reader as appropriate also to Euphorbos. Menelaus's spear destroys

---

[12] *Iliad* 8.306–8.
[13] 'Tenor' and 'vehicle' are the terms coined by I. A. Richards in *The Philosophy of Rhetoric* (Oxford 1936), lecture 5, to denote the two ideas present in any metaphor (e.g. 'life's but a walking shadow', in which 'life' is the tenor, 'shadow' the vehicle). The tenor is thus the main subject or purport of the discourse, the vehicle the borrowed or metaphorical image. Richards argues that 'the co-presence of the vehicle and tenor results in a meaning (to be clearly distinguished from the tenor) which is not attainable without their interaction'. It seems to me that these terms may usefully be extended to cover the simile, where, especially in Virgil, it is clear that the total meaning of the discourse when enriched by the simile is different from the meaning without the simile or indeed of the separate meanings of discourse and simile, in so far as these can be isolated.
[14] *Iliad* 17.53–60.

him as suddenly and as violently as the wind had blasted the young tree.

The incorporation of such scenes and moods into the world of the *Iliad*, scenes and moods from ordinary life and its set-backs, life going on far from Troy and at the same time as heroes are dying, is one of the tasks of the reader in creating the total meaning of Homer's war epic. Life does not stop when a hero dies. But the simile has another strange tangential point which may strike the modern reader. The sapling was reared in a lonely place, and Euphorbos has gone to the loneliness of death. It is in any case an over-simplification to say that Homeric similes are independent of the scenes they decorate; although Homer's art is sequential not simultaneous, I believe that, if the simile was the poet's display piece, it was the audience's chance, too, to exercise its powers of holding in the mind two separate but co-ordinate pictures, the one enriching the other.

Virgil goes further: but how? The death of Euryalus moves the reader partly because Nisus was there when his friend died; in the narration the simile links the dying hero to his friend who then makes his last death-charge. The three lines about the flower separate the friends in death yet also unite them, in a perspective of grief. The simile also – and deliberately – places the end of this passage inside that world of art which, in his epitaph, the implied author declares shall immortalise the story as long as Rome lasts. The simile enacts 'whatever my songs can do'. The poet's epitaph becomes more than a directive to the implied reader; it challenges and transcends its own confines; it looks beyond those past readings to all possible future readings, including ours, which have outlasted Roman power.

When in book x Virgil came to describe the death of Pallas he had moved far into his Iliadic narrative, into the very heart of his Patrocleia. There is no simile, no empathetic perspective of friendship. Pallas dies far from any friend, with only the gloating Turnus to despatch his soul. The poet's epitaph this time comments directly on the end of the poem and on the end of every reading of it. The time will indeed come for Turnus to regret killing Pallas, it will come in xii, and it is to this end of his epic and our reading of it that the poet specifically refers. The pathos of Pallas's death is felt most strongly in the epiphonema 'this was your first day of war, and your last'. There is no mediating presence, no Nisus, no Anchises speaking of Marcellus in the Elysian fields and associating the dead-unborn youth with flowers. There is an unfinishedness in this death, not just because of the account with Turnus which will be settled in xii. The full pathos of response is held back for the funeral in xi. The reader will there need the fullest empathy of grief. A flower-simile in x would have made Pallas's death a repetition of Euryalus's. But in xi, when the dead Pallas is lifted on to the bier, Virgil likens him to a soft violet or drooping hyacinth, picked by a maiden, its beauty cut off from earth's nourishment, but not yet faded. This is a more elaborate version of the Homeric flower-simile in ix. There are more tangents: Pallas had not yet lost his beauty, he was picked off, but the virgin-reaper is a transference, for virginity belongs to Pallas, not to Turnus, and the flexibility of Latin word order aids the transference:

> qualem uirgineo demessum pollice florem
> seu mollis uiolae seu languentis hyacinthi,
> cui neque fulgor adhuc nec dum sua forma recessit,
> non iam mater alit tellus uirisque ministrat.

> *Just like a flower a girl has picked,*
> *A violet maybe or a drooping lily,*
> *Its sheen, its graceful shape still linger,*
> *But it draws no life now from the earth that bore it.*

This is the world of erotic elegy: Virgil alludes to the closing simile of Catullus 11, in which the poet's rejected love is compared to the flower on the edge of the meadow caught by the casual ploughshare. Virgil had said a pessimistic farewell to the world of erotic pastoral in his tenth *Eclogue*:

> nunc insanus amor duri me Martis in armis
> tela inter media atque aduersos detinet hostis.
>
> *Now by love's uncontrollable force am I held*
> *In war's cruel arms under the fire of the foe.*

The madness of love has driven the disconsolate Gallus, as in his eleventh poem Catullus was driven by his unfaithful mistress, to war. Nisus and Euryalus have remained lovers in a world of war and conflict: the fragile, pessimistic eroticism of pastoral has not merely survived transplantation into heroic epic, it has flowered and flourished in the stronger context.

The flower-similes distance the reader from the narrated act of death. The analogy between human mortality and the mortality of flowers, grass, leaves, is one of the oldest figures in 'wisdom' literature, found in Homer and in the Old Testament. The cutting and picking of flowers is a common-place of shared experience, as is their destruction by nature. An epic about war turns deaths into commonplaces, may even seem to be in danger of exploiting death for narrative sensation. Nor is the reaction 'it's only a story' an adequate defence. The mimetic analogy with historical experience is too insistent for that. We may not want to linger in our reading too long on the chronicled deaths. But we are invited to linger on the flower-similes. They operate as narrative figures, breaking up an assault on the reader's sensibilities which might become insupportable. Thus the similes are not just self-indulgences of the poets, whether of Homer elaborating or adding to a rich traditional repertoire of illustrative vignettes, or Virgil refining and extending this tradition in accordance with the Alexandrian tastes of his implied reader. The juxtaposition of simile and narrative requires the reader to construct a meaning for the entire epic in which the sensibilities are fully stretched. Words like *seu*, *qualem*, signalling the start of a simile, alert the reader to change, but to spend too long on the similes, or to extrapolate them, is to sentimentalise one's response. The single flower, momentarily isolated, forces us to think of a single death, in the series of deaths repeated infinitely through legend and history.[15]

3. Siege

The story of Nisus and Euryalus forms the centrepiece of book IX, which, like so many books of the *Aeneid*, has a triadic structure. The long final section, describing the assault on the Trojan camp, marks the first narrative of general fighting in the *Aeneid*. It is written in the poet's grandest epic style. It offers not only a re-enactment of the *Iliad*, but also a continuation of it. History repeats itself, but in each repetition a new element is found. There is development and extension. Early in the passage, the Volsci, allies of Turnus led by Camilla, mount the first assault on the camp, and the Trojans find themselves once again in a situation with which they are only too familiar.

> adsueti longo muros defendere bello

They are

> *Well used to defending their walls in a long war*

The spondaic line, as so often in the *Aeneid*, slows down the action and the reader: there is a narrowing of focus. The reader feels the static weight of perpetual defensive campaigns pressing on the Trojans; behind the single verse is the whole of the *Iliad*, and with it something else – the implied Augustan reader's awareness of Rome herself having passed through a historical time of what must have seemed perpetual defensiveness, against Etruscans, Gauls, Carthaginians, and the enemy within herself.

The attack culminates in a striking passage in which Turnus is actually shut up inside the Trojan gates by Pandarus,

---

[15] For a critical discussion of the death of Euryalus see W. R. Johnson, *Darkness Visible* (Berkeley 1976) 59–66. On the flower-simile, see D. West, 'Multiple Correspondence Similes in the *Aeneid*', *JRS* 59 (1969) 47.

perhaps an allusion to the wooden horse in which the Trojans had foolishly and fatally shut their enemy within their own gates. This time, however, there will be a reprieve. Another mighty spondaic line marks Pandarus's efforts to secure the gates:

> portam ui multa conuerso cardine torquet
> obnixus latis umeris, multosque suorum
> moenibus exclusos duro in certamine linquit;
> ast alios secum includit recipitque ruentis,
> demens, qui Rutulum in medio non agmine regem
> uiderit inrumpentem ultroque incluserit urbi,
> immanem ueluti pecora inter inertia tigrim.

> *With mighty force he turns the gate on its hinge*
> *Using his shoulders, leaves many of his own army*
> *Outside the walls, unprotected in the struggle,*
> *But others he shuts in with him as they rush headlong,*
> *Fool, not to see that charging in their midst was King*
>   *Turnus,*
> *And he actually shut him inside with them,*
> *Like shutting a tiger in with cattle.*

Book IX begins the *aristeia* of Turnus. The model for this is the *aristeia* of Hector in the Trojan breakthrough in *Iliad* XII. But the relation between Aeneas and Turnus and their Homeric archetypes Achilles and Hector is a complex one. Turnus plays both roles; so does Aeneas. The fluctuation of the Homeric roles is an important element in the structure of Virgil's Iliad. And there is a good reason for it. For this is a war which nobody loses. After the defeat of Turnus the two sides, Latins and Trojans, indigenous and immigrant, will become one nation. Thus the Homeric concepts of victory and defeat are in a sense irrelevant in the *Aeneid*, or they are transcended. As a Trojan, Aeneas avenges the death of Hector and is a second Hector, but this time a victorious one. Turnus is, in the words of the Sibyl's prophecy to Aeneas in *Aeneid* VI, a second Achilles born in Latium awaiting a second Troy: but this time, if he is Achilles, he will die, as indeed did Homer's Achilles, whose self-awareness that by staying in Troy he is doomed (he often threatens to go home but cannot resist playing out his hand against fate) adds much to the tragic power of the *Iliad*.

In book IX, the absent Aeneas is playing the role of the absent Achilles which in Iliadic terms works in with Turnus's replaying of the role of Hector on the offensive. Yet when Turnus finds himself inside the enemy walls he naturally recasts himself as Achilles, for the Trojans are now on the defensive as the Greeks were temporarily during Hector's *aristeia*. When Pandarus taunts him

> This is not the stronghold of your native Ardea.
> You are in the enemy camp and you can't get out

his reply comes pat:

> You'll be able to tell Priam that you found here
> another Achilles.

But Turnus's triumph, like that of Hector in the *Iliad*, is short-lived. As Achilles returned, so will Aeneas.

Virgil's Trojans have just escaped from the most famous military defeat in the ancient world. Their role as challengers in Latium (for so they have now unwillingly become) must have seemed to the Italian leaders fairly incredible, and naturally elicits various unflattering sneers at their military record, most notably in the taunts of Turnus's brother-in-law Numanus in the last section of book IX. He refers sneeringly to the Trojans' defeat at the hands of the Achaians, and asks them if they are not ashamed to face a second disaster, not this time at the hands of the Greeks but of a much tougher people, *patiens operum paruoque adsueta iuuentus*, 'young, used to hard work and roughing it'. If the Trojans could be beaten by the Greeks, who in Augustan times were not regarded as a race of warriors, how can they have the nerve to take on the Italians? All this is addressed to the implied Augustan reader. Virgil's account of the tough (*duri*) Italians in Numanus's speech carries the same moral implications as the portrait of the hard-working Italian farmer in his second *Georgic*; there is the same contrast between simplicity and effeminate luxury.[16] Just as the farmer is the antitype of the city-dweller with his fine house and dependence on foreign luxuries, so the Italian is the antitype of the Trojan, who is effeminate in dress, oriental in origin, devoted to the worship of strange gods and goddesses, especially the Magna Mater (Great Mother): it is a deliberate irony of the poet's that earlier in IX we have seen the women of Latinus's city, under the influence of Juno–Allecto, behave in the uncontrolled and orgiastic fashion now attributed to the Trojans, who are first called *Phryges* (a people despised by the Augustans for their effeminacy) and then *Phrygiae*, Phrygian women. So in the *Iliad* Thersites sneered at the Achaians as women, and Priam after Hector's death referred with contempt to his other sons as heroes of the dance-floor. Paris's preference for love-making over fighting is also mentioned in the *Iliad* several times, notably in III,[17] and the metamorphosis of Aeneas himself into a second Paris, ready to take another man's wife, is another element in the manipulation of figures in the poem. Aeneas must move through the roles of Paris (discredited) and Hector (defeated), and finally reassume the role of Achilles, ousting Turnus.

So Turnus will see the role of Achilles slip from his grasp when victory seemed certain. What defeats him is finally Aeneas, but before that, his *caedis insana cupido*, 'crazy lust for slaughter'. The madness of war, symbolised earlier in VII by the visitations of Allecto, sweeps over the victorious hero; instead of concentrating on strategy, he behaves like an old-fashioned Homeric hero obsessed with self-displaying prowess. He kills many Trojans, but in Roman eyes this *aristeia* is magnificent but it is not war. The reader will think continually of the ten-year siege of Troy, ended not by any *aristeia*, but a ruse, an intelligence strategy.

Virgil modifies the *Iliad* in many ways, not the least important of which is that he passes judgement, through the

[16] *Georg.* 2.458–74. For bibliography see Williams (ed)., *Georgics* (1979) 173.
[17] *Iliad* 2.235, 24.261, 3.54–7.

Aeneid, on its attitudes to warfare. The Trojans in Italy put to good use the lessons of Troy. The Rutuli just made the same mistakes as the old heroes, failing to follow through advantages, obsessed with personal glory. If only, says Virgil, Turnus had simply opened the gates and let his army in, 'that day would have been the end of the war – and of a nation'. But he did not. When in book x Aeneas kills Mezentius, this is not mere *aristeia*: he is the most dangerous enemy leader after Turnus and must be eliminated; when Camilla is slain only Turnus stands between Aeneas and victory. But Turnus makes no comparable killing in ix. Instead, he wears out his strength in strategically valueless slaughter. Mnestheus rallies the Trojans at the end of the book. His words carry a grim warning: if they lose this siege too, where next can they find refuge, what other walls can they hide behind? The appeal coincides with a divine intervention: as with Achilles in *Iliad* xx, a victory for Turnus now would be 'beyond what is fated'.[18] The strength in battle which Turnus is losing as the day wears on is now taken from him by Juno; the hero's power flags; he retreats, plunges into the Tiber and is carried back to his comrades. This leap into the Tiber is a 'pre-echo' of Horatius Cocles' famous leap. Cocles is depicted on Aeneas's Shield, along with Cloelia, an Etruscan hostage who also escaped into the Tiber and swam to safety.[19]

Turnus's retreat (the first of his two escapes by water, the second being in x) is itself an Iliadic turn in the fortunes of war. In *Iliad* viii, the 'unfinished battle book', in which the Trojans first succeed in counter-attacking during Achilles' absence – the start of Zeus's fulfilment of his promise to Thetis – Hector nearly breaks through despite the opposition of Hera; but night falls, too soon for the Trojans, welcome to the Achaians. The surge of fighting in viii is ineffectual and confused, the real break-through for Hector not coming until later. The triumph of Turnus in ix is the triumph of Hector, first the

---

[18] *Iliad* 20.30 (ὑπέρμορον). The words of Zeus are 'I fear that [Achilles] may storm the wall beyond what is fated.'
[19] *Aen.* 8.649–51.

unsatisfactory and interrupted attack in VIII, then the resumed and greater *aristeia* of XII, XV and XVI. In XV the exhortation of Nestor to the Achaians to acquit themselves like men is the model for Mnestheus's exhortation in *Aeneid* IX. In the *Aeneid*, the Rutulian attack in the Trojan camp is interrupted by the divine intervention of Iris.[20] Turnus, exhausted by personal vendetta, retreats at the moment of potential triumph (another Homeric echo: Ajax under fire in *Iliad* XVI). In the ebb and flow of attack and counter-attack which articulate the enormous narrative of the *Iliad*, the unfinished battle book of *Iliad* VIII offers a check to the Trojan offensive which surges forward again through the central books of the poem. Virgil has a much shorter narrative span for his Iliad, four books, into which he compresses the broad outline of the Homeric conflict from books VIII to XXII; his structure of movement and counter-movement is sharper, less wayward, tighter, he pays scrupulous attention to the laws of cause and effect and to military probability. He does not try, nor would he have been able, to represent the multiplicity of views, voices, characters, perspectives, the sheer density of Homer, a poet working with an enormous mass of traditional material in which the emphases continually shift within and around the narrative core, never quite lost sight of for long, the choice or perhaps the invention of Homer himself, the story of the wrath of Achilles.

The endings and beginnings of books in a *carmen perpetuum* ('continuous poem') are of special significance. They expect, and bear, close scrutiny. They carry the reader across gaps, allowing him either to pause in his reading or to continue. They articulate changes in time and place. They pick up echoes, anticipate or confirm parallels and correspondences, bring into the mind images and symbols from an earlier point in the narrative or from a later point recalled from earlier readings. The river Tiber is an important symbol in the *Aeneid*. It is the Simois and Xanthos of the Italian Iliad, in the

---

[20] Iris also figures in *Iliad* VIII, though it is not she who interrupts Hector's *aristeia* but nightfall, which supervenes during an argument between the gods.

prophetic words of the Sibyl *multo spumantem sanguine*, 'foaming with much blood' (its fellow river is the Numicus, where Aeneas's death and translation occurred). It is the way by which Aeneas reaches the site of Rome. It forms the pastoral transition of the opening passage of *Aeneid* VII. It dominates the first section of VIII, in which Aeneas prays for protection to the personified and manifest Tiberinus:

> O father Tiber with your sacred stream,
> Receive Aeneas and keep him safe from peril at the last.

Now at the end of IX it receives Turnus, washes his wounds, bears him back safe to his comrades. The word *laetum* is strikingly and perhaps strangely applied to Turnus in the last line of IX; it was a key word for the receptive, eager and optimistic Aeneas of book VIII. But Virgil needs to emphasise that the river of Italy receives and succours all her sons, indigenous no less than immigrant. Structurally, the end of IX takes us back to the pastoral opening of VII and completes the third quarter of the epic and the first half of the Iliadic *maius opus*. It makes a strong and historically significant reference to the river as a source of succour. It offers a decrescendo in the narrative leading us briefly away from the war and preparing us, by a strikingly dramatic transition, to read the opening of X, the council of the Olympian gods, which grandly ushers in the last movement of the poem.

Thus in *Aeneid* IX Virgil has begun his Iliad, his *maius opus*, and also the task of writing the Homeric wrath theme out of his Iliad. But in writing out the wrath theme he did not write out wrath. There is much wrath in the last books of the *Aeneid*, and Aeneas himself does not escape it, but it is the wrath of Achilles against Hector, not against Agamemnon. When in *Aeneid* X Aeneas returns to the fight he returns in triumph at the head of fresh Etruscan troops. Homer's Achilles also returned to the fighting in *Iliad* XX, at the head of his Myrmidons. But he returned after and because of Patroclus's death. Aeneas returns from an absence prompted not by wrath and pique and refusal to fight (unthinkable in a hero renowned alike for *pietas* and military prowess) but by military necessity. He has been behaving not like a sulking Homeric hero but like a Roman *dux*. And he returns to the war before the death of Pallas. Indeed he cannot prevent that death; it lies heavy on his heart throughout the sombre eleventh book. Pallas has been entrusted to his protection. But he did not cause his death, as Achilles' wrath had let Patroclus die. Virgil had to write the wrath theme out of his Iliad, for the enormous and paranoid egotism of Achilles was inappropriate to a Stoic hero and father-figure of the Roman nation.

4. The council of the gods

Knauer has argued[21] that the model in Homer for the scene on Olympus with which *Aeneid* x opens is the scene between Achilles and Patroclus at the start of *Iliad* xvi. Certainly *Aeneid* x corresponds structurally to *Iliad* xvi. In his telescoped and speeded-up Iliad Virgil has reached his Patrocleia. There are a number of parallels. But there are also significant modifications. Achilles does not return in the Patrocleia, though the appearance of Patroclus on the battlefield in his armour (which causes many of the warriors to believe Achilles has indeed returned)[22] constitutes a kind of mock- or shadow-return of the hero. In *Aeneid* x Aeneas returns, in a grandly resonant passage, at the head of his Etruscan allies, *before* the death of Pallas. The catalogue of these new Etruscan allies corresponds to the catalogue of the Myrmidons who follow Patroclus into battle in *Iliad* xvi. At a moment of crisis in both poems reinforcements are introduced into the narrative.

But it is clearly important to understand why Virgil needed a change of scene to Olympus at the start of his Patrocleia. It is as valuable to study the differences between the openings of the two books as to draw attention to their structural

[21] *Die Aeneis* 296–8.   [22] *Iliad* 16.278–83.

resemblance. Indeed, it is possible to over-stress the structural parallel here. There is an unsurpassable human sadness in the encounter between Achilles, who will not fight, and Patroclus, who will fight and die. Patroclus weeps because the Achaians are losing good men. He begs Achilles to act, or, if he is forbidden by pride or scruple, to allow *him* to lead the Myrmidons, who are fresh and unweary (like the Etruscans whom Aeneas will lead into battle in x). Proleptically, Patroclus's tears dominate the opening of *Iliad* XVI; it is characteristic of him (we think of his selflessness in *Iliad* XI when he pauses in his mission to Achilles to administer first aid to the wounded Eurypylos) to weep for others, though himself doomed (Homer says that his request to Achilles was a prayer for his own death); and it is equally characteristic of Achilles to respond to his grief without any reference to a possible fault on his own part. He compares his friend's grief to the tears of a small child on a walk, wanting to be picked up by its mother – one of those Homeric similes whose simple humanity surprises and delights the modern reader – and he wonders whether Patroclus has had bad news from home; only then does he consider that the tears might be occasioned by the deaths of many of the Argives – 'through their own transgression', he adds with characteristic defiance and self-righteousness.

One of the most effective transitions in the entire *Iliad* occurs at 16.100ff., when the poet shifts the scene from the colloquy of Achilles and Patroclus back to the battle.

> Now as these two were talking thus to each other, meanwhile
> the volleys were too much for Aias, who could hold no longer
> his place. The will of Zeus beat him back . . .

At this point in the narrative Hector fires the first ship and Achilles orders the Myrmidons into battle under the command of Patroclus. There follow a catalogue of Achilles' fifty ships, and the celebrated prayer of Achilles to Zeus for success in the counter-attack and the safe return of Patroclus ('the father granted him the one prayer and denied him the other'). The battle which is to claim the lives first of Sarpedon and then of Patroclus is now fiercely resumed.

Virgil broadly follows this structure in *Aeneid* x. The council of the gods is followed by a return to the siege as we left it in ix: the transitional verses

> Interea Rutuli portis circum omnibus instant
> sternere caede uiros et moenia cingere flammis
>
> *Meanwhile the Rutuli at every gate threaten*
> *To destroy men with death and ring the walls with fire*

echo a phrase from ix, but now in a different sense: then the walls were ringed with watch-fires, now it is the fire of the enemy. The Trojans, among them the young Ascanius, are on the defensive. This is the moment for Aeneas's spectacular re-entry into the narrative. In a few rapid lines the narrator summarises Aeneas's activities since the end of viii: after leaving Evander, he went to the Etruscan king Tarchon who put his fleet at the heaven-sent foreign leader's disposal, fulfilling the oracles. There follows the catalogue of the thirty Etruscan ships. Through the night Aeneas sails, as he had sailed through the night to Pallanteum in viii, Pallas at his left side (*sinistro adfixus lateri*, another grim proleptic touch). As dawn breaks, the nymphs who were once his old Trojan fleet, now miraculously transformed, swim out to meet him and escort him in. They tell him the bad news of the war. Aeneas prays to the Great Mother for a successful outcome to the second day of fighting. The scene is now set for the Virgilian Patrocleia. For the rest of x, fighting is continuous. The return of Aeneas, splendid on the deck with flashing shield, prefiguring Augustus himself at Actium (as depicted in viii on Aeneas's prophetic Shield), and the encounter with the nymphs who escort him ashore, forms the end of the first section of the book, completing the opening council of the gods. The supernatural ends the first section, the divine began it. Death and mortality will dominate the rest. Virgil needed the scene on Olympus and the marvellous episode of the nymphs to separate the fighting of his Patrocleia from the fighting in IX. The nymphs also serve as links back to IX and indeed back to VII and VIII, the two voyages to the mouth of the Tiber and upstream to Evander's settlement. Both these earlier landfalls are now reinforced in the account of Aeneas's third and final voyage home; in a fine symbolism, his old Trojan ships, now metamorphosed, pilot his new fleet in; the Trojan *nostos*, completed, has become miracle and myth; military reality now lies in the future, with the real nations, Latins and Etruscans; just as the Trojan fleet was metamorphosed, so, soon, will the Trojans themselves be transformed into Italians, and both their Odyssey and their Iliad will be over.

Into this structure Virgil has incorporated the Homeric council of gods which opens *Iliad* XX, the *aristeia* of Achilles. Virgil has telescoped his *Iliad* into four books and a few days of fighting. He begins the *aristeia* of Aeneas in book X. The pathos which colours Achilles' return to battle in Homer's *Iliad*, so movingly articulated at the start of book XVI in the scene between him and Patroclus, has no place in Virgil's story. There is a loss in human sympathy, a gain in moral clarity. And because Virgil has written out the wrath theme, because his hero returns to the war before, not after, the death of his Patroclus, nothing corresponding to the opening scene of *Iliad* XVI would be appropriate. Aeneas and Pallas, to start with, are not boyhood friends united in *Blutbrüderschaft*: they only met in *Aeneid* VIII, when Evander entrusted his son to Aeneas, a relationship of disciple to master, son to father.

Structurally, some other episode, a massive and pivotal opening statement, was necessary. The council of the gods was the answer to the problem. Such councils are a feature of Homeric epic; moreover, Virgil uses the episode to make some comments on the nature of human destiny and history which underpin the moral structure of the entire epic.

The closest parallel in the *Iliad* to Virgil's council is that in

Iliad xx (though there are also, as we shall see, allusions to *Iliad* IV). Achilles is in the full spate of his furious *aristeia*. Zeus expresses a fear (which in Milton's God becomes authorial irony) that Achilles may storm the walls and take Troy 'contrary to what is fated'. He sends forth the gods to war, himself sitting apart. After this scene we return to the fighting and it is now that Homer's Aineias makes his most significant entry into the poem. He wants to engage Achilles, but is divinely prevented from doing so, 'for it is appointed to him to escape, that the race of Dardanus perish not . . . thus shall the might of Aineias reign among the Trojans, and his children's children, who shall be born in the aftertime'.[23]

The gods, who removed Homer's Aineias from the fighting, for if he had faced Achilles he would have been killed, now, in the Virgilian Iliad, send him out against the second Achilles, Turnus. The polyvalent allusions of secondary epic allow Aeneas to appear as a second Achilles, as a second, this time victorious, Hector, and as himself, saved from Troy to fight another day, preserved by Homeric guarantee which enabled later mythography to link Rome directly to Troy.

Book x opens with resounding dactyls: the language is grand and Ennian. The reader who paused at the end of ix where Turnus was carried gently, washed and refreshed, back to his comrades, crosses an invisible gap in narrative space and time.[24]

> Panditur interea domus omnipotentis Olympi
> conciliumque uocat diuum pater atque hominum rex,
> sideream in sedem, terras unde arduus omnis
> castraque Dardanidum aspectat populosque Latinos.
>
> *And now stands open the house of omnipotent Olympus,*
> *And the father of gods and men summons a council*

---

[23] *Iliad* 20.300–8.
[24] The transition is not unlike that between the middle and last sections of *A Passage to India* discussed above, 68–70.

> *To his throne in the stars, whence on high he all the earth,*
> *Even the camp of the Trojans and the Latin people, surveys.*

Jupiter demands an explanation of the present conflict: *quae contra uetitum discordia*, 'What is this civil war in defiance of my veto?'; *abnueram*, 'I forbade it', he says. Throughout epic, there is a narrative tension between the will of the supreme deity, co-ordinate with destiny though in Homer and Virgil capable of being considered separately, and human free will (or the will of other deities). Temporary checks to the will of the supreme deity may be afforded by others, gods or heroes, but in the end the story of the *Iliad* is the story of how 'the will [or design] of Zeus was accomplished'; the *Aeneid* reveals the historical process as the unfolding of destiny, foreknown to Jupiter and his agents. Milton's God, though he had forbidden (*abnuerat*) the eating of the tree of knowledge, saw beyond the fall to the redemption, so that ultimately the tension between his will ('what I will is Fate') and human free will is resolved.

Jupiter's brief speech is followed by long and important speeches by Venus and Juno. Their rhetorical confrontation creates a pause in the narrative of action. We stand back as history is made, to consider its motivating causes, its effects and implications. Venus's speech is full of pathos and irony. She uses a familiar technique: a speaker affects to put an extreme case against himself and his cause, hoping for a refutation and the confirmation of his real secret desires. Can Venus really believe, as she says she does, that the reiterated promises of fate by oracle, deity and shade throughout the poem, all of them in conformity with the will of Jupiter, whom she addresses as *hominum rerumque aeterna potestas*, the very personification of 'everlasting dominion over men and their affairs' – can she really believe that any power, even Juno, can alter those decrees and change the course of destiny? She appears, or affects, to believe it, and, indeed, to believe that the diversion is already being accomplished. Diomede, she believes (in error, as we learn in XI) is about to rise up against his ancient foes, including, no doubt, she says, herself, once wounded by him at Troy. She no longer hopes that the Trojans will gain their promised *imperium*; let them be defeated, let Aeneas resume his wanderings –

> et quacumque uiam dederit Fortuna sequatur
>
> *whatever path fortune provides, let him take it*

– she asks, or affects to ask, only (with a renewal of pathos) that her grandson Ascanius be saved, *positis inglorius armis exigat hic aeuum*, 'let him put off his armour and live inglorious with me'. Then, in a travesty of history which the implied reader will read ironically, 'Let Carthage rule in Italy, there will be no opposition there.' And her last thought is the bitterest irony of all: so traumatic an escape from Troy, so much suffering by sea and land, has it all been for nothing? The Trojans had better have stayed in the ashes of their dead city.

What response from Jupiter – and the reader – is to be elicited from this exercise in self-indulgent hypothesis? When in book I Venus watched the Trojans, storm-tossed and far from the goal of their *nostos*, she had addressed Jupiter in a speech similar in its tone of plaintive reproach, a speech likewise starting with an appeal to Jupiter's omnipotence, *o qui res hominumque deumque aeternis regis imperiis*, 'o thou who rulest the affairs of men and gods in everlasting dominion', and affecting to be resigned to a reversal of the irreversible course of history. Jupiter had answered reassuringly:

> parce metu, Cytherea, manent immota tuorum fata tibi
>
> *Spare your fear, Cytherea, the destiny of your Descendants has not changed*

There then followed Jupiter's and the implied author's unfolding to the Augustan reader of a 'destiny' which was already history or quasi-history. Now, in book X, Venus hopes for the same comfort and reassurance from Jupiter. She does not get it. The tragic context of the Virgilian Iliad requires a different set of responses. The modern reader must experience a sense of crisis, a possible turning of fortune's wheel. Epic is in its larger movement a narrative of the expected; but there must be smaller movements, currents and cross-currents of the unexpected, on which all fictions thrive. If Jupiter can begin a speech *quae contra uetitum discordia?*, if Milton's God can begin a speech 'Nearly it now concerns us to be sure / Of our omnipotence', then the implied author may be trying to generate in his reader a shock of moral dislocation, something more than a twist of the narrative, the shadow across the pure serene of the divine will. Venus's rhetoric articulates the reader's moral bewilderment.

The parabola of the poem's movement is now at the furthest point it ever attains from the golden vision of peace and reassurance unfolded by Jupiter to Venus in book I. Nothing, in the context of book X, seems further away than the time when

> Fast in their iron frame
> Shall the gates of war be shut, and locked inside, war-madness
> Chained, bound, squatting on her arsenal,
> Bloody-mouthed, shall snarl . . .

Now the gates of war have been opened, *Furor* is free and stalks the plains of Latium. And it is with that same *furor*, *acta furore graui*, driven by the weight of wrath, that Juno bursts into speech as soon as Venus has finished, as Hera had done in *Iliad* IV when Zeus spoke on behalf of the Trojans. Virgil has made some use of this earlier Homeric council, which had ended with an uneasy truce between Zeus and Hera, the gods agreeing on only one thing, that the war is to continue, each deity jealously guarding his own sphere of influence. In Virgil's council, Juno's indignant appeal for her sphere of influence ('You, Venus, can act within your province, am I to be forbidden to help the Rutuli?') is an echo of Hera's indignation in *Iliad* IV.

The war in Latium cannot end until Turnus is dead and Aeneas and Latinus can make and keep a peace treaty. To this end, Juno's powers may be further exercised. Neither the demands of the narrative nor those of historical necessity can permit Venus to be comforted.

Jupiter's arbitration at this point is crucial, as is the day of fighting which will follow upon Aeneas's return, the day of the Virgilian Patrocleia. The fighting which starts with the dawn marked at 10.256–7 continues until the beginning of XI. When the nymph Cymodocea escorts Aeneas to land and reviews for him the military situation she says

> crastina lux, mea si non inrita dicta putabis,
> ingentis Rutulae spectabit caedis aceruos.
>
> *Tomorrow's light, if you can take my words as valid,*
> *Will see a great slaughter of the Rutuli.*

The day of book X, then, is crucial, and in Jupiter's arbitration Virgil comes as close as he ever comes to expressing the concept of free will. The nymph gifted with prophetic powers can see something of what the day will bring forth, but Jupiter's statement makes it clear that the future is not rigged in such a way that heroes are mere automata.

> Since between Italians and Trojans there can be
> No peace, nor your strife find an end

(that is, the strife of Venus and Juno),

> Then, what each man's fortune is today, the hope each pursues,
> Trojan or Rutulian, let him carve it out, I'll make no distinction,
> Whether this siege is because of the destiny of the Italians
> Or the mistakes and bad tactics of the Trojans.

> Nor are the Rutuli exempt by me from fate. For each
> Whatever he sets his hand to will bring him toil and fortune.
> King Jupiter is the same for all men.
> Fate will find the way.

In *Iliad* xx the gods, with Zeus's permission, go forth to prepare for war, while Zeus himself sits apart. This is the point in the narrative when Achilles' renewed might seems invincible and when the poet, wishing to postpone the climactic encounter between Achilles and Hector, introduces the abortive encounter between Achilles and Aineias. Apollo inspires Aineias to offer his opposition to Achilles. Hera counters by proposing renewed support for Achilles.

> For all of us have come down from Olympus to take our part
> In this battle, so nothing may be done to him by the Trojans
> On this day.

But Poseidon arbitrates and leads the gods out of the battlefield – to which they do not return in earnest until book xxi after the fight between Achilles and the river-god has already brought Hephaestus into the conflict. 'Let us go apart and watch', says Poseidon, 'and leave the battle to men.' This is a similar situation to that in *Aeneid* x. Jupiter will not on this day permit any intervention or himself take sides in the war. It began without him, let it end without him. We may contrast the intervention of God through his Son in the holy war against Satan in *Paradise Lost* vi (685–703):

> Two days, as we compute the days of heaven,
> Since Michael, and his powers, went forth to tame
> These disobedient, sore hath been their fight
> As likeliest was, when two such foes met armed.
> For to themselves I left them, and thou knowest,
> Equal in their creation they were framed,

> Save what sin hath impaired, which yet hath wrought
> Insensibly, *for I suspend their doom*,
> Whence in perpetual fight they needs must last
> Endless, and no solution will be found.
> War wearied hath performed what war can do,
> And to disordered rage let loose the reins,
> With mountains as with weapons armed, which makes
> Wild work in heaven and dangerous to the main.
> Two days are therefore past, the third is thine.
> For thee I have ordained it, and thus far
> Have suffered, that the glory may be thine
> Of ending this great war, for none but thou
> Can end it.

Milton presents the war in heaven as a stalemate, to be broken on that significant third day by the Son. God did not will the war but once it had happened it was subsumed into his will by having happened, since all history must be seen as thus subsumed. Jupiter in the *Aeneid* presented to Venus in book I a solemn unrolling of the book of destiny, a history which he does not repudiate in book x even though he does not, either, restate it. What he does is to assert, uniquely here, his impartiality: the doctrine 'fate will find the way' carries a bleak dignity. The deity puts off the burden of human responsibility, it becomes man's existential choice, on the plains of Latium man in his lonely destiny must enact history.

Thus the central conflict of the *Aeneid*, between the pro-Trojan Venus and the anti-Trojan Juno, remains in suspense. On this crucial day (*hodie*) the conflict must work itself out without divine interference.

In *Iliad* xx, the strange episode of the rescue of Aineias from Achilles is managed by Poseidon himself 'lest the son of Kronos [Zeus] be angry if Achilles slay him, for it is appointed to him to escape, that the race of Dardanus perish not . . .' In *Aeneid* x Juno is allowed to rescue Turnus temporarily from the battle, but Jupiter makes it clear that her interference and Turnus's respite are only a delay in waiting death, *mora praesentis leti*:

> But if you think you can change the whole course
> Of the war, you nurse a vain hope.

Neither in *Iliad* xx nor in *Aeneid* x is the confrontation between the two principal heroes destined to take place. This still leaves room for manoeuvre for the gods in both epics. There actions, or the rhetoric of their refusal to act, shape the narrative.

The crucial day of *Aeneid* x thus corresponds to the day in *Iliad* xx before the final confrontation of Hector and Achilles. In the *Iliad* Aineias has to yield to Achilles. In Virgil's Iliad, Aeneas will finally confront the 'second Achilles' of the Sibyl's prophecy, and himself take over that role. The stone which in *Iliad* xx Aineias picked up but never threw at Achilles becomes in *Aeneid* xii the stone which Turnus picks up but never throws at Aeneas.

> The wheel is come full circle: I am here.[25]

But first there is the same 'day of suspense' to be lived through, while the gods fiddle with a mechanism they cannot stop or alter, for they are part of it.

> And all sway forward on the dangerous flood
> Of history which never sleeps or dies . . .[26]

Both the Homeric and Virgilian episodes illustrate the difference between the power of Zeus/Jupiter and that of the other gods. In Homer these are passionate and warring, immortal versions of the heroes whose causes they espouse. Occasionally, as with Poseidon, god of the sea, they take on a larger, more elemental and symbolic significance, as do Virgil's Juno and Venus. Venus in particular, mother of Aeneas and hence of the Roman people, the *Aeneadum genetrix*

---

[25] *King Lear*, act v, sc. iii, 174 (Edmund to Edgar).
[26] W. H. Auden, 'August for the People', *Look, Stranger!* (1936) no. 30.

of Lucretius's great prologue to the *De Rerum Natura*, presiding deity of generative fruitfulness and sexual love, had a special and beneficent function in the Roman cosmic system.

The key words of *Aeneid* x, however, are Jupiter's, and they require the reader to give them the greatest possible emphasis. *nullo discrimine habebo*, 'I shall make no distinction.' A Pallas for a Halaesus, a Lausus for a Pallas – Jupiter's arbitration takes its toll of both sides alike. Just as Achilles' prayer in *Iliad* XVI for Patroclus was only partly successful, for Zeus refused Patroclus a safe return, so Aeneas in *Aeneid* x prays for success on the crucial day of battle which follows his return at the head of his Etruscan 'Myrmidons'. But his prayer is only partially successful, for he will lose his Patroclus. Immediately after his prayer, the fateful day is introduced in rushing syllables.

> tantum effatus et interea reuoluta ruebat
> matura iam luce dies noctemque fugarat . . .
>
> *He spoke no more, meanwhile rolled back and rose*
> *The day, light strengthened, night despatched.*

The day that now dawns is not just a day in a mythical past. The poet's use of the historic present helps the reader to see that 'today' as any and every day, a paradigm of life as it must be lived through by us all. If Jupiter can proclaim a suspension of divine interference on one day, he can suspend it on any or every day. Men can no longer assume divine aid or divine hostility. They must act alone. They will find out soon enough whether their actions, the consequences of free will, have won divine approval or provoked divine outrage.

5. The return of Aeneas

The return of Aeneas is one of the great focal points of the narrative, both when one is reading it and in any retrospective view of the work. The atmosphere of the marvellous returns with him, from the eighth book, when his arrival by river at the site of Rome, the gleam of bronze, the painted prows, strike the very landscape with awe, as well as the celebrants at the Great Altar of Hercules, backwoods colonists confronted with the legendary magnificence of Troy. Now on another ship, standing high on deck like Augustus at Actium, Aeneas sails once more into the story to the wonder of those who see him. To the Rutuli and their leader it seems as if the whole sea is rolling towards them, *ea mira uideri*, 'a marvel to behold'.

Virgil sustains and enhances this epiphany of Aeneas with a Homeric simile, of cranes against a stormy sky. And from the hero's helmet stream flames, as from Augustus's head at Actium, a dramatic hyperbole further ornamented by another simile, of a baleful star or comet portending disaster to the enemy, though Virgil characteristically broadens the reader's sympathy with a generalisation so that Sirius is said to bring diseases to wretched mortals. Thus an atmosphere of magic and wonder surrounds each of Aeneas's three arrivals in Latium which articulate the divisions of the Virgilian Iliad. First, the arrival at the mouth of the Tiber, in VII, its pastoral peace reflecting the hitherto untroubled peace of Latinus: Aeneas is then *laetus*, joyful, but this mood of peace and happiness is shattered almost at once. His second arrival, in VIII, at Pallanteum, *in rebus egenis*, a suppliant for aid in a Greek city, as prophesied by the Sibyl, brings him support and comfort, and book VIII ends in joy and wonder again as he puts on the Shield of History, last and most significant pledge of divine providence. Once more he departs on the next stage of his mission, to the Etruscans, while the military situation deteriorates. This third epiphany, also by water, is a prefiguration for the implied reader of Augustus at Actium. He holds up the Shield, and for the first time the Trojans feel a sense of possible victory, *spe suscitat iras*, 'hope reawakens aggression'.

This is the crucial day on which Jupiter has decreed that 'fate will find the way'. The renewed optimism of the Trojans is balanced by a renewed determination on the part of Turnus, and the conflicts of the day will swing to and fro, neither side being able to make a decisive breakthrough. Jupiter's words, *sua cuique exorsa laborem fortunamque ferent*, 'For each, whatever he sets his hand to will bring him toil and fortune', underpin the conclusion of Turnus's *hortatio* to his soldiers as the Etruscan fleet approaches the shore.

> What you longed for in your prayers has happened.
> This is the break-through.
> Be men, and this war is in your grasp. Let each man now
> Think of his wife and home, let each man now recall
> The great and glorious deeds of our ancestors. Let us take them here
> On the water's edge, as they disembark, vulnerable, insecure.
> Fortune favours the bold.

Jupiter's proclamation of divine impartiality is wholly consonant with a comment of the poet when contemplating the destinies of Lausus and Pallas: 'the great ruler of Olympus by no means suffered these two to challenge each other; hereafter did their fate await them, at the hand of a mightier foe'. The reader elicits from the narrative itself a bleak awareness of a deity who has chosen not to intervene in history, but to let its processes work themselves out: 'what I will is fate'. The authorial comment comes from the omniscient narrator, and carries strong Homeric precedent; the *Iliad* contains many such proleptic reflections, taking the reader to a point beyond that which the narrative has so far attained. Jupiter's proclamation of non-intervention is in itself a defining element of the narrative structure seen in retrospective overview as though from the end of the poem.

At the crisis of his brief *aristeia*, Pallas, face to face, not with another untried youth (Lausus) but with Turnus, prays to Hercules, his father's old guest-friend at Pallanteum and erstwhile saviour of the city from Cacus:

> si qua fors adiuuet ausum
uiribus imparibus
>
> *Hoping for help from chance, bold but
In might unequal*

he thus resembles Troilus at Troy, as depicted on the walls of Juno's temple at Carthage and seen there by Aeneas in book I:

> infelix puer atque impar congressus Achilli.

Just as Troilus, 'unlucky boy', was 'no match for Achilles', so Pallas is no match for Turnus. Hercules, powerless to help, weeps. It is his father, Jupiter, who speaks next; eloquent and evocative words which bring back the death of his own son Sarpedon at the hands of Patroclus in *Iliad* XVI, a death which was followed by Patroclus's own.

> Determined each man's day, brief and irrecoverable
> the time
> Of life for everyone. But to extend glory by deeds,
> This is the work of virtue. Under the high walls of
> Troy
> There died so many sons of the gods, yes and
> among them
> Sarpedon, my son. Turnus too by his own
> Fate is called; he is come to the end of his time.

Just as Patroclus draws his spear from Sarpedon 'together with his spirit', so too does Turnus draw his spear from Pallas.

Pallas's courage – he not only faces the enemy but chides his faltering comrades as they run away from the pursuing Latins – is a re-enactment of Sarpedon's when he chides his fellow Lycians in *Iliad* XVI. In Pallas's death are combined the deaths of both Sarpedon and of Patroclus: in the shifting kaleidoscope of war, the tragic events of Homer's Patrocleia are re-enacted and conflated. Sarpedon's death is a major event in the *Iliad* for two reasons. First, he is Zeus's son and provides a test case as to whether Zeus will go so far as to save him from death. But human mortality, in this tragic epic, is stronger than the power of the gods. Secondly, Sarpedon's death carries a further tragic irony in that he dies at the hands of Patroclus, who is himself doomed, the last victim of the death-littered promise of Zeus to Thetis – the greatest and most fatal act of Hector's *aristeia*. Virgil relies on the power and relevance of intertextuality when he makes Jupiter recall the *Iliad* for the implied reader: a modern reader ignorant of the *Iliad* will here miss an essential element in the reading of *Aeneid* x. Jupiter recalls Sarpedon's death at that very moment in the *Aeneid* when Pallas is praying to Hercules for protection against Turnus's attack. Thus the two most important deaths in *Iliad* XVI are transposed and assimilated into *Aeneid* x. When Turnus pulls the spear from Pallas's flesh, Virgil echoes Homer's words at the moment when Patroclus pulls his spear from Sarpedon's flesh: the dying Pallas assumes for a moment the figure and role of Sarpedon. But as soon as Turnus takes Pallas's baldric, Pallas 'becomes' Patroclus and the reader initiates the ultimate Iliadic confrontation between Turnus, wearing the baldric, and Aeneas, the avenging Achilles.

Virgil's proleptic comment on the end of his poem has already been noticed: *Turno tempus erit* . . .

> For Turnus the time will come when he will pray
>   for Pallas
> To be unharmed, give anything for that, and loathe
> This day, these spoils . . .

The reader will remember for how brief a time Hector wore Patroclus's armour, which was Achilles' own, and this memory will itself cast a shadow over the narrative of Virgil's Iliad. He will remember too Zeus's sombre soliloquy as he watches Hector put on that armour: 'you have killed this man's dear friend who was strong and gentle, and taken the armour as you should not have done'.

The violence of Aeneas after Pallas's death has troubled modern readers who wish to see the *Aeneid* as 'civilised poetry'. But Aeneas's role as an Achillean avenger cannot be contained in the mode of civilised poetry. When Aeneas refuses Magus's plea for mercy, for all its Italian operatic eloquence –

> per patrios manis, et spes surgentis Iuli
> te precor –

he answers him as Achilles answered Lycaon in *Iliad* XXI when he told him that until Patroclus's death he had spared the lives of many Trojans, 'but now none shall escape death'.

Turnus's killing of Pallas touched Aeneas closely, for Evander had entrusted him to his protection:

> sub te tolerare magistro
> militiam et graue Martis opus, tua cernere facta
> adsuescat, primis et te miretur ab annis.

*Let him learn under your leadership to endure
Campaigning and the burden of war, watching your
  deeds
While he is young, have you as his ideal.*

Evander's words, his guest-friendship, return to Aeneas's mind when he hears of Pallas's death. What time has he had to teach him the art of war? Thus the motive for his Achillean fury and violence in 10.510–65 is again a transformed and purified version of the wrath of Achilles. Homer's Achilles feels savage and bitter grief for Patroclus's death; his anger against Agamemnon has led inexorably to that death. No similar trait of character in Aeneas is shown by Virgil to be the cause of Pallas's death. He was unlucky; he was fated to meet Turnus; this element in the narrative was structurally central to Virgil's Iliad. But by introducing Pallas into the story through his father Evander Virgil has emphasised a psychological force which springs as much from his own Roman convictions about *pietas* as from Homeric ones. Indeed, the two poets share a deep humanity and a sense of the love between father and son. In *Iliad* XXIII, the ghost of Patroclus reminds Achilles that his father Peleus took him into his house when still a child and made him in due course his son's squire. In *Iliad* XXIV Priam appeals to Achilles by reminding him of his father. In *Aeneid* X when Aeneas kills Lausus, *mentem patriae subiit pietatis imago*, 'there came into his mind the image of his own love for his father'. Such emotions do not belong exclusively to any one cultural tradition; they are part of our common humanity, without its share of which no poetry can be great. When Liger begs Aeneas for his life after Aeneas has killed his brother Lucagus, *per qui te talem genuere parentes*, 'by the parents who made you what you are', Aeneas says to him 'Die; let not brother desert brother.' But Liger had told Aeneas *he* was going to kill *him* and had taunted him with a sneering reference to his divinely engineered escapes from Diomede and Achilles at Troy.[27] Part of Virgil's intention in the *Aeneid* is to remind his readers that Rome's originator was as renowned for fighting as for *pietas*. We must not forget that for all his impartial humanity and notwithstanding the nobility of the character of Hector, Homer was a Greek poet, and for him most Trojans were to some extent tainted with the fault of Paris — lack of military discipline, effeminacy; Aeneas was after all the son of Paris's special champion, Aphrodite. In the *Aeneid* his reputation as a warrior, not only supreme among the Trojans since Hector's death but the equal of Achilles himself in warlike prowess (and his superior in *pietas*), must be established. He is amply shown by Virgil to be capable of pity. He does not show pity consistently in the fighting; he remains an epic hero, romanised but not 'civilised'. Some of those he kills exist only at the moment of their meeting with him, in the manner of the *Iliad*.[28] His 'arrogant and sarcastic speech'[29] when he kills Tarquitus is closely modelled on that of Achilles when he kills Lycaon in *Iliad* XXI. Achilles says:

[27] *Aen.* 10.581–3; *Iliad* 5.311ff., 446ff., 20.290ff. An interesting example of how Virgil 'plants' his allusions to the Homeric text. Liger shows an acquaintance with Aeneas's military record which is a metaphor or surrogate for the implied reader's knowledge of Homer. As Aeneas himself observed (l. 459–60) *quis iam locus . . . quae regio in terris nostri non plena laboris?* What Liger 'knows' is the *Iliad*: it is not the events which signify but their Homeric record.
[28] See J. Griffin, *Homer on Life and Death* (Oxford 1980) 103–43.
[29] Williams (ed.), *Aeneid VII–XII* (London 1973) on 10.557ff.

> 'Lie there now among the fish, who will lick the
>   blood away
> from your wound, and care nothing for you, nor
>   will your mother
> lay you on the death-bed and mourn over you, but
>   Skamandros
> Will carry you spinning down to the wide bend of
>   the salt water.
> And a fish will break a ripple shuddering dark on
>   the water
> As he rises to feed upon the shining fat of Lycaon.

Aeneas says:

> 'There now, dread warrior, lie. Nor shall your dear
>   mother
> Bury you deep in your fatherland:
> You shall be left to the birds of prey, or as you
>   drown
> The waves shall take you away and the fishes lick
>   your wounds.

There are in heroic epic as many ways of killing as there are of dying. And in the twentieth century it hardly needs saying that war breeds and is bred by violence; that in war acts of kindness and pity are still performed, but that if they were the rule rather than the exception there would be no more war.

Like Homer, Virgil is aware of the need for *uariatio* in a long stretch of battle narrative. At the height of Aeneas's *aristeia*, when *furor* rages on the plain of Latium, Juno asks Jupiter's permission to rescue Turnus from the battle. We have noted that Homer's Aineias was himself rescued from battle 'so that the race of Dardanus might not perish' in *Iliad* xx, but Virgil has also assimilated another structural parallel, the rescue of Hector from Achilles later in the same book. There, as here in *Aeneid* x, the warrior fated to die is given a brief and poignant reprieve. Hector is caught up in a mist by Apollo, which postpones his doom but does not alter it. What is postponed, we may say, is the moment at which the reader comes to Hector's death. The poet manipulates this postponement by inserting digressions, extensions and elastications of narrative temporality. Thus the amount of 'real' time separating the reader, at a particular point in the narrative, from the climax of the hero's death, may be several weeks or a single day. When the climax does finally occur, it must seem to the reader that no further postponement would be tolerable. The decisive act must finally be accomplished. When the reader looks back over the act, and the various postponements and digressions which preceded it, it will seem inevitable that it was reached when it was reached, and not earlier.[30]

In *Iliad* v Apollo made a phantom Aineias when the real Aineias was threatened by Diomede. There are resonances in that episode which are heard again in Virgil. It is Diomede, now settled in Italy, to whom Turnus has sued for help against Aeneas and, as we learn in xi, sued in vain. Virgil has also made use of the second rescue of Homer's Aineias in *Iliad* xx when he is confronted with Achilles: Poseidon sheds a mist over Achilles' eyes. This follows a dialogue between Poseidon and Hera, in which Hera reiterates her implacable hatred of the Trojans, while Poseidon shows concern for Aineias both because of his piety and because he knows that 'it is appointed to him to escape that the race of Dardanus perish not'. Virgil thus blends two different Iliadic motifs: that of the temporary reprieve of a hero who is doomed, and the saving of a hero not fated to die within the temporality of the epic narrative.

Virgil's description of the phantom Aeneas follows another Olympian dialogue, between Jupiter and Juno, which begins Homerically but in tone and treatment develops far beyond its model in *Iliad* iv, a passage already used by Virgil in his great opening council in x. This second council (10.605–32) starts with Jupiter saying to Juno, as Aeneas's irresistible *aristeia*

---

[30] Cf. Tolstoi, *War and Peace* ix. i: 'Each man lives for himself, using his freedom to attain his personal aims, and feels with his whole being that he can now do or abstain from doing this or that action. But as soon as he has done it, that action performed at a certain moment in time becomes irrevocable, and belongs to history, in which it has not a free but a predestined significance.'

continues, 'Of course you were thinking it is Venus who is propping up the Trojans, not their own prowess.' Zeus in *Iliad* IV had taunted Hera when he said 'Aphrodite is helping Paris, but Menelaus's divine protectors are conspicuously absent'. Zeus also alluded to Aphrodite/Venus's assiduity in the Trojan cause, but what he said in *Iliad* IV was plain fact. In *Aeneid* X Venus is not helping Aeneas.

Homer's Hera answered Zeus angrily, taunt for taunt. Virgil's Juno is deeply aware of Turnus's approaching doom and of the long delayed but inevitable triumph of the Trojans which she has so constantly and bitterly opposed. Her answer is full of pathos and self-pity. 'You no longer love me; if you did, you would let me rescue Turnus.' She would like to believe, against all the evidence of fate, that Jupiter will alter destiny itself and save Turnus altogether, but she leaves herself a way out: a temporary reprieve will be better than nothing and, on the narrative level, is exactly what is now needed to keep the action in suspense and to allow the irruption of Mezentius into battle as Aeneas's chief enemy in Turnus's absence, an irruption which leads to his and his son's deaths at the hands of Aeneas, and provides the climax and conclusion of book X.

> 'If what you are asking is a delay and for the doomed
> Young hero respite, snatch him from immediate fate.
> That much is granted. But if some deeper motive
> Lurks in your plea, and you think you can change the whole course
> Of the war, you nurse a vain hope.'

And Juno:

> 'What if, that which lies reluctant on your lips,
> You granted in your heart, and Turnus should live?
> No. Death's burden waits for him, innocent of crime. Else I

Am mistaken and deceived. Oh, if only my fears
   were false,
And you would — for you can — change your
   decree.'

The council of the gods in *Iliad* IV shows the Homeric gods in their worst light, with Zeus yielding to Hera's insatiable desire to destroy Ilion ('perhaps if you were to enter the gates and eat Priam and his sons raw, your anger might be assuaged'), but yielding reluctantly, and demanding in exchange the right to destroy some other city without demur by Hera. Zeus's personal feelings for Troy are counter to what is destined. Virgil's Jupiter is wholly committed to destiny, his will fully co-ordinate with it. At the end of the Homeric council the two warring armies are reported by Homer as saying helplessly 'Either the war will be resumed, or Zeus will establish peace': that is, at this point the war might end or not end. The cynical and immoral debate on Olympus determines that it shall continue. If it did not, there would be no *Iliad*. The poet and reader must therefore assent to the gods' will.

Virgil's dialogue between Jupiter and Juno serves a different purpose and its tone is quite different. True, Jupiter's opening words seem deliberately calculated to provoke Juno, but their irony is not so much taunting as illustrative of Jupiter's all-seeing power over the minds of gods and men alike. 'I know what you are thinking now,' he says to Juno; 'you are thinking that all this is Venus's doing, not the result of Trojan prowess, and' (blandly) 'you are right.' Jupiter refers to Juno's Homeric obsession with Venus's championship of Troy, a resentment which has its origins in the judgement of Paris:

> manet alta mente repostum
> iudicium Paridis spretaeque iniuria formae
> et genus inuisum et rapti Ganymedis honores

> *deep in her heart it sticks,*
> *The judgement of Paris, her beauty spurned,*
> *That hated race, Ganymede grabbed and exalted*

Ganymede, Zeus's cup-bearer, of whom Juno is also jealous, was a Trojan too: her hatred of the Trojans, which troubled Homer's Zeus because he could not share it yet also could not alter the city's doom, becomes in the *Aeneid* an *idée fixe*. In Homer Hera won; in the *Aeneid* she loses, yet what she loses ultimately is her hatred and her obsession. She becomes free of the past.

Jupiter's words to Juno are more than an ironic dig. They show his power to read her thoughts. She does blame Venus; like all obsessives she would prefer to attribute an event to her obsession than to its true cause, in this case Trojan prowess, with Aeneas stimulated to *furor* by his grief for Pallas. Jupiter articulates Juno's fears, her heart-sickness, as her answer shows:

> Why, fair consort,
> Do you provoke a heart sick with fear at your sad words?

The word I translate 'provoke' (*sollicitas*) Williams renders 'taunt', in order to strengthen his sense of the passage's irony, but it means 'trouble' or 'disturb'.[31] Juno has a premonition of the end: yet, as people do when they know in their hearts that something is inevitable yet retain a secret, half-real, half-pretended reservation that even now, against all the odds, it may yet turn out differently, so she too leaves a tiny crack of light, in her heart the door of fate is even now not quite shut on Turnus, there is still time for all-powerful Jupiter to change his mind, the impossible can still happen, the inevitable need not occur. The psychological insight of this passage is acute and powerful, more Dantesque than Homeric.[32]

The episode of the phantom Aeneas is a strange piece of writing in Virgil's most fantastic and imaginative style, owing as much to Lucretian theories of *imagines* as to Homer. Juno endows the phantom with

---

[31] See *Oxford Latin Dictionary* s.v., where the sense of 'taunt' does not appear.
[32] For Dante's insight into other minds, see e.g. *Inf.* 13.25–7, *Purg.* 21.103–11.

> words without substance,
> Speech without intelligence, the power of
>   movement,
> Like the ghosts supposed to hover after death,
> Or phantom forms which trick the sleeping brain.

The simile is weirdly effective, and the reader who has read the last book of the poem will pick up also a proleptic shadow of the final scene, in which the real Aeneas confronts a Turnus who moves to the horror of death like an automaton in a dream,

> But he cannot feel himself run or move,
> Or raise his hand or shift the great stone,
> But as in dreams, in a night of heavy sleep,
> We seem desperately to need to run,
> Yet at the moment of crisis we fail, our tongues
> Have no voice, our bodies no responses,
> We are paralysed and cannot cry or speak,
> So from Turnus, whichever way his courage tried
>   to break out,
> The dread goddess withheld power. Confused
>   images
> Trouble his mind . . .

In *Iliad* XXII the failure of Achilles to catch Hector and of Hector to escape Achilles is likened to a dream in which the pursuer never catches the pursued and the pursued never escapes. Virgil has taken this familiar dream-experience of frustrated movement (whose persistence seems to indicate the survival of an archetype) and developed it in terms of a traditional epic motif. But in *Aeneid* XII the use of the first person plural (*uidemur*, 'we seem') makes the reader identify with the experience as one he has shared and thus draws him into empathy with Turnus's final paralysis of will. So in this earlier passage in X, the episode of the phantom, another Homeric motif, is brought into the human light of shared dream-experience for the reader through the simile. The ghosts supposed to hover after death, the phantom forms which trick the sleeping brain, are phenomena which Lucretius explained materialistically so that men would no longer be afraid of them.[33] The epic phantom, the automaton in the form of Aeneas, may be related by the reader, through the common ground of the simile, to his own experience; and because the simile takes us into the world of dreams the reader can make sense of this episode in terms of the final confrontation between the real Aeneas and a Turnus who, outlawed now by Jupiter himself, has become a kind of phantom or automaton, no longer able to command his old heroic *uirtus*, a man already dead.

One final point must be made about this passage. The phantom Aeneas, apparently in fearful flight, hides on board one of the Etruscan ships; thither Turnus pursues it, Juno breaks the mooring, and the ship drifts out to sea. The humiliated and badly shaken Turnus considers both suicide and an attempt to swim ashore, but Juno carries the ship safely round to land and deposits Turnus back in the city of his father. This scene echoes the end of IX when Turnus was carried to safety by the Tiber. This is his second escape by water, and it is his last. Its manner, the deception of the phantom, continues to haunt him in book XI and contributes something to the growing sense of despair which comes over him as the poem, and his own life, draw to a close.

His removal from the battle-scene marks the transition to the final triad of book X, the *aristeia* of Mezentius, *contemptor deum*, 'despiser of the gods'. The poet signals the change by the emphatic *at*:

> At Iouis interea monitis Mezentius ardens
> succedit pugnae . . .
>
> *But now it was Jupiter's thinking that sent Mezentius*
> *Berserk into battle . . .*

He comes in to replace Turnus, keeping the contest even: Juno's temporary protection of Turnus is balanced, briefly, by

[33] Lucretius, *DRN* 4.722–76.

his deeds of prowess. The final triad is strongly Iliadic in its proliferation of similes and its presentation of Mezentius as a traditional epic hero, only concerned with single combat and personal glory. Aeneas kills his son Lausus (a Lausus for a Pallas) and finally Mezentius himself (a surrogate for Turnus, who has lived to fight again, in XII). But the reader leaves the Iliadic world again for the world of Italian sentiment in the touching lament of Mezentius for his son: it is an anticipation of the grief-laden eleventh book, when Evander learns of Pallas's death. It is one of Virgil's finest soliloquies, deeply felt and strongly written, and ending in a characteristic expression of feeling towards which the poet is always responsive, the longing for the end of life, which is quite foreign to the philosophy of the *Iliad*.

> Now I live still, and am not yet gone from the
>   light and from men,
> But I am going.

Alongside these lines must be placed two other sentiments in this final *aristeia* of book X, which serve to relieve and distance us from the violence and grandeur of war. First, there is a couplet depicting the gods watching the conflict from Olympus; they feel an unhomeric and wholly Virgilian empathy for a conflict so evenly balanced that both sides labour in vain: it is a summing up of the pointlessness of war.

> The gods in Jupiter's house feel pity for the
>   pointless anger
> Of either side, and for all the efforts of men . . .

The second example of pathos occurs in the account of the death of Mezentius's young son Lausus – a Lausus for a Pallas, the very embodiment of that bleak and evenly balanced state of the war in book X: *nullo discrimine habebo*. Before Aeneas kills Lausus he is attacked by Mezentius but the latter's spear misses Aeneas and strikes Antores. This hero, once a comrade of Hercules (presumably a younger companion) who had joined Evander's brigade, is nowhere else mentioned by Virgil. In his epitaph

> Unlucky, he is brought down by a wound meant for another. He looks up
> To the sky, and dying remembers Argos, his beloved land.

Virgil has finely transferred a poignant motif of the *Iliad*, that of the hero dying far from home. But Virgil's empathy is distinguished from the Homeric handling of the motif by the word *reminiscitur*: it is not merely that the poet introduces the idea of a hero dying far from home, leaving the reader to respond to the pathos of the situation; he identifies the last feeling of the dying man as a nostalgia, so that the reader's sense of pathos is that of Antores himself.

Virgil also gives its full weight of pathos to Lausus's loyalty to his father Mezentius, that typical embodiment of war lust. Mezentius, *contemptor diuum*, acknowledges only one god, his right hand, *dextra mihi deus*, he says, with a terrifying self-sufficiency, and when he strikes a foe down he says, 'but as for me, let the father of gods and men see to that', thus expressing his indifference to divine mercy. Jackson Knight translates 'the so-called father of gods and men', presumably because the Latin is an Ennian phrase (*diuum pater atque hominum rex*) so that Mezentius's use of it is a kind of sneer, like an atheist quoting the Bible. The picture of the raging Mezentius forms the final grim tableau of book x: his *furor*, his challenge to his son's slayer, a kind of suicide, in fulfilment of his pledge not long to outlive his son, leave the reader as though himself in the middle of a battle, in which hatred, revenge, bloodshed and death are the sole objects of human courage and endeavour.

Readers of the *Aeneid* do not always attend sufficiently to Virgil's indications of narrative time. In x, a day which began at 257 with the return by sea of Aeneas at the head of his Etruscan reinforcements, has ended with the deaths of Pallas, Lausus and Mezentius, and many others. The previous day

(9.459 – 10.256) had been a day of Trojan disaster, following the night raid and the deaths of Nisus and Euryalus, a re-enactment of the siege of Troy, a day without Aeneas. The day now ended has reversed this fortune and the two days have thus together illustrated and exemplified 10.755–9, where the struggle was even and death fell impartially on both armies while the gods watched with pity the swing and balance of war as the whole grim tragedy of the *Iliad* was played out again over the peaceful fields of Saturn's Italy and the shadow of the age of heroes passed across the land.

6. The funeral of Pallas

Book XI is the only book of the *Aeneid* to open with a dawn-formula. The mood of this opening is in strong contrast to the deliberately controlled savagery of the end of X, the defiant death-speech of Mezentius and the remarkable cluster of violent and aggressive words in the final lines:

> '*hostis amare*, quid *increpitas mortemque minaris*?
> nullum in *caede nefas*, nec sic ad *proelia* ueni,
> nec tecum meus haec pepigit mihi foedera Lausus.
> unum hoc per si qua est uictis uenia *hostibus* oro:
> corpus humo patiare tegi. scio *acerba* meorum
> circumstare *odia*: hunc oro, defende *furorem*
> et me consortem nati concede sepulcro.'
> haec loquitur, *iuguloque* haud inscius accipit *ensem*
> undantique animam diffundit in arma cruore.

> '*My bitterest foe, why do you have to crack death-threats
>   at me?
> I wouldn't have gone to war if I'd scruples about killing.
> And when you killed my son there were no concessions,
> But if there are such, for the defeated, then I ask only
>   this:*

> Let my body be buried deep. I know my own people's
>   hatred
> Is waiting on every side. Protect me from their fury
> And let my son and me share the same sepulchre.'
> He spoke; and deliberately offered his throat to the sword
> And drained his soul out on a stream of blood.

Hated even by his own men, redeemed only by his love for his son, Mezentius dies. It is as though in his arrogance he deliberately shares with his killer the responsibility for his own death. Now 'the monstrous anger of the guns' gives place to a solemn ritual, the burial of the dead, which takes up two days of a twelve-day truce. On the third day (11.210) there is a war council of the Latins, occupying the central section of the book, whose structure follows the usual triadic pattern. This third day, which ends with the end of the book, sees the renewal of battle: the final section is dominated by the *aristeia* of Camilla.

Thus book XI offers a great variety of tone and incident. The opening is dark and majestic, with a drum-like, leaden repetition of the word *maestus* ('gloomy', 'sombre'), a form of which is found eleven times in the book (nine times in the other three war-books, IX, X, XII, put together, and fourteen times in books I–VIII). The central section is a rhetorical debate in which Turnus and a new character, Drances, play large parts, while the final section is varied and relieved by the presence of Camilla, the first part played in the poem by a woman since the 'Bacchic' scenes in VII.

The last three books of the *Aeneid* are the most complex in structure and the richest in variety of mood and incident. They make enormous demands on the reader's concentration. It is the reader who must relate the divisions of the narrative to each other and gradually construct as complete a meaning as possible for the whole. Meanwhile, the reader will become increasingly aware not only of a narrator who links the various parts of the poem, but also of an 'implied author' who becomes, in the last three books, a more and more considerable and indeed dominant element in the poem's 'meaning'. The more use Virgil makes of Homer's *Iliad*, the more the modern reader is driven back to that source and the more he has to make an assessment of Virgil's dependence on, and divergence from, his model. It is like having to read two epics at once.[34]

The breaks and intervals between books, and between triads in each book, become charged with greater significance as the reading proceeds. We have already noticed the gap between the end of ix, Turnus carried *laetus* back to his own troops, and the grand opening of x

> panditur interea domus omnipotentis Olympi
>
> *And now the gates of omnipotent heaven are opened*

in which Jupiter proclaims his refusal to take sides. Throughout book x the implied author was never far away, directing the reader to the shifting fortunes of the narrative, making him ask what divine indifference means in terms of human misery – does it differ much from divine interference? Jupiter's lofty statement

> rex Iuppiter omnibus idem.
> fata uiam inuenient.
>
> *King Jupiter is the same for all men.*
> *Fate will find the way.*

is separated by paragraphs of violence and death from 10.758–9, where

> the gods in Jupiter's house feel pity for the
>   pointless anger
> Of either side, and for all the efforts of men.

In that passage, antithesis follows antithesis, and the repetitions and pairings of words comment on the action narrated,

---

[34] On the idea of intertextuality, as distinct from 'simple allusion or reminiscence', see Culler, *Pursuit* 100–18.

indeed do more than comment; they make of it a rhetorical representation which brings the narrative to a virtual standstill and stalemate. Both sides attack, both are winning, both are losing, neither will yield. Juno watches on one side, Venus on the other, and in the middle of the conflict a pale Fury out of hell keeps the war going. Just so, at the battle of Actium on Vulcan-Virgil's vatic shield, we have seen, and Aeneas has seen, the gods ranged on either side, with the war-god raging indiscriminately at the heart of the conflict, Civil Strife, Bellona and the Furies at his side.

A conflict which neither side can win for a long time, a war of attrition, is a *donnée* of Homer's *Iliad*, and accounts to a considerable degree for the psychological tensions so brilliantly drawn in the first two books of the *Iliad*, the quarrel between Achilles and Agamemnon and the latter's weak and ill-judged testing of the troops. Virgil's Iliad lasts only a few days, yet in this brief time he includes this aspect of the Trojan war, its sense of stalemate, frustration, and tension. In Homer's *Iliad* there is no final end to the war, though the death of Hector, the Trojans' only real champion, acts as a symbolic prefiguration of that end. But Hector's death is not the end of Homer's narrative. In book XXIV Achilles gives back Hector's body to Priam, a personal decision made not (as Achilles characteristically insists) in response to Priam's supplication ('I myself am minded to give him back to you') but in conformity to the expressed concern of Apollo ('Achilles has destroyed pity') and the will of Zeus, who refuses to interfere directly but sends Thetis to plead with her son: a symmetry which mirrors the situation in book I. This gesture of reconciliation ends the story of the wrath of Achilles in a mood of love and pity but is far from prefiguring – indeed its tone and mood contradict – the end of Troy as we see it in *Aeneid* II, when the Greeks (now without Achilles) showed no pity to their conquered foes. This is why an epic about the wrath of Achilles 'means' to every reader something much more complete and all-embracing than the proclaimed subject might suggest. The motif of the eventual fall of Troy, repeated prophetically several times in the poem, helps to create in the reader a sense of a larger meaning which demands a response to the total context of the Trojan war, from its remote first cause, through the sacrifice of Iphigeneia, the quarrel with Agamemnon, the deaths of Patroclus and Hector, and so down to the coming of the Amazon, the death of Achilles, the wooden horse, and the sack of the city.

In the *Aeneid* the death of Turnus and the end of the war in Latium are the same. But they are not the end of the whole story or of the significance of the *Aeneid*. Through various prophetic passages the poet brings into the narrative events which lie beyond the heroic age, events which Aeneas, gazing on the Shield, delights in as pictures, while ignorant of their meaning. In a curious way, this too has become prophetic: for Virgil's implied Augustan reader, those events whose meaning Aeneas could not understand were his own history, but the modern reader will identify with Aeneas, delighting in images whose historical meaning he may not be able to reconstruct. Yet he must take his unfamiliarity with Roman history into his reading of the *Aeneid*; as he may also, perhaps, have to take his unfamiliarity with the Bible into his reading of *Paradise Lost*. 'An epic', said Pound, 'is a poem containing history', and by history we may also understand legends, myths and traditional tales as well as 'what happened in the past'. The modern reader may bring to his reading of secondary epic ignorance of the past, so that, indeed, the epic becomes all that he knows of the past: the *Aeneid* will contain for him, as it did for many in the times when Greek culture was forgotten, the whole of the *Iliad* and the fall of Troy and the subsequent *nostoi*. It will also contain the triumph of Augustus.

But 'meaning' for a reader of literary epic does not stop with knowledge of facts, legends and Homer. For the reader of the second half of the *Aeneid* – and that reader will additionally achieve a retrospective sense of books I–VI different from any he would have gained had the second half not been attempted – what may now come across most intensely is the poet himself, not the epic narrator of a Romanised Homeric conflict, but the

THE FUNERAL OF PALLAS

commentator and moraliser on a spectacle of misery, carnage and 'impartial' disaster for both sides. A heroic poem expressing hatred of war is not wholly surprising: many passages in the *Iliad* express an intense and possibly traditional nostalgia for peace as it was before the Achaians came, while others depict the waste and madness of war. But in the *Aeneid* such sentiments dominate and colour the entire narrative. The presence and sensibilities of the empathising poet emerge more and more strongly as the reader encompasses the closing books of the epic.

Indeed, by the end of x, the reader's own sense of the war-narrative as a rhetoric of violent images has become more intense and more restless. After the deaths of Nisus and Euryalus in ix, have come the deaths of Pallas, Lausus, Mezentius; the last word of x is blood, the last image that of blood spurting from Mezentius's throat over his armour, the last speech that of Mezentius, proud, bitter, contemptuous, ready for Aeneas's sword, asking only, as Hector had once asked, for safe burial: the whole scene forms, in terms of epic narrative, a scene from an imaginary theatre of cruelty and of the absurd. Aeneas does not answer Mezentius in the violent and characteristically rejective fashion in which Achilles had answered Hector. He gives, indeed, no answer, and the book ends abruptly, as does xii, with an act of almost ritualised bloodshed.

From that ending of x to the dawn which opens xi the reader has to bridge an eloquent gap or blank in the narrative. Indeed, the first line of xi

> Oceanum interea surgens Aurora reliquit

with the echo of *interea* from 10.1, *Panditur interea . . .*, serves a similar kind of narrative bridge-function. Aeneas, as this day dawns, though troubled by Pallas's death, his thoughts wholly on the dead and the need for burial (*sociis dare tempus humandi* in line 2), does first his duty as a Roman: he gives thanks to the gods for victory as the new day starts. We may recall the beginning of book viii when after a troubled night

Aeneas faces the rising sun and prays to the river-god Tiberinus for protection, before he goes upstream to Pallanteum. Aeneas *imperator* has become Aeneas *pontifex*, *pius* Aeneas, as he is again, supremely, in the final book. The narrative now slows down to the rhythm of a funeral cortège, as we settle to a deeply felt slow movement in the symphony, a long-drawn-out, solemn funeral march.

The opening of XI is both a continuation of, and a break from, the end of X. We paused in our reading as the blood of Mezentius flowed from his throat. The new day comes up with the new book, a coincidence found nowhere else in the poem, and we at once enter the troubled mind of Aeneas. We see Aeneas carry out the construction of a trophy, a practice current in the armies of Virgil's own day, a Romanisation of epic warfare, which also has an epic grandeur appropriate to a bronze-age warrior. With barbarous and grim splendour a huge oak lopped of its branches is decked in the armour of Mezentius, *contemptor diuum* in life but in death subject to the proper rites imposed by his conqueror and antithesis, *pius* Aeneas. Aeneas then reviews the military situation and gives a brief *hortatio*:

> 'This is a great achievement, men; be of good courage,
> For what still waits. Here are the spoils of war, a proud king's
> Weapons. Mezentius is in my hands now. Here he is.
> Now to march on Latinus and his citadel . . .
> Meanwhile let us commit the unburied bodies of our comrades
> To earth, the only honour of the underworld.
> Go,' he said, 'and to those noble souls who with their blood
> Have won for us this land, pay the last tributes
> Of honour, and to Evander's town of mourning let Pallas

Be sent home, for the black day of death
Which took him, found him not without courage.'

The narrative moves away now from the dead Mezentius, the primitive and crude trophy, to the long intense description of the funeral of Pallas, a passage displaying all the techniques of the literature of pathos. We follow the narrative, and the cortège, through Aeneas's eyes; his immense sense of desolation which we experience, his sense of Evander's loss. It is Aeneas who superintends the placing of the body on the bier, and he who pronounces, in the second paragraph of book XI, the funeral oration.

This speech is one of the focal points of the entire poem, around which some of its central moral and emotional attitudes are organised. Through it the reader may direct his sense of the narrative away from the grand heroic gestures of the epic of action, the necessities by which things happen and by which they are as they are, towards that which was not to be, towards the intuition of loss and pain. Like all great literature, the *Aeneid* frequently enacts the things which were not enacted, says the things which were not said, whereby the reader constructs an alternative world in which 'If only Pallas had not died' (but he had to) becomes 'Pallas did not have to die', and then (momentarily) 'imagine a world in which he did not die'. For a while, one of the poem's most important characters still lives in that other world – Evander does not yet know of his son's death. The rhetoric of *consolatio* becomes in terms of the narrative a means by which the reader may construct a meaning for the entire poem which depends on negation, not affirmation. The key words of Aeneas's speech are words of negation, disappointment, loss, failure, an ironic awareness of the gap between heroic boast and human destiny: *non haec, spe . . . inani, exanimum, nil iam caelestibus ullis debentem, uano . . . honore*, and the ubiquitous *maesti, meastum, maesto, maestus, maesta*, the declension of sorrow.

Aeneas begins his oration with words in which the implied

reader secures another secondary epic allusion to Homer. In *Iliad* XVIII Achilles laments Patroclus:

> Ah me. It was an empty word I cast forth on that day
> when in his halls I tried to comfort the hero
>   Menoitios.
> I told him I would bring back his son in glory to
>   Opous . . .

Aeneas addresses Pallas as *miserande puer*, words he heard his father use, in the Elysian fields, about another young hero who died before he was 'put on', whose premature death, indeed, is foretold even before he is born, thus deepening the sense of mortality which underlies Virgil's use of the idea of reincarnation. The words *miserande puer* belong to Marcellus, but also to Nisus and Euryalus and now to Pallas and so to every young man of whom these characters are types.

> O young man, most pitiable, did Fortune grudge
>   you
> To me, though she came smiling? You were not to
>   see
> Us in our kingdom, nor to your father ride home
>   victorious.
> No. This was not the promise I gave Evander your
>   father at our going
> When he embraced me and charged me to begin an
>   empire
> But told me in fear of dangerous foes and a tough
>   war.
> And oh, perhaps even now, led on by hope's fool's
>   light,
> He is saying his prayers and piling with offerings
>   his altar,
> And here we are, and his son lifeless with nothing
>   left
> Of obligation to any god, and so with empty
>   pomp,

> Comrades in sorrow, we bring him home.
> Ah so unlucky, soon to see this bitter death.
> Is this our homecoming, our long awaited triumph?
> Was this my grand assurance? Oh Evander, at least
>   you shall not
> See him defeated by the wounds of shame, nor
>   pray
> A father's prayer for death because your son has
>   saved
> His life but not his honour. But oh, how great
> A rock, how great a refuge, is lost to you,
> My son, and to Italy.

Achilles, after mentioning his vain promise to Patroclus's father, does not refer again to Menoitios; instead, he foretells his own death at Troy and makes a pledge to kill Hector. It is characteristic of Virgil to sustain a single large and universal image of pathos; to invite us to feel, not only with Aeneas but through Aeneas with Evander. Aeneas, having been a surrogate father to Pallas, speaks as a father and for a father, a father as yet ignorant, like Andromache, in *Iliad* XXII, who hadn't yet heard the news and was preparing Hector's warm bath for his return from the battle, 'while he', says the poet, 'far from warm baths was cut down by Pallas Athene at the hands of Achilles'. The pathos of this famous piece of dramatic irony is transformed by Virgil into a different scene: the ignorance is the same, but an intensely Roman act of prayer and *pietas* replaces the domestic task; Aeneas puts words of awareness and tragic grief proleptically into Evander's mouth just as Homer invites his audience to feel with Andromache in those terrible last moments of ignorance before she learns the news. In *Aeneid* XI when Evander hears the news and goes out to meet the cortège, his own words are made by the poet to begin with an echo of Aeneas's

> non haec, o Palla, dederas promissa parenti
> *This was not the promise you made your father, Pallas*

cf. Aeneas:

> non haec Euandro de te promissa parenti
> discedens dederam . . .
>
> *This was not the promise I gave Evander your father
>   about you
> At our going. . .*

Then the reader anticipates Evander's grief, carries his sense of the poem's unfolding meaning beyond Evander's immediate unawareness, to realise the full significance of this protracted episode. Moreover, Aeneas's speech gives the reader a further chance to link the meaning of the narrative across the break between books x and xi, for while it is true, as we saw, that x ends in violence and blood, the dying hero Mezentius, *contemptor diuum*, has already put into the poem an intensely moving version of a father's sense of agony at his son's death. He feels a kind of guilt in survival, at having not yet gone from the light – 'but I am going'; and he turns to address his horse Rhaebus, in another marvellous transformation of Homer, in words which are peculiarly Virgilian in their pathos:

> Rhaebus, we have lived a long time, if anything
> Mortal can be said to live long . . .[35]

Even the proud, now vanquished foe, second only to Turnus among the Latin chiefs, whose symbolic figure, a lopped trunk decked with arms, stands as the first gaunt image of book xi, even Mezentius has in the author's direction of the narrative close of book x made a contribution proleptically to the long perspectives of pathos through which the reader of book xi must now pass. Evander, too, expresses the by now

---

[35] The transformation is characteristic. Hector encourages his horses before battle at *Iliad* 8.184ff. without considering the possibility of failure. Mezentius says that if horse and hero do not return together victorious then they will die together. For the motif of horses weeping for their masters cf. *Aen.* 11.89 (Pallas's horse) and *Iliad* 17.426ff. (Achilles' horses weep for Patroclus); but again there is a characteristic transformation, for Mezentius's horse does not only mourn for Lausus, but (as it were) for Mezentius himself, whose death is not far off.

familiar Virgilian sentiment of 'contempt for the light'. And he expresses a further sentiment which links his speech back to the opening image of XI:

> You too would now be standing, a huge trunk on the field,
> If your ages and strengths had been equally matched,
> Turnus.

The death of Mezentius, his lopped image, must stand for the time being for the death of Turnus, Pallas's slayer; yet Mezentius is not wholly disjunct from the pathos of Pallas's funeral and Evander's and Aeneas's grief; his own lament for his son is, as it were, held over from book X and allowed to permeate the reader's sense of the unfolding of the brief, tragically charged Virgilian Iliad. Pallas's death now makes Turnus's confrontation with Aeneas certain; the Iliadic structure, and the sentiment, require it; the reader expects no other end. Only the death of Camilla is to be encompassed; otherwise, the rest of the poem is dominated by Turnus.

Aeneas's last words of ritual despatch over Pallas are among the briefest and most eloquent of all his speeches.

> nos alias hinc ad lacrimas eadem horrida belli
> fata uocant: salue aeternum mihi, maxime Palla,
> aeternumque uale.
>
> *We from this place to other tears by war's same dreadful doom*
> *Are called. For ever and for ever, noblest Pallas,*
> *Hail and farewell.*

These formulaic words echo both Achilles' farewell to Patroclus in *Iliad* 23.19 and Catullus's words over his brother's tomb (101.10). Thus ends the first part of book XI. The majestic funeral tone, the repetition of *maestus*, continues to dominate the passage which follows, until Evander and his dead son face each other and the dreadful reality is brought home to the reader, who now reads through Evander. As the funeral cortège winds its way towards Evander and that final outburst of grief, *maestam incendunt clamoribus urbem*, other Iliadic themes are being interwoven into the narrative. The funeral of Pallas signals a twelve-day truce for the general burial of the dead. The Iliadic models are the truce after the fight between Ajax and Hector in book VII together with the truce granted at the very end of the *Iliad* by Achilles. Neither of these models corresponds exactly in structure to that in *Aeneid* XI. Aeneas plays the Achillean role of truce-granter, but he has not yet killed his Hector, and the moral argument is that of the implied author. Aeneas replies to the request of the Latin ambassadors in carefully chosen, emphatically rhetorical words which require the reader to consider not merely epic precedent but also moral justice.

> Do you ask me for peace for the dead?
> Indeed I should have wished to extend it also to the living.
> I only came here because fate said it was my place.
> I have no quarrel with your people. It was your king who
> Rejected my guest-friendship, preferring Turnus and war.

The point is taken up, speciously, by Drances, a Latin leader who hates Turnus and flatters Aeneas with rhetorical flourishes:

> O great in fame, greater in action,
> Hero of Troy, with what praise shall I lift you to the sky?
> Shall I start with your moral scruples or your military prowess?

Drances now goes on to say that he will try to persuade Latinus to resume his alliance with Aeneas and repudiate Turnus. In the debate which follows, Drances comes out as an opponent of war, but he does not thereby emerge as trustworthy or admirable, any more than Belial does when he counsels peace in the debate in Pandemonium.[36] Drances' praise of Aeneas is a reworking of a familiar formula, almost a cliché of his character, equal in renown for *pietas* and for prowess, an epic vaunt used by Aeneas himself, for example, at 1.544; here the smooth flattery might suggest a sneer if Drances did not hate Turnus so much.

It is sometimes said that early in XI Virgil is at pains to reinstate Aeneas in the reader's eyes after showing him, in book X, subject like other men to *furor* in the extreme and catastrophic situation of battle. Williams goes so far as to speak of Aeneas being here in his normal frame of mind[37] after the frenzy he showed in X, but the reader's memory is not so short that he can forget. It is the reader's task to make sense of inconsistencies in behaviour, if this is what they are, and of the gaps between books and episodes. If there are judgements to be made, the reader must make these too, and change them as he reads. One might read the poem, to give an extreme instance, in such a way as to place most emphasis on the battle scenes ('this is what Aeneas really enjoys, all the time he has been controlling himself, now all his *furor* is released'): the exemplary story of Hercules and Cacus in VIII, in which the saviour hero showed *furor* against his enemy, then becomes paradigmatic of the entire epic. One might reduce such passages as Aeneas's speech to Drances and the other Latin representatives about the truce (11.108–19) to propagandist rhetoric on the part of the Augustan author, inserted to ensure that the founder of the *gens Iulia* has clean hands. One might read the hero's frequent protestations – 'I would not have come here if fate had not sent me', etc. – as mere self-justification, no more convincing than his words to Dido ('It is fate, not my own will, that took me from you'); Dido's

---

[36] *Paradise Lost* 2.106ff. The 'peace party' in Milton's council is represented by both Belial and Mammon. Satan's rejection of their advice and determination to continue his opposition to God are modelled on Turnus's proud and contemptuous rejection of Drances' *nulla salus bello* argument: see esp. *Aen.* 11.411–15.

[37] 'Here we see him as he really is'; Williams on 11.100ff.

silence in the underworld may then express the reader's own lack of conviction about the validity of 'this' Aeneas.

It is probably not surprising that some critics, faced with a work as complex as the *Aeneid*, should seek to simplify it. This is partly the result of the poem's having been too long a school book. The modern reader is too seldom able to manipulate the multiplicity of viewpoints it contains, the shifting of the narrative from narrator to hero to other characters, the continually changing perspectives, the variety of pace and tone, the way the episodes can stand alone and must yet relate to each other, the gaps between passages and between books, the elaborate time-structure which takes the reader backwards and forwards around a 'now' which is both Virgil's Augustan present and the reader's own time, the 'now' when he reads: the fact that so much of the poem is written in the historic present facilitates this synchronic structure. The episode being read will always seem to draw into itself all the perspectives of the whole epic. All this makes the *Aeneid* a very modern piece of fictional narrative, which can only be properly understood if the reader is aware of his own role and responsibility: to make sense of the poem from all its parts and from the interstices between them. Any judgement we pause to make, struck by the force of a particular scene, and the apparent contradictions which (in a naive reading) this judgement seems to set up, must be seen as partial, true perhaps, but for the time being. Any judgement which decides that Aeneas the apologist, the statesman, the man of *pietas* is 'normal' and Aeneas the frenzied is abnormal has in a sense fallen victim to a propagandist or 'ennobling' interpretation of the poem, in which the battle-scenes are distasteful reminders of the unpalatable realities of *imperium*. War is uncivilised, and a 'civilised' poet cannot really 'mean' what he writes about war: true, but the poet's discourse on the insanity of war (shared by his whole generation, sick of *discordia*), operates within a narrative in which war becomes a grand rhetorical topos. We must not so etiolate Virgil as to remove from him all zest for heroic narrative. I believe, too, that for Virgil the *Iliad*

THE FUNERAL OF PALLAS

remained a great masterpiece; in attempting a recension of it in terms of his own nation's legendary past, he did not intend a repudiation. Whether its object is to sack a city or to found one, war remains insane; he that wills the end must will the means. And the greatness of the end, the positive act of founding a city as distinct from the negative act of destroying one, does not automatically glorify the means. For the modern (as distinct from the implied Augustan) reader, even the end, *urbs condita*, is now subject to the ironies of history: 'Alaric has avenged Turnus.'[38]

After Evander's farewell to Pallas, the scene changes back to the battlefield and the sombre burial of the dead. A new day dawns at line 182, marking the end of one of the shortest narrative days in the poem (182 lines). The funeral cortège has taken, as it would have had to do, a whole day to wind its way back to Pallanteum. The day now dawning is ushered in with a characteristically Virgilian and deeply appropriate version of a familiar topos:

> Aurora interea miseris mortalibus almam
> extulerat lucem referens opera atque labores.
>
> *And now dawn to miserable mortals her kindly*
> *Light had revealed, bringing back toil and labour.*

Behind the panoply and rhetoric of the funeral and of the war council about to take place, the life of man is all the time as wretched as it was in *Iliad* XVII, when all heroic grandeur was reduced to zero in the meditative words of Zeus to an immortal horse. Here the epexegesis, *opera atque labores*, extends and reinforces the sense of mortal man's unending tasks. The new light shows up the desolate spectacle of the battlefield, the building of pyres, the ritual of the Trojan cremations, the lamentations until nightfall. Two days are allotted to the burial; after describing the Trojan rites the poet turns to the Latins, and depicts their mourning in slow spondaic measure:

[38] W. H. Auden, 'Secondary Epic', in *Homage to Clio* (1960).

> tunc undique uasti
> certatim crebris conlucent ignibus agri.

*And all around the devastated fields
Are lit by fitful and conflicting fires.*

The women of Latium in particular are already in profound reaction against the war:

> dirum exsecrantur bellum Turnique hymenaeos;
> ipsum armis ipsumque iubent decernere ferro.

*They curse the dreadful war and Turnus's marriage
  contract.
Him they bid fight, let him decide the war with his
  sword.*

They will recall now, with (and for) the reader, how they let Amata, fury-driven, lead them into a Bacchic frenzy, crying vengeance in the name of that same marriage contract. Soon now we shall see them file repentant into Athene's temple.

The long first section of *Aeneid* XI ends at last at line 224, having reached its climax in the passage showing the grief-stricken 'city of most wealthy Latinus', *praediuitis urbe Latini*, the unusual adjective powerful with irony. The language is highly wrought, with elaborate alliterative patterns (the repeated 'c' at lines 207–9, for instance), the repeated verb *maerentes, maerentem* (root of *maestus*) emphasising the extent of a shared and protracted grief, *longi luctus*. The entire passage is modelled on the lamentation for Hector and funeral truce in *Iliad* XXIV (with the earlier and structurally less significant truce in *Iliad* VII) yet, as so often in the last part of the *Aeneid*, Virgil moves further from the tone and spirit of the *Iliad*. In structure and thematic focus, his *Iliad* is modelled on Homer's, with a Patrocleia and with careful assimilations of the deaths of Sarpedon and Euphorbos. But each action in the *Aeneid* generates an immense charge of emotional discourse which slows the reader down in a way he is not slowed down in the *Iliad* even by the funeral of Patroclus or of Hector. The normal pace of reading the *Iliad* is fast; even the passages of extended pathos and sensibility do not decelerate this pace noticeably. The normal pace of the *Aeneid* is slow; the heavier hexameter, the longer descriptions, the proportion of feeling to action, all contribute to this. The interaction in the *Aeneid* between events and responses is an extreme and fascinating example of expressionism.

The miserable mortals on whom another day of toil and labour dawns become specifically the *miseri Latini . . . matres miseraeque nurus*, the miserable mothers, brides and sisters of dead warriors; Homer's formula 'wretched mortals' is not now a piece of traditional gnomic wisdom, the proper response of man to his mortality, but a sense of the intolerable burden which living and action place on human sensibility. The pressure to end this war, after only a few days, is already overwhelming, for it is more than a story-book war. It is for the implied reader a paradigm of historical civil war. In the *Iliad*, after nearly ten years, an attempt to end the war by single combat between Paris and Menelaus is aborted by divine intervention. The only heroes who 'must' die in order to produce the narrative of the wrath of Achilles, are Patroclus and Hector. No other important heroes die in the poem.[39] In the *Aeneid*, Aeneas must get rid of all his rivals as surely, and with as firm a basis in historical necessity, as Octavian had to.

The quarrel over Helen is not the 'real' theme of the *Iliad*. Virgil not only wrote the wrath theme out of his Iliad. He assimilated the motif of the rape of Helen into his Patrocleia and his version of the Achilles–Hector confrontation. In the *Iliad*, we see Helen not so much as a *casus belli* but as its chief and most self-aware victim. As an element in the narrative, she belongs with the effects not the causes of war. Though in no way blamed by the Trojans, she knows how the poet will project her into the future. She foresees the Iliad.[40]

In the *Aeneid*, Turnus sees Aeneas in Iliadic terms as Paris to

[39] See F. Ferrucci, *The Poetics of Disguise* (Cornell, Ithaca 1980) 22–3.
[40] See above, Prologue, 19–22.

his Menelaus, an effeminate oriental seducer, the dancing-master and chorus-boy of Hector's and Priam's taunts against the hero whom Aphrodite loved and rescued from Menelaus's spear. But the motif of the marriage-contract is a true *casus belli* in the *Aeneid* since whoever marries Lavinia succeeds to the throne of Latium. Helen's recovery carries no territorial guarantee to her rescuers, whose aim is plunder and destruction, not empire. The Trojan war is vendetta and the saving of 'face'. It is not through Paris or Menelaus or the bumbling Agamemnon, but through the story of Achilles, Patroclus and Hector, that Homer brings tragic intensity and meaning to the ten-year siege. For Virgil, the 'cause' of his *Iliad*, the silent and all but invisible Lavinia, seems mere pretext. The Latin war must be fought so as paradigmatically to lay the foundations for that past on which Virgil's Rome is constructed. The ultimate cause of the war is to be found in history itself.

The inevitable finality of Troy's fall, from which the *Aeneid*, and the Roman foundation legend, takes its beginning, lies far beyond the end of Homer's *Iliad*, yet that end is included in the poem by Homer, in the famous prophetic words of Agamemnon and Hector:

> For I know well this thing in my heart and mind:
> the day will come when holy Ilium shall be destroyed
> and Priam and the people of Priam of the good ash spear.

For Virgil that inescapable 'cause', now past, reverberates through the narrative as part of the effect of the Italian Iliad: the winning of the gods back to the city of *pietas* which they seemed once to have abandoned – back to the new Troy, Rome.[41]

---

[41] Professor Kenney has suggested to me that Homer's words about the coming fall of Troy are 'echoed and inverted' at *Aen.* 1.283–5, when Jupiter foresees the ending of Greek power: *ueniet lustris labentibus aetas | cum domus Assaraci Phthiam clarasque Mycenas | seruitio premet ac uictis dominabitur Argis.*

uenit summa dies et ineluctabile tempus
Dardaniae. fuimus Troes, fuit Ilium et ingens
gloria Teucrorum; ferus omnia Iuppiter Argos
transtulit.

The last day and inevitable time has come
To Ilium. We are past, Troy is past, and our mighty
Glory. So cruelly Jupiter has taken all
Over to the enemy.

At the end of the *Aeneid*, the last stage of the working out of destiny through the will of Jupiter does indeed involve the final disappearance of Troy; the Trojans, who throughout their wanderings, and throughout the poem, have striven to keep alive their traditions and identity, must now surrender them; the grim words of Panthus, recalled by Aeneas to Dido, come true at last. With Turnus's death the ghosts of Hector and Priam are finally laid to rest, and the very name of Troy, sounding out like a musical figure for the last time at 12.828 (the last word spoken in the epic by Juno) vanishes for ever. If Jupiter changed sides and deserted Troy, Juno now changes sides herself to become a tutelary deity of the Roman people and one of the divine guardians of the Capitol. This is the magnitude of the finality which the Virgilian Iliad sets out to achieve. Not only Homer's Troy, but in a sense Homer's *Iliad* is subsumed in the *Aeneid*, to such an extent that for a long time it usurped its model as the supreme epic of heroic warfare. The rediscovery of the original *Iliad* in the Renaissance and in the centuries which followed, had the effect of putting the *Aeneid* back into the transforming intertextual relation to the *Iliad* which Virgil had always assumed and intended.

7. The council of war

The second triad of book XI describes the council of war held by the Latins at which they first receive the ambassadors despatched in VIII to seek aid from the Greek settler Diomede, survivor of the Homeric *Iliad*. It is a typical gesture of secondary epic to introduce him into the *Aeneid*, and a striking piece of moral irony to introduce him as a non-combatant, for he was one of the greatest heroes of the Achaians. But Diomede has had enough of war. His message is first related briefly in indirect speech by the poet as narrator; it is then that Latinus summons a council, a scene parallel to the council of gods at the beginning of x, introduced in a passage of parallel grandeur (11.231–8):

> deficit ingenti luctu rex ipse Latinus:
> fatalem Aenean manifesto numine ferri
> admonet ira deum tumulique ante ora recentes.
> ergo concilium magnum primosque suorum
> imperio accitos alta intra limina cogit.
> olli conuenere fluuntque ad regia plenis
> tecta uiis. sedet in mediis et maximus aeuo
> et primus sceptris haud laeta fronte Latinus.

> *King Latinus breaks down under the heavy strain.*
> *The gods' anger, so many newly dead –*
> *Aeneas must be the man of destiny*
> *Sent by the declared will of heaven.*
> *And so he calls a council of all his chiefs.*
> *They come through packed streets to the great hall.*
> *There, eldest in years, first in authority,*
> *Much troubled in countenance, Latinus takes his place.*

Between Latinus and Jupiter there is both parallel and contrast. The king is traditionally in epic an earthly figure of the king of men and gods, Zeus/Jupiter, but whereas Jupiter, although displeased with events, is still in control even when proclaiming that events shall take their course, Latinus, equally displeased, is not in control. Yet both Jupiter and Latinus are themselves opposed to this war; Latinus is too weak to oppose Turnus, Jupiter refuses to arbitrate between Venus (longing for peace, but on her terms, like Drances in the council) and Juno (a figure of Turnus).

The envoy Venulus now gives in full and direct speech the long and powerful rejection by Diomede of the Latin call for military aid against the Trojans. It provides a chance for the poet to engage the reader in a résumé of the Trojan war and its aftermath from the viewpoint of the victorious Greeks: the sufferings of the war itself, the dead, the disasters which attended the homecomings of many of the surviving heroes (notably, in ascending order of fame, Neoptolemus, Idomeneus, Agamemnon). All this is presented as the justifiable punishment of sinners. Zeus at the beginning of the *Odyssey* also rehearses the fate of Agamemnon, distinguishing it from the undeserved sufferings of Odysseus, though to Virgil Odysseus, as the hero ultimately responsible for the sack of the city, is specially culpable. Homer thought of his two opposing sides primarily in terms of their respective champions – the Trojans had Hector and Aineias, but the Greeks had a string of mighty warriors, and their superiority won them victory. Between Homer and Virgil came the rise of the city and nation states, the sense of events as collectively brought about, the formalisation of national characteristics (adumbrated already by Homer as a patriotic Greek poet). For the Roman poet, Trojan piety (Homer's Zeus admired the Trojans for their religious observances) is reinforced with the heroism of Hector while the military superiority of Achilles is transposed to the new Roman nation through Aeneas, supreme in prowess as in *pietas*, and by an infusion of the fighting blood of the tough (*duri*) Italians. Just as the defeated Trojans retained their *pietas* in exile as the Jews retained theirs, a kind of national badge, so the defeated Latins will retain their best characteristics when the war is over. In Diomede's speech it is, therefore, the impiety of the Greeks which must be stressed, as it was in book II, in which Aeneas was the narrator: both he and Diomede are made by the implied author to present, so to speak, an agreed version of the sack of Troy as an act of moral outrage. In particular, the famous account in II of the killing of Priam by Pyrrhus, who first killed Priam's son Polites in front of his eyes, is presented as an act of monstrous impiety. The king is in his palace, in the sanctuary of his own altar, an altar full of Roman significance, like all the altars in the *Aeneid*.

Virgil's council of war is an assimilation of three Trojan councils in the *Iliad*. In *Iliad* VII Antenor proposes the return of Helen, 'for we are fighting having falsified our true pledges', a reference to the oaths sworn in book III by both sides to leave the outcome of the war to be decided by Paris and Menelaus. In the council, Antenor's proposal is overruled. Structurally, this council is important for Virgil since it occurs in the context of a truce for the disposal of the dead, a truce which, while not crucial to the story of the *Iliad* at that point, *is* crucial to Virgil's narrative at the point reached in book XI. The truce willingly granted by Aeneas, granted along with a heartfelt wish to extend that peace also to the living, forms the prelude to the truce in book XII which the Rutuli break, thus becoming violators, like the Greeks at the sack of Troy – for the breaking of oaths, like the sanctity of altars, was central to Roman *pietas*; these violations carry for Virgil's implied reader a force and horror absent from the world of Homer's *Iliad*.

But Virgil has assimilated to his council not only that from *Iliad* VII but also that in *Iliad* XVIII, which is a longer episode and offers an important analogy with *Aeneid* XI, for in it two opposing views on how the next stage of the war is to be conducted are put forward, and again the more prudent and sensible one, the 'Antenorian' one, is rejected: this time its exponent is Polydamas, who advises the Trojans to stay inside the walls and not go out and risk the fresh and dangerous aggression of Achilles beside the ships. Not for the first time, the brave but foolhardy Hector rejects this counsel: the motif of the impetuous hero overruling the voice of prudence occurs several times in the *Iliad*.

The third council of war in the *Iliad* which has contributed to *Aeneid* XI is that in *Iliad* II, in which Agamemnon tries to persuade the Greeks to go on fighting by suggesting that they ought to go home. This devious plan backfires on him and in any case seems illogical when he has just had a dream of certain victory, but it is characteristic of his weak generalship:[42] elsewhere in the *Iliad* he seriously proposes retreat and is answered with contempt by Diomede and Odysseus.[43] In *Aeneid* XI Latinus advises peace but is unable to sway the war-party. From *Iliad* II Virgil takes the attack on Agamemnon by Thersites, the only common and ugly man mentioned by Homer in his heroic poem. His advice to withdraw is rejected with contempt by Odysseus, as is Drances' by Turnus. Thersites' view, and his presence in the poem, may perhaps represent, as Willcock suggests, 'new political strivings', the ruling class having become suspect by Homer's time with 'discontent beginning to find a voice'.[44] Certainly Drances' rancour and his dubious ancestry suggest that Thersites may have served as a model. The content of his speech is closer to that of Thersites than to that of Polydamas, for he does not just counsel more prudently than Turnus, as Homer says Polydamas counsels more prudently than Hector: he counsels surrender, blaming the war on Turnus as Thersites blamed it on Agamemnon.

Gilbert Highet has pointed out[45] that Drances' speech works quite differently from Thersites'. As he rightly says, it is more dignified, more intellectual, more effectively incorporated into the narrative. But why is this so? Highet does not offer an explanation. In part, the answer must be, as noted above, that Virgil has assimilated other councils from the *Iliad* besides that in book II: Drances is certainly not a straight transcription of Thersites. But in addition, Virgil's rhetoric functions in a

[42] Willcock, *Companion* 18.   [43] *Iliad* 9.26–8, 14.74–81.
[44] Willcock on *Iliad* 2.212, and *Companion* 20.
[45] *The Speeches in Vergil's Aeneid* (Princeton 1972) 248–51.

more complex way than Homer's. In the speeches in *Iliad* 1, for example, Achilles, though he does not speak at random, seems to speak in the very heat of anger and temper: the poet cleverly makes him seem to speak 'off the top of his head': this is the great achievement of the monumental composer working with oral techniques at the beginning of the age of literature, whereas Virgil's speeches are codified in accordance with five hundred years of rhetorical theory and practice and belong at the centre of all Graeco-Roman culture.

Thersites' speech is also motivated differently from that of Drances. Homer tells us that he talked in a disorderly fashion and in order to make the Argives laugh. In fact they do laugh, but only when he is beaten by Odysseus. The reader may, I suppose, read this passage so as to construct a meaning unfavourable to the heroes – an allegory of how the upper class keeps down the lower by force? The silencing of Thersites by Odysseus when he hits him with his staff and raises blood on his back is felt by the rest of the company to be a good thing, and Homer gives us a general reaction in the form of speech one to another. Homer often gives us his implied author's reactions to what he tells us as narrator (as in the council scene in book XVIII where he comments on the foolishness of the Greeks in rejecting Polydamas's strategy in favour of Hector's), and the fact that he can criticise Hector, the most sympathetic character in his story, validates his criticism of Thersites and makes it harder for us to dismiss it, even though we find the suppression of minorities by force distasteful. Homer has introduced Thersites into his aristocratic poem and also rejected him. His inclusion, and his rejection, are elements in the poem's enormous versatility and polyvalence; his treatment is, perhaps, an unresolved element in the poem's archaic value-structure.

The confrontation between Drances and Turnus is crucial to the *Aeneid* in a way that none of the Homeric war-councils are, or can be (given the poem's psychological and narrative modes), least of all Thersites' outburst, which occurs too early in the poem to have any significant effect on the action. In

Aeneid XI the choice between peace and war is presented to the reader for almost the last time in the poem. We are at a point in the second half of the poem which corresponds structurally to that reached in the first half at book V, where (as in XI) Aeneas is approaching a climax in his labours (the visit to the underworld, the duel with Turnus). In both V and XI he celebrates the funeral of one close to him, and for whom he feels deep personal grief – his father Anchises and his surrogate son Pallas. Anchises' death is in a sense negated by his role in VI as expounder of spiritual and historical truth, while Pallas's death is not negated but avenged by the death of Turnus and the peace which can then, and only then, begin. The end of V, too, the death of the sympathetically drawn figure of Palinurus, has affinities with the end of XI, the death of Camilla (both characters are in some sense deceived against their better judgement).

In *Virgil: A Study in Civilised Poetry*, Brooks Otis[46] works out a more elaborate and less convincing correspondence between XI and III. To go back in reverse through the six books of the 'Odyssean' *Aeneid* is to reduce the poem's powerful linear thrust and its significance as a narrative text. By the time we reach XI, we do not want a reading which will involve references back to III, a book which is part of Aeneas's narrative at Carthage, when he is far from his Odyssean, let alone his Iliadic goal. But we may make some gesture of recall towards V, for then we were in sight as readers of a goal in our act of reading, no less than Aeneas is, and was, in sight of a goal as protagonist. A moment of destiny is all but within the grasp, a decisive act towards which Turnus himself is now directing the narrative by the sheer force of his determination to fight. From now until the end, Turnus is the central focus of the narrative, and we see events, and respond to them, increasingly through his eyes. By putting the case for peace into the clever but ill-motivated speech of Drances the certainty of renewed conflict is guaranteed by the heroic and

[46] Otis, *Virgil* 363.

indeed Achillean response of Turnus which makes his bitter hostility to the very end of the action inevitable. Indeed, behind all the other Iliadic models of councils which pervade this scene in book XI, we become more and more aware of the undercurrent of the most important confrontation in the entire *Iliad*, that in book I between Agamemnon and Achilles. Turnus's violent response to Drances' smooth and plausible argument contains something of the violence and angered pride of Achilles: thus late in the *Aeneid* the wrath theme makes a kind of return to the story; it is the last Achillean gesture of a hero who must soon resign his role of Achilles to Aeneas and assume the role of Hector, but a Hector who has forfeited sympathy by an Achillean anger which will stay with him now till he is killed, the last trace and vestige of a traditional heroic prowess history has doomed. It is here that the ambivalence and interest of Turnus's character lie. He is wrong to keep the war going, he represents an outdated concept of personal heroism, he leads an army composed largely of similarly inclined heroes dedicated to personal glory – of whom Camilla still survives as the most appealing figure. Yet he is also the focus, through the Iliadic *Aeneid*, as Dido was through the Odyssean *Aeneid*, of a structurally and morally significant antithesis. The reader does not want to walk out on Dido or Turnus, any more than he does on the great flawed fallen heroes of later fiction, in Milton or Conrad, to name two writers who offer heroic narratives with strong sets of antithetical value-structures, both indispensable to the narrative.

The last fifteen lines of Drances' speech are an eloquent, authorially ironic plea to Turnus to make peace, or, if his desire for personal glory will not let him, then to face Aeneas man to man, and not sacrifice other lives in the cause of his marital quarrel. This motif of 'it is not our cause' again echoes the first scene of the *Iliad*, but now, in the Virgilian manipulation of Homeric roles, Drances has momentarily put Turnus into the figure of Agamemnon, or rather his brother, and speaks as Achilles once spoke to his commander-in-chief:

'the Trojans have not wronged me, it is your honour and Menelaus's which was wronged and which we are defending here'. For Turnus is not only Achilles who will soon become Hector, he must also take on himself the burden of the discredited and effeminate figure of the seducer Paris (thus freeing the Trojan Aeneas from the taint of this role) trying in vain to retain a bride whom destiny has not permitted him: the final duel in XII is the abortive duel between Paris and Menelaus from the *Iliad* fought now to a finish, as well as a re-enactment of the duel between Achilles and Hector; the two plots of the *Iliad* come together, Helen/Lavinia is won, Patroclus/Pallas avenged.

Drances' eloquence mounts to the words *nulla salus bello, pacem te poscimus omnes, Turne*; Drances here names Turnus for the first time in a speech full of criticism of him.

> There is no safety in war, peace is what all of us,
> Turnus, want from you . . . feel for your
>   followers,
> Set your pride aside. You have been beaten.
>   Surrender. We have seen enough
> Of death, enough of us have died, we have made
>   desolate so many acres.
> Oh yes, so long as Turnus can marry a princess he
>   can
> Leave us, humble souls, to lie out there, unwept,
>   unburied,
> Dead. And what of you? If you have the might
> And martial force your father had, stand face to
>   face
> With him your challenger.

Turnus replies by pouring scorn on Drances as a mere talker, not a doer, and reminding the council of his own achievements inside the enemy camp before the return of Aeneas. He makes no mention of the loss of Mezentius or of his own pursuit of the phantom Aeneas, presumably the defeat to which Drances referred, but it would seem natural for an 'Achillean' hero to dwell on his successes, and of course he includes the killing of Pallas, a boast both hubristic and full of proleptic irony; he will pay in full and in person for the destruction of the house of Evander. It seems possible, too, that Turnus is still too baffled and confused by the episode of the phantom and his adventure on the ship at the end of x. He was, in any case, not running away from but, as he supposed, pursuing his arch-foe, so he might feel himself in no way '*pulsus*', beaten, an accusing word of Drances, which, according to the rules of rhetoric, he quotes in order to repudiate it: not, understandably, by trying to explain what for him remains an inexplicable cause of shame (and the reader will feel sympathy here, knowing that the gods had 'Homerically' weakened the hero by interfering with his sense-impressions and his power over the external world) but by dwelling on the victories he has achieved, on the Trojan losses (for the storm of loss has broken over both armies equally, another echo of Jupiter's warning that if this war is fought 'against' his will, both sides will have to accept the blows of impartial fortune) and on the still unbeaten battalions of his army, Camilla and her Volsci, another piece of proleptic hubris. He is still ready to make peace if this is really the best way – 'but oh, if we had anything of our old courage' we should not think of it. In some famous lines adapted by Virgil from Ennius he reminds the council of the changing fortunes of war:

> Many a day's labour of men's mutable lifetimes
> Has brought change for the better, many a day has
>   gaming Fortune
> Deluded men, then turned again and restored them
>   to solid ground.

These words may also be a covert reference to his own mysterious return to land from his involuntary sea-journey in pursuit of the phantom Aeneas.

Finally, Turnus agrees to face Aeneas in single combat if this is decided on as the best course – *solum Aeneas uocat? et uocet oro,*

'Aeneas is challenging me alone? Pray let him challenge . . .' – and this takes us back to *Iliad* III, in which Paris, after being taunted by Hector, agrees to face Menelaus. The Iliadic tension begins to increase.

But all this debate is swiftly brought to nothing by the news that Aeneas has renewed the attack, the truce having expired.

8. Camilla's last stand

At this point in his narrative, with a new Trojan offensive about to start, Virgil makes an indispensable allusion to Homer's *Iliad*, and one for which the reader has been prepared since *Aeneid* I, when Aeneas gazed with grief and nostalgic pride at the murals in Juno's temple at Carthage depicting scenes from the Trojan war. The presentation of Troilus's death at the hands of Achilles (a pre-Iliadic episode) has already engaged the reader as the type of a pervasive Virgilian motif, the death of the young hero at the hand of a more experienced one. But now another scene is re-enacted: the incident in *Iliad* VI in which the matrons of Troy take gifts to Athene's temple and pray to the goddess to break the shield of Diomede, depicted at *Aeneid* 1.479–82. The goddess rejected their prayer, for she was not only on the side of the Greeks but had, in *Iliad* V, specifically encouraged Diomede, kindled flame from his helmet, head and shoulders, and launched him on his *aristeia*, which was to include the wounding of Aphrodite, Aineias's mother. Those murals at Carthage also showed the Amazon Penthesilea, killed, in a post-Iliadic period of the war, by Achilles. The implied reader is invited to reconstruct these episodes in preparation for the *aristeia* of the 'Amazonian' leader of the Volsci, Camilla, singled out by Turnus in his speech to the war council as a great ally whose forces were still virtually intact, and for her death, which removes Turnus's last remaining hope and prepares him and the reader for the final confrontation with Aeneas.

The reader thus enters a richly associative and transforming phase of the Virgilian Iliad. The author places significant parallels like signposts, which control the reader's response, and his awareness of what the structure and direction of the narrative must be. Now, in *Aeneid* XI, the women of Latium, led by Queen Amata, repair to the temple of Athene and pray to the goddess, as their Trojan counterparts had done before, that the spear of their most dangerous foe, this time Aeneas, might be broken. The role of Diomede has been transferred to Aeneas, for now it is the Latins who are hard-pressed and fearful. Moreover, the silent allusion to the 'suppressed' figure of Diomede, already implied in the scene on the murals at Carthage, is transformed in its new context by the very fact that Diomede himself, the Homeric original cause of that fearful women's prayer, has just been written out of the *Aeneid*. His heroic role, therefore, devolves, like other Homeric roles, upon Aeneas, as a number of lines from different starting-points converge towards a single terminal point. Aeneas becomes the focus and end of several heroic perspectives: one by one these are, so to speak, eliminated (or assimilated to him); the omens for Turnus grow more unfavourable; with each new allusion to Homer the implied author offers his reader an increasingly inescapable sense of the 'intertextuality' of his poem and the *Iliad*. One more turn of the screw now: the mention of Lavinia among the suppliant women is crucial to Virgil's motif of a second Iliad in Italy, for she is called here (11.480) *causa mali tanti*, 'cause of so much evil', the very words of the Sibyl in her prophecy to Aeneas in VI, when she warns him to prepare for a second Troy, with Lavinia in the role of Helen.

Thus in a few highly charged transitional lines between the end of the Latin council and the renewal of the attack, Virgil draws together several motifs and directs the reader to recall the pattern of a cyclic recension of the *Iliad*: to recall also, perhaps, the fourth *Eclogue* which tells how, before Saturn's peace returns to the world, there must be a renewed era of heroic warfare: 'and once more shall Achilles come to Troy'.

The word *iterum*, once more, is a signifier of cyclic prophecy,[47] and it is not surprising to find it also in the Sibyl's prophecy to Aeneas in VI:

> causa mali tanti coniunx iterum hospita Teucris
> externique iterum thalami.
>
> *Once more to the Trojans shall a foreign bride be the*
>   *cause of so much evil,*
> *Once more the alien marriage bed.*

The transition from the war council to the renewal of the war is one of the finest passages in the *Aeneid*: here, perhaps, the reader can best approach an understanding of the presentational mode of Virgilian epic. The transition is from speech to narrative, but the reader must unify both modes into the symbiosis of a single text. For too long there has been a tendency for the reader to see the two modes as in some sense disparate literary operations, to regard the rhetoric of long speeches as less relevant to our expectations as forward-readers of fictional narrative. The reader has been persuaded to find the speeches too formal, elaborate and static (whereas Homer's seem more accessible because apparently arising spontaneously from the traditional 'tale') and to be impatient for the 'real' action to be resumed. This may help to account for the relative unfamiliarity of the second half of the *Aeneid*, in which the interdependence of speech and tale becomes increasingly evident and increasingly important.

The speeches contribute as much to the reader's final experience of the work as does the narrative of action, and the contribution is made in the same way. We ought not to seek, or need, different reading techniques for the two modes, but to find a single technique for a single text. Whatever we decide to be the value and significance of this text, and of our reading of it, our formulation is likely to be in some sense a formulation about the nature of human discourse as a

---

[47] Christian as well as Sibylline: *et iterum uenturus est cum gloria iudicare uiuos et mortuos.*

description and analysis of human conduct. Human nature emerges as much from what men say as from what they do, often more: Virgil's speeches offer the reader statements about the role of language itself in human behaviour. We learn from them more about the psychology of professed purpose, human defensiveness and aggression, the concealing and revealing of motive, the power of generalising issues and conflicts. Our understanding of 'reality' through fiction depends on how we interpret modes of articulation. Reality becomes that which is expressed.

While the council is still unresolved between peace and war, while the proposal of Turnus, that he will meet Aeneas in mortal combat if that seems best, is still on the table, Aeneas sets the war going again, for the sooner it starts again the sooner it will end. The Latin council has actually delayed for the reader that ending of the war and the epic which must now be pursued. Yet the delay was not digressive and it is a pity to skip it. In the words of Richard Lanham, 'the rhetorical interlude perpetually analyses the kind of statement the narrative plot is allowed to make'.[48] The speeches now ended give a clearer perspective to the narrative. Drances' dissembling plea for peace, Latinus's weakness, Turnus's old-fashioned heroic egotism, confer significance on the resumed battle and separate it from the long funeral passage. Three blocks of text: funeral, speeches, military action: all part of the same reading experience, continuous yet articulated by felt transitions of mood and mode, as sentences are articulated into clauses and paragraphs into sentences.

We move into the book's last triad, the *aristeia* and death of Camilla. Turnus had specifically mentioned her in his speech, in two glorifying signal-verses:

> est et Volscorum egregia de gente Camilla
> agmen agens equitum et florentis aere cateruas.

---

[48] R. Lanham, 'Theory of the Λόγοι: the Speeches in Classical and Renaissance Narrative', in *To Tell a Story* (Clark Library Seminar Papers, Los Angeles 1973) 89–90.

And we still have Camilla, the noble Volscian,
And the cavalry she commands, brilliant with bronze.

It is on her that the narrative now focuses. She is to engage the enemy cavalry while Turnus lays an ambush for Aeneas and the infantry. She is a composite figure whom Virgil, in his characteristic synthetic manner, contrives to make wholly original; she is in part the Amazon of the continuation of the *Iliad*,[49] and here we have been prepared for her by the reference in the passage depicting the murals in Juno's temple at Carthage in book I:

> ducit Amazonidum lunatis agmina peltis
> Penthesilea furens mediisque in milibus ardet,
> aurea subnectens exsertae cingula mammae
> bellatrix, audetque uiris concurrere uirgo.

> *Leading the crescent-shielded Amazon ranks*
> *Penthesilea blazes conspicuous,*
> *Golden-girdled, one bare breast,*
> *Woman-warrior, man-challenging maid.*

Some of the key words in this passage recur in the description of Camilla in XI: she too is an Amazon, she too has one side of her breast bare (*exserta*), she too is conspicuous in gold and can be seen in the midst of the battle (*medias inter caedes exsultat*), she too is *uirgo* and *bellatrix* (7.805). Later in XI she is actually compared to Penthesilea and the phrase *lunatis agmina peltis* is repeated from 1.490. Moreover, the placing of the picture of Penthesilea at the very end of the catalogue of murals in book I is a brilliant stroke, for it leads straight into the appearance, for the first time in the poem, of Dido, herself, like Camilla, and like Penthesilea, *regina*, bearing on her shoulders, also like Camilla, the quiver of the huntress Diana, to whom she is compared. Camilla is a protégée and devotee of Diana, whose virgin servant she is: the name, like its masculine form

---

[49] The story of Penthesilea was included in the *Aithiopis* of Arktinos, the poem in the Trojan cycle which followed chronologically after the *Iliad*.

Camillus, means the servant of a god, and Virgil calls her *dia Camilla* ('divine'): the archaic adjective occurs nowhere else in his work. Furthermore, when the goddess Venus appears to her son Aeneas in book I she assumes the form of a virgin huntress and is likened to Harpalyce of Thrace, of whom Servius says that her father was exiled and killed, and that she had to take to the woods and live rough: Virgil himself refers to her swiftness of foot and her horsemanship. All these characteristics also belong to the magical pastoral side of Camilla, of whom in the Catalogue of Italian Leaders in VII Virgil writes, in a beautiful passage to which the reader ought now to refer back, that she is

> bellatrix, proelia uirgo
> dura pati cursuque pedum praeuertere uentos.
> illa uel intactae segetis per summa uolaret
> gramina nec teneras cursu laesisset aristas,
> uel mare per medium fluctu suspensa tumenti
> ferret iter celeris nec tingeret aequore plantas.

> *A maiden warrior, in battle*
> *Tough, faster on foot than the winds.*
> *She might glide over cornfields and leave the crop*
> *Intact, never harm the tender shoots in her passing,*
> *Or over the sea skim lightly, on the rolling*
> *Waves upborne so swiftly, never so much as wet her feet.*

Thus Camilla assimilates several figures from elsewhere in the poem. Like Dido, she is a royal foe of Aeneas with whom we feel some sympathy; she resembles Dido, as she also resembles Turnus, with whom, in their brief scene together in XI, she clearly has a sympathetic understanding. Her death removes a major obstacle for the Trojans, yet we feel the poet's empathy when she dies. The verse which describes her death is also used of the death of Turnus and is the very last line of the poem: this seems to be an echo of the common Homeric epitaph for Patroclus and Hector. Her death is brought about by Arruns, who has no other role in the *Aeneid*, and who is later himself killed by Opis, Camilla's protectress; this parallels and modifies the wounding of Patroclus by Euphorbos and his subsequent death in *Iliad* XVII at the hands of Menelaus. She thus also subsumes yet another version of the figure of Homer's Patroclus, and prepares the way for the 'Iliadic' death of Turnus in book XII.

But she also has affinities with Harpalyce, a pastoral figure who may have been treated by Callimachus. According to Servius, Callimachus, who wrote much aetiological poetry, said that the name Camillus signified in Etruscan Mercury, chief messenger and minister of the gods.[50] Mercury in Virgil's descriptions is noted for his swiftness. The famous passage in *Aeneid* IV in which Mercury is despatched by Jupiter to warn Aeneas against Dido emphasises his speed and his power to fly over land and sea. In *Aeneid* VII Camilla is only said to look as though she *could* perform such miracles, an oblique allusion by Virgil to the grace and lightness with which he himself has endowed her. His subjunctives do not let us read this miraculous lightness as something counter to any natural law, instead they idealise a very human woman:[51] but the hint of the supernatural enters the reader's understanding of her.

Camilla's strange pastoral unbringing has affinities with the legend of Harpalyce. She is also assimilated to the figure of another Italian chieftain catalogued in *Aeneid* VII, Virbius, also associated with Diana, and with Hippolytus, who also took a vow of virginity: Virgil curiously makes Virbius Hippolytus's son:[52] there are common elements of virginity, pastoral isolation and rural hardship in both legends. These elements are developed in the account depicting Camilla's early life. Her father Metabus, driven into exile like the father of Harpalyce, needing to cross the river Amasenus in spate and hampered by his baby daughter, swaddled her in cork, tied her to his spear and threw her across, committing her to the protection of Diana. Camillus is recorded as having used corks to cross the

[50] See Austin on *Aen.* 1.317.
[51] W. Fowler, *Virgil's Gathering of the Clans* (Oxford 1918) 85–6.
[52] Fowler, *Virgil's Gathering* 79–81; Fordyce, *Aen. VII–VIII* on 7.761ff.

Tiber[53] and Virgil may have recalled and assimilated the incident. Other details of her life may have come from the legend of Harpalyce.

The dark fate which forced Aeneas to war is relieved and lightened by the story of Camilla, the acme of Italian heroism. Yet behind the glittering conclusion, the lust for gold which overcame her as it overcame Cleopatra (and we see the same *auri sacra fames* in the picture of the gold-necklaced Gauls, Rome's enemies in historical times, on Aeneas's Shield[54]), there is more violence, and her death, a reworking of the Euphorbos–Patroclus passage in the *Iliad*, returns us to the world of the *Iliad*. Camilla's last words to her companion Acca are nevertheless powerful, simple and self-dramatising in a manner wholly unhomeric in tone and recalling strongly the death of Dido.

> I can do no more, Acca my dear. Now the sharp wound
> Undoes me, and about me all things blacken in the dark.

The news of her death reaches Turnus when he is on the point of ambushing Aeneas. He abandons the rocky pass he had commanded and returns to the plain, in time to see Aeneas ride through safely. Another nightfall ends the day's fighting and postpones the final duel until the last book; as the Trojans pitch camp we are taken back to two nightfalls in the *Iliad*, that in book VIII, after the short battle which inaugurated the run of Trojan victories, and that in XVIII, when Patroclus is dead and Achilles poised to return to the battle. Turnus might have faced Aeneas now, had night not fallen – Virgil has postponed the final encounter, the last climax, in the manner of Homer, who often used the oldest trick of all story-telling, that of holding back the climax, a technique essential to any extended narrative.

Thus the situation to which we return as the eleventh book

[53] Plutarch, *Vita Camilli* 25.   [54] *Aen.* 8.659–62.

ends and the last begins is essentially Iliadic, but the treatment is less and less Homeric. Structurally, the Turnus who confronts the reader in his violent and frustrated anger after Aeneas has escaped his stratagem is a Homeric figure: in the shifting and variable mutations of the Virgilian Iliad he is poised between the roles of Achilles and Hector as between victory and defeat. In the simile of the wounded lion roused to fresh attack, we are returned, by a remarkable transition, through our fresh memory of Camilla, to the now distant opening of *Aeneid* IV and the figure of Dido as with unsated love–fury she prowls through her city;[55] her dialogue with Anna corresponds structurally to Turnus's dialogue with Latinus. The opening words of both IV and XII offer the same image of a wound, the first a metaphor, the second a simile working as a symbol.

> at regina *graui iamdudum saucia* cura
> *uulnus* alit . . .
>
> (4.1–2)

> *Poenorum* qualis in aruis
> *saucius* ille *graui* uenantum *uulnere* pectus
> *tum demum* mouet arma leo . . .
>
> (12.4–6)

Not only are *saucius* and *graui uulnere* common terms, but *iamdudum* matches *demum*, conveying a strong surging forward to a long delayed but now inevitable end, while the detail *Poenorum* in XII adds a further associative touch (an African queen, an African lion). With the death of Camilla, the last heroic Italian warrior who could stand worthily at his side, the remaining vestige of glamour and sympathy vanishes from Turnus, and he must face at last single combat with Aeneas to decide the fate of Italy. The simile of the lion is used by Homer of Diomede in *Iliad* V and again of Achilles against Aineias in XX. Here Turnus is for the last time Homerically on

[55] Cf. Pöschl, *The Art* 109–38.

the offensive: Virgil stresses the force of his *uiolentia* with a rare verb, *gliscit*:

> haud secus accenso gliscit uiolentia Turno
>
> No differently[56] is the violence of Turnus kindled into a blaze.

Turnus's dialogue with Latinus, which opens XII, again assimilates two passages from Homer's *Iliad*, one from the first part – the planned combat between Menelaus and Paris in III – and one from the later part, when Priam tries to dissuade Hector from facing Achilles. As so often in his telescoped and assimilated Iliad, Virgil fuses a pre-Patroclean and a post-Patroclean passage: the two great quarrels of the Homeric *Iliad*, that between Paris and Menelaus and that between Achilles and Hector over Patroclus, reappear. Nor, as we shall see, does Virgil entirely lose sight of that other quarrel, between Agamemnon and Achilles, the so-called wrath theme, the germ of Homer's *Iliad*.

9. War and peace

In *Aeneid* XII Virgil manipulates the roles of Hector and Achilles for the last time. In *Aeneid* VI the Sibyl had foretold that a second Achilles already born in Latium would engage Aeneas in a second Trojan war. Thus Aeneas must become an avenging Hector, destined to reverse, this time, his earlier defeat. In the *Iliad* Achilles' death is a *donnée* of the poem, although not part of it. In book IX he says that he has the power to choose between two destinies – either to die at Troy or, returning home, to live long and ingloriously. The *Iliad* itself is 'about' this choice, and indeed about the *Angst* and stress of all human choice: it is an existential poem. Achilles' decision to stay in Troy, and his awareness of what he has chosen,

---

[56] This formula signals the return to the subject after the simile.

reverberate through the poem. His approaching death is unforgettably articulated in book XIX when the horse Xanthos speaks.

But Virgil reaffirms Turnus's affinity with the doomed Hector by stressing his ignorance of his own fate. He is prepared to take risks; he thinks he has a chance of victory until near the end of XII. Homer's Hector, too, had acted with the impetuous, obstinate valour of a man who can't give up. He had expressed, as indeed also had Agamemnon, that tragic prescience of the city's destined fall which colours every reading of the poem, but of his own future he says only that no man can escape his destiny, and encourages his wife with cheerful words. When Turnus sets aside the plea of his despairing mother-in-law never to be, Amata, the implied reader will hear again the pleas of Priam and Hecuba in *Iliad* XXII, and, behind that, more faintly and distantly, the despairing foreboding of Andromache in VI. Turnus calls Amata *mater*, thus emphasising the Homeric echo and adding pathos to a claimed relationship which, in his obstinate pride, he still clings to. The reader will also remember the counter-effective divine protection exercised by Venus, which recalls, yet far outshines, the concern of Thetis for Achilles.

Virgil's Aeneas is a man set apart by a destiny of which he himself seems uncertain. Venus knows that her son will die and be deified within three years of the settlement of Latium, a tradition assumed for the implied reader. But Aeneas himself does not know this. His faith in his destiny is not based on any immense pride and self-regard (Achilles) nor on the soldier's assumption that either the bullet has your name on or it doesn't (Hector), but on a remote, bleak, awareness of a process of historical necessity wholly indifferent to the individual will. Even when a future beyond his personal fate is revealed to him, the future of the Roman nation (as the future doom of Troy was known to Agamemnon and Hector), he shows little understanding of it. In the Elysian fields he had wondered sadly how any human soul could bear to go through life's sorrows a second time, and his only question to

Anchises, characteristically, concerned Marcellus, the young, flower-decked hero, untimely dead. And the magic Shield gives him pleasure as an artefact, but he cannot understand its significance.

For the reader of *Aeneid* XII, constructing as he reads a prefiguration of the Augustan settlement which lies outside Aeneas's grasp, there is an impatience, now, to reach the poem's end, to see Italian *uirtus*, for all its spectacular audacity and fire, yield to a stronger force, that of historical necessity, 'what will be in the long run', that which awaits its time, the embodiment of Trojan *pietas* and patience in adversity. The qualities of toughness and endurance, of which Numanus had boasted that the Italians had the monopoly, was all the while building as the greatest strength of the Trojans: *durate*, Aeneas had said in his first words to his storm-wearied company in book I: 'endure'.

Now the time has come, and in Turnus's angry and impetuous arming, the reader too feels a sense of urgency, or impatience for the poem's last dawn, when the duels between Paris and Menelaus, Hector and Achilles, will recur. But the killing of a rival suitor is also an Odyssean motif, and a distant memory of that other Homeric ending may come into a reading of *Aeneid* XII. In the scenes between Amata and Latinus domestic elements are as important as dynastic ones. The motif of *nostos*, homecoming, so strong in *Aeneid* VIII when Aeneas sailed up the Tiber to the site of Rome, is not wholly lost sight of.

The arming of Turnus is a full-scale epic episode based on several Iliadic exemplars, but postponed by Virgil until this last book, and now of much greater impact and significance than the very grand but display-conscious and, in terms of any military outcome, largely gestural arming of Agamemnon in *Iliad* XI; while the arming of Paris for his abortive duel with Menelaus in *Iliad* III strikes the reader almost as a kind of dressing-up. The other two Iliadic armings are those of Patroclus, full of pathos, and of Achilles, full of wrath, but also of foreboding, for it is on this occasion that the horse

Xanthos prophesies his coming death. These two are the crucial armings of the *Iliad*, and it is these which carry for the implied reader of *Aeneid* XII the strongest resonance. But the arming of Turnus is more decisive even than these, for it is the immediate prelude to the end of the war, and its true thematic function is to prefigure the battle of Actium. *nunc . . . nunc tempus adest*, says Turnus, 'now, now the time is at hand': that time of which the poet himself had warned, in book X, when Turnus killed Pallas: *Turno tempus erit . . .* We are at a crisis and turning-point more significant than anything in the *Iliad*: it is time as *kairos* that is at hand, not time as *chronos*.[57]

> For Turnus the time will come when he will pray
>   for Pallas
> To be unharmed, give anything for that, and loathe
> This day, these spoils . . .

This is the time that has now come.

Aeneas's arming is no less powerfully presented:

> Nec minus interea maternis *saeuus* in armis . . .
>
> *No less cruel he, in his mother's gift of arms . . .*

Later, when the war breaks out again in defiance of the treaty, at the instigation of Juturna, Turnus's sister and Juno's agent (her name is a word-play on the other two names), Virgil tells how anger invades both armies and both leaders:

>   non segnius ambo
> Aeneas Turnusque ruunt per proelia; nunc, nunc,
> fluctuat ira intus . . .
>
>   *with no less energy*
> *Aeneas and Turnus charge into battle. Now, now*
> *Is the surge of wrath . . .*

That repeated *nunc, nunc*, picks up the *nunc, nunc, tempus adest*

---

[57] On the distinction see F. Kermode, *The Sense* 46–50.

of Turnus's arming, words addressed to his own spear, perhaps echoing Mezentius's defiant *dextra mihi deus et telum* in x. In this last book we are taken back to book VII and the first outbreak of war-madness in a structure of returning symmetry: the Virgilian Iliad ends as it began.

But the next day sees the treaty between Aeneas, still armed, still with the drawn sword, still *imperator*, and Latinus. Just before it is solemnised, Juno authorises Juturna to overthrow it, so that the reader follows the very grand and majestic account of the ritual with a kind of incredulity. The Homeric model is in *Iliad* III – the treaty solemnised between Agamemnon and Priam before the duel between Menelaus and Paris. Aeneas's prayer at the treaty-making is a version of Agamemnon's: both invoke the Sun, the Earth, Zeus/Jupiter and the Rivers; both give undertakings about what they will do if they lose and if they win (in that order). Aeneas says that he thinks the latter more likely; Agamemnon does not actually say this, but he spends longer on what will happen if he wins than on what will happen if he loses. Virgil also assimilates the opening words of Aeneas's oath to a second oath of Agamemnon's, in the reconciliation between him and Achilles in XIX, when he swears that he has not touched Briseis. Just as that reconciliation is the prelude to Achilles' *aristeia*, and Hector's death, this one is the prelude to Aeneas's *aristeia* and Turnus's death.

With Latinus's oath Virgil introduces a new motif from the *Iliad*, one which contributes further to the sense of tension and unease generated by the scene between Juno and Juturna:

> By that same earth, Aeneas, sea and sky, I also swear
> And by the sun and moon and by two-headed Janus,
> And by the power of the infernal gods, and by the shrine of Dis.
> Hear this, o father of gods and men, who keepest treaties with the power of the thunderbolt.

My hand on this altar, these sacred fires between
   us, and the gods, I so testify:
Never shall come the day for the Italians to break
   this peace, this treaty,
Whatsoever shall befall. No force shall bend my
   will,
While I have any power, no, not even if it should
Pour the whole world into the sea, the heavens into
   hell.
As this sceptre of mine (for he held his sceptre
   now)
Shall never again put forth leaves and give men
   shade
Once cut from the woods and its mother earth,
   trimmed by the knife,
Once a tree, now the hand of the artificer has
   decorated it
With bronze, to be borne by the elders of Latium.

Those last words are the words of Achilles' oath in the quarrel scene in *Iliad* I, when he swears to Agamemnon that the time will come when he will be wanted in battle and will not be there. Achilles' threat comes true in the course of the story, just as Virgil's *Turno tempus erit* comes true when Turnus faces Aeneas wearing Pallas's baldric. Virgil has assimilated two aspects of Homer's Agamemnon. First, in relation to Priam, swearing a treaty before the duel between Helen's 'suitors'; secondly, in relation to Achilles, both in the reconciliation between them in *Iliad* XIX and in the quarrel which set in motion the wrath theme. *Furor*, war-fury, stalks the plain of Latium as once it did the plain of Ilium. Virgil's Aeneas must not sulk, quarrel or withdraw: he must subsume the roles of Menelaus, rightful suitor, and Agamemnon, commander of the armies of victory, and assimilate these roles to those other roles, of Hector and Achilles: Hector to Turnus's Achilles, Achilles to his Hector. But the words of Achilles, the wrath-hero, are now adapted to Latinus, a figure in part of Priam, the old king, unable to control events.

Thus in the final scenes of the Virgilian Iliad, the implied reader must reconstruct the Homeric cause of that tragic death which alone could bring the absent champion back into battle and turn the tide of victory against the defenders. In the *Iliad* itself, the wrath theme is the pre-emptive narrative cause of the greater quarrel, between Achilles and Hector over Patroclus, itself a paradigm of the Trojan conflict as a whole. This final confrontation in *Iliad* XXII eclipsed the duel between Menelaus and Paris, so early in the poem, an expected ingredient of a Troy-tale but not causally linked to the wrath theme.

All these motifs and parallels, then, Virgil has blended into one: nowhere else is his extraordinary 'esemplastic' power, to use Coleridge's remarkable word, so much in evidence. Wrath dominates *Aeneid* XII but it is not the wrath only of Achilles dishonoured by Agamemnon, though that is alluded to in Latinus's oath, and though that quarrel, also over rivalry for a woman, reinforces the quarrel over Helen: the two stories parallel each other.

Latinus's oath is immediately nullified by the swift and sudden intervention of Juturna, which like that of Allecto in VII induces a fresh outburst of war fever. The throwing down of the altars, the defiling of the sacred vessels, the acts of sacrilege which follow the oath, are like the carnage in the *Iliad* which follows Zeus's promise to Thetis. Structurally, both oaths are followed by a renewal of fighting (there is no real fighting in the *Iliad* until book IV). It is to the situation, then, with which Homer's *Iliad* started that Virgil directs the reader as he reaches the twelfth book. The circle is almost complete.

It is at this point that one last crucial placing reference to the Trojan war is offered to the implied reader of *Aeneid* XII. We are taken back once more to the murals in the temple of Juno at Carthage in the first book: thus *Aeneid* XII completes not only the circle of Homer's *Iliad* but the circle of the *Aeneid* itself, a complex double structure of ring-composition. Among the other murals Aeneas had seen Priam unarmed stretching forth his hands in supplication over Hector's corpse, *tendentemque manus Priamum conspexit inermem*. Now in XII when the war breaks out again in defiance of the solemn treaty Virgil writes

> At pius Aeneas dextram tendebat inermem.

Aeneas had been *pius* when he swore his oath, with drawn sword: that sword had become ceremonial; it awaited only Turnus. Now Aeneas is a second Priam, unarmed, suppliant, begging that the treaty be not dishonoured, in a deeply Roman appeal against wrath and on behalf of law:

> o cohibete iras! ictum iam foedus et omnes compositae leges . . .
>
> *O control your wrath. Now is the treaty struck and all The laws enacted . . .*

In his oath to Latinus Aeneas had already promised that the indigenous laws of Latium would remain in force even if the Trojans were victorious:

> paribus se legibus ambae
> inuictae gentes aeterna in foedera mittant.
> sacra deosque dabo; socer arma Latinus habeto
> imperium sollemne socer.
>
> *In equal laws let both
> Nations undefeated make an everlasting covenant.
> I shall set up our gods. Let my father-in-law Latinus hold
> His ancient powers.*

Latinus shall keep his *imperium*: the Roman concept of a duumvirate is strongly felt here, but in the defeat of Latinus after the breaking of the treaty the implied reader may also have to consider the kind of necessity whereby in defiance of all the proclaimed republican principles which stand against allowing all power to flow into one man's hands, Augustus himself nevertheless after Actium assumed all power and established the Principate.[58] And Aeneas's religious mission – *sacra deosque dabo* – which was his sacred trust since he left Troy with the household gods and his father, symbols of *pietas* towards gods and men and the essential feature of the legend of Aeneas – becomes here a formulation of the powers of the head of state as *pontifex maximus*. In the final scene of the poem Aeneas must accept *imperium* and the role of lawgiver as well as *religio* and the role of *pontifex*. The breaking of the treaty has made this necessary. The Italians have shown themselves deficient in *pietas*, as did the Greeks when they sacked 'the holy citadel of Priam': the denotative 'holy' is that of a patriotic Greek poet, Homer himself, and if he was using a traditional formula that only confirms the persistence of the idea of Trojan *pietas*.

The spectacle of Aeneas stretching forth his unarmed hand in supplication against the sacrilege of treaty-breaking and the horror of war completes the cycle of the second Iliad. Aeneas must re-enact the role of Priam before he re-enacts that of Achilles, an Achilles whose wrath is that anger without which no man can fight at all. Sergeant-majors who incite their recruits to scream furiously at the dummies they run at with fixed bayonets act correctly in abnormal circumstances. To kill in cold blood is not in the nature of most men, and epic heroes are not psychopaths. Aeneas's *furor* is the direct outcome of war and is a direct response to it; Achilles' anger in *Iliad* 1 was a matter of personal pique over the spoils of war. Virgil's Iliad must enact a transcendence of the old heroic code of personal honour and material gain; Turnus must finally discredit that code, but so also must Aeneas himself. And perhaps what is to be discarded must first be discredited.

> Nec minus interea maternis saeuus in armis
> Aeneas acuit Martem et se suscitat ira . . .

[58] See Syme, *The Roman Revolution* (2nd ed., Oxford 1952) 297. It was largely due to Virgil's artistry that the story of Aeneas and the battle of Actium took on a similar colouring as official myths of the Augustan principate and became parts of the same larger-than-life epic narrative.

> *No less cruel he, in his mother's gift of arms,*
> *Whetted the knife of war and roused himself in*
> *   wrath . . .*

When the treaty was solemnised Aeneas laid aside his wrath; afterwards, that wrath re-invades him as much as it does Turnus:

>   non segnius ambo
> Aeneas Turnusque ruunt per proelia; nunc, nunc
> fluctuat ira intus . . .

The allusion to Priam in the treaty-scene further enriches our reading of the final scenes of *Aeneid* XII and deepens our understanding of what Virgil himself meant by the wrath of war. In *Aeneid* II Aeneas had described to Dido how Priam, before he was killed by Pyrrhus on that last dreadful night of Troy, said that even Achilles had not threatened him but was abashed, respected the rights due to old age and the suppliant, and had returned the body of Hector. The conduct of the Homeric Achilles in *Iliad* XXIV provides the necessary and confirmed conclusion to the poem of his wrath. The chain of events which started with the quarrel in *Iliad* I – Achilles' withdrawal, Zeus's promise to Thetis, the Trojan counter-attack, Hector's *aristeia* and Patroclus's death, Achilles' reconciliation with Agamemnon, his *aristeia*, the revenge-killing of Hector and the dishonouring of his body – ends when Achilles, of his own free will, and not under divine coercion, though with strong divine prompting, surrenders Hector's dead body to Priam as, in book I, he had refused to surrender Briseis's living body to Agamemnon.

But Aeneas, when he kills Turnus, is not only acting out again the Patroclus-motif: he must also avenge the murder of Priam. The wounding of Aeneas the suppliant is thus a crucial element in the poem's final scenes. It transfers to the Latins the guilt of the Greeks on the last night of Troy. They too have thrown down altars and overturned shrines, now they have tried to kill an unarmed man, *pontifex* not *imperator*, and only divine intervention heals the priest-king's wound. At the miracle of healing the surgeon Iapyx speaks some significant words. Once again, as in the *Iliad*, Aeneas is preserved for the future of his race.

> non haec humanis opibus, non arte magistra
> proueniunt, neque te, Aenea, mea dextera seruat:
> maior agit deus atque opera ad maiora remittit.
>
> *No human help is here, and by no master's art*
> *Are these things done; not by my hand, Aeneas.*
> *A greater god acts here, to greater work sends you forth*
>   *again.*

The greater work which now awaits Aeneas will itself complete the *maius opus*, the greater work undertaken in *Aeneid* VII by the implied author, of which book XII is the fulfilment.

In the renewed conflict which now follows many more men are killed. The poet in his own person asks, stepping outside his own narrative, as he had at the start of book I,

> tanton placuit concurrere motu,
> Iuppiter, aeterna gentis in pace futuras?
>
> *Was this great conflict your will,*
> *Jupiter, between nations destined for eternal peace?*

The implied reader recalls the eleventh line of the *Aeneid*: *tantaene animis caelestibus irae?*, 'Is there in heavenly spirits so much wrath?' Jupiter had said in book X that the war between Latins and Trojans, indigenous and immigrant nations, civil war (*discordia*), was against his will (*abnueram*). He thus appeared to permit what he had not willed. This theological paradox persists throughout epic narrative. Men will their own acts, but within a pattern of destiny foreknown by the gods, resisted by some of them (Juno, Satan), and glimpsed by some mortals in moments of foreboding or revelation, by most men, never.

Virgil's questions are the beginning and end of the poem: 'Is there in heavenly beings so much anger?' 'Was this great conflict your will, Jupiter?' create a theological framework within the confines of which the narrative moves. But the questions – how can the gods permit, even encourage, world-evil – present the questioner in a role other than that of empathising narrator, and identify the poem's most significant 'undecidability'. If the *Aeneid* is a kind of pagan saint's legend, the reader must be expected to assent, as a believer, to the hero as a man operating in a universe in which historical necessity and divine providence move to their appointed end. If the poem is to be read as a poem of ideas, a spiritual pilgrimage for the reader as well as the hero, then the poet as metaphysician becomes more important in any construction of a total meaning for the poem than the epic narrator; the doubtful, speculative questions offer a morally ambiguous ideology which is bound to cast its shadow over any reading of the end of the poem. Indeed, if the reader is to assent to the implied author's ideological and moral uncertainty, it must alter his sense of the poem as a whole. The implied author has, after all, chosen to remind us of his opening question as we reach the poem's last narrative stretch. He need not have done this. The presented world of the poem must include this moral doubt, and the reader is included in that doubt. The gods do not merely allow men to enact history as Jupiter proclaimed in book x. By their own discords, they create the tensions within which that history must be enacted.

The last question of the poet – 'Was this great conflict your will, Jupiter?' – occurs in the poem's last invocation, itself cast in the form of a question.

> Quis mihi nunc tot acerba deus, quis carmine caedes
> diuersas obitumque ducum, quos aequore toto
> inque uicem nunc Turnus agit, nunc Troius heros,
> expediat?

What god, now, I wonder, could unfold in song

> *So many bitter things and diverse deaths and falls*
> *Of princes, over all the field*
> *By Turnus now despatched, now by the Trojan hero*
> *. . .*

The invocation is a gesture towards Homeric authorial convention. Before long stretches of narrative, especially those containing many names, an appeal to the remembering Muses signals to the hearer a guarantee of the accuracy of the sequence and a correct attribution of the various achievements. It also implies that the poet himself is following tradition rather than composing in his own right. But Virgil uses the tradition quite differently. He implies the unwillingness, if not the powerlessness, of any god to assist in the chronicling of such bitter and tragic events. It is as if, the epic now moving to its end, the implied author is casting doubt on the epic tradition itself, with its divine apparatus, its aiding Muses, its never-failing machinery. It is not the historical but the moral credibility of the last events which seems beyond earthly chronicle and beyond divine inspiration. Could Jupiter himself underwrite so sad a story of the death of kings?

The paragraph beginning with this doubtful invocation, with its triple *nunc* (*now* who can tell what happened *now* . . .) ends with some lines already quoted:

> non segnius ambo
> Aeneas Turnusque ruunt per proelia; nunc, nunc
> fluctuat ira intus, rumpuntur nescia uinci
> pectora, nunc totis in uulnera uiribus itur.

The two heroes are compared to forest fires converging on dry brushwood, and to mountain rivers. They are alike in their destructive power, in their violence, in their lack of control. The whole emphasis of the paragraph is on the indistinguishable conduct of the two sides and the two leaders.[59] The triple *nunc* at the end of the passage encloses it inside a

---

[59] In *Iliad* XVIII, Hector 'becomes' Achilles when he puts on his armour (taken from the dead Patroclus). The two heroes are mirror images of each other. See Ferrucci, *Poetics* 26–8.

narrative 'present' which, in the poet's own 'now', is total and inescapable. The elemental blindness of irrationality is like fire and water. In natural disaster there is only a timeless 'now'. So in the double *aristeia* of the two heroes: often the reader cannot quickly identify the killer, either by the *hic* or *ille* which designates him, or by the undifferentiated catalogue of victims, most of whom simultaneously enter and leave the poem, like names on a list of the fallen. I believe we can see here an authorial intention which has not been fully recognised. Servius was the first to notice a confusion:[60] but suppose it to be deliberate? Suppose the implied author to be saying that total war cannot be contained within decorous epic conventions? Suppose that, ultimately, it does not matter who kills whom? Suppose that, like Jupiter, the poet makes no distinction between the two sides? On such hypotheses a view of war emerges which is closer to that of Wilfred Owen than to Homer: that emphasis on *nunc* does not allow the implied reader to pretend that this all belongs in the remote past.

> If you could hear, at every jolt, the blood
> Come gargling from the froth-corrupted lungs . . .
> My friend, you would not tell with such high zest
> To children ardent for some desperate glory
> The old Lie: Dulce et decorum est
> Pro patria mori.[61]

But there is one victim of *furor* who stands out in these final scenes. Though briefly narrated, and without direct speech, the suicide of Amata is crucial to Turnus's final isolation. Moreover, there are uneasy echoes of another queen's suicide. Now both leaders have this on their conscience; once more, the scales are balanced, *Tros Rutulusne fuat, nullo discrimine habebo*: Jupiter's words come grimly home again to the reader. Both queens die, what is more, as a direct result of thwarted dynastic ambition.

---

[60] Servius on 10.747–54: *hoc loco est confusio in aliquibus nominibus. Nam quis sit Troianus, quis sit Rutulus, ignoratur.* M. Willcock, 'Battle Scenes in the *Aeneid*', *PCPS* (1983) 87–99.
[61] Wilfred Owen, 'Dulce et Decorum Est'.

Just as in book X Jupiter abandoned the war to the heroes who must fight it, who must enact history, so now he abandons Turnus, or Turnus thinks he does. Amata, too, had killed herself under a delusion, that Turnus was already dead. And perhaps he is, as good as dead: *di me terrent et Iuppiter hostis*, he says; 'the gods terrify me, Jupiter himself is my enemy'.[62] He sees that he has crossed the permitted bounds of his power, into an isolation comparable, perhaps, in its pagan context with the isolation of Marlowe's Dr Faustus. Turnus in the closing scene of the epic retains the bravado which has been his most conspicuous characteristic, but the despair of those six words (he speaks after that only once more, to surrender to Aeneas and ask that his body be returned for burial, in the conventional and formal manner of the old-style Homeric hero) is absolute. It is a despair already articulated by his sister Juturna, who, lamenting her immortality, asks

> Could any abyss of the earth be deep enough
> To open and swallow me and send me to the shades?

Turnus himself had used some of those same 'Faustian' words in his soliloquy in book X when he was carried away on the ship in his vain pursuit of the phantom Aeneas: but only some of them. He had not then fully experienced the longing to die now articulated by Juturna. In this growing atmosphere of despair Virgil more and more reminds the reader of parallels between Turnus and Dido. And because there is a parallel with Dido there is also one with another suicide of an enemy of Rome, Cleopatra, and thus Aeneas in his hour of victory will complete his prefiguration of Augustus at Actium and, with whatever reluctance or show of reluctance, accept supreme power. The single combat was not only a device to spare more lives; it was a means of ensuring that the survivor was without a challenger and could now proceed to dispose as he wished the total power which had come to him, by the will of the gods.

[62] W. Fowler, *The Death of Turnus* (Oxford 1919) 152–6.

There is a strong sense in any reading of the poem nowadays, and this has perhaps been true ever since the Renaissance, that Turnus and Dido are tragic victims in the classical mode, hubristic, flawed by *hamartia*, proclaiming a self-deluding innocence. Turnus's farewell reads like an operatic aria, as indeed does Dido's, with its final dramatic gesture, *sic, sic iuuat ire sub umbras*, as she stabs herself on the words *sic, sic*. Turnus too makes a self-dramatising and self-justifying statement:

>   uos, o mihi Manes
> este boni, quoniam superis auersa uoluntas.
> sancta ad uos anima atque istius inscia culpae
> descendam magnorum haud umquam indignus
>   auorum.

> *O shades below, to me*
> *Be good, now that heaven's will has turned from me.*
> *I shall to you a holy soul and innocent of blame*
> *Go down for ever worthy of my great forefathers.*

Turnus proclaims his innocence, not as a general moral claim, but as a specific repudiation of the one fault no hero can carry: cowardice. It is an act of bravado, or propitiation to the gods of the underworld, *dis manibus*, and perhaps a belated defence against Drances' rankling accusations in XI. Turnus has always put himself first, and does so to the end: again, he acts like a pagan Faustus, and the reader may now perhaps also recall Juno's defiance of the Olympian will: 'if I can't persuade the gods above, I'll stir up hell'. Aeneas has never put himself first, he has acted throughout *non sponte sua*, as Augustus also claimed he acted, not by his own will but by that of the people of Italy who asked him to be their leader.[63] Dido had put her own political and sexual needs first; so did Cleopatra. The end for which Aeneas has laboured is not merely outside himself: it lies beyond his son's lifetime, in remote centuries which will

---

[63] *iurauit in mea uerba tota Italia sponte sua, et me belli quo uici ad Actium, ducem depoposcit* (*Res Gestae Diui Augusti* 25.2).

only start to evolve with Romulus. Only beyond two myths can Roman history begin. That end lies, too, beyond the poem as narrative, yet it is an essential part of any reading of it, since the reader is not meant to be bound by Aeneas's perspectives, but to see beyond them. And how is the reader to be stopped from seeing also beyond Virgil's?

Yet the grandeur of Turnus's egotism, in his daring to cross the permitted limits of his world, the courage which shines through his egotism, will not vanish wholly from history, and (like Faustus's soul) 'ne'er be found'. It will persist in many acts of personal *uirtus* in time of danger throughout Rome's history, acts depicted on Aeneas's Shield, associated with Romulus, Horatius Cocles, Cloelia (of whom Camilla is the type), Manlius, Cato. Turnus's grandeur dominates book XII as Dido's had dominated book IV.

The settlement between Jupiter and Juno in XII is a mirror of the scene between Jupiter and Venus in I: a mighty instance of returning symmetry or 'ring-composition'. The smile with which Jupiter turns to Juno

> olli subridens hominum rerumque repertor

mirrors the smile with which he had reassured Venus in book I that all in the long run should be well

> olli subridens hominum sator atque deorum

The words are a clear signal from the implied author that the reader is approaching the end.

> This nation which shall arise from Italian stock
> Shall in its piety transcend both men and gods.
> You shall see it.
> And no nation shall honour you as they shall.

Here is the famous transformation of Juno from inveterate anti-Trojan to guardian of Rome, a member, with Minerva and Jupiter himself, of the 'Capitoline triad' of deities who symbolised *imperium sine fine*. 'You can't beat us – join us': *uidebis*, 'you shall see it', is a joke of the implied author (and part of the joke is that he speaks now with the voice of Jupiter) to the Augustan reader. Not *uidebis* but *uides*. The future becomes present and completes a meaning. Not 'the meaning': for the modern reader cannot make that particular syntactical change. For him, the implied future is already past. Yet he may, reaching this end, suspend syntax, with that future not yet mediated into history, 'something evermore about to be', held in a past remoter from him than Troy was from the Augustans.

The end of the *Aeneid* is not 'just' the death of Turnus, abrupt, perfunctory even, with its repeated curtain line already used for Camilla as Homer had used Patroclus's for Hector. Homer saw that Hector's death could not be the end of the *Iliad*; there had to be a resolution of the wrath theme, the long decrescendo of the games and the ransoming of Hector's body to Priam, alone in the tent with his son's killer.

The *Aeneid* has two endings. The sending of Turnus's soul is the narrator's last task, the god's last sad act of chronicle vicariously and reluctantly performed.

> What god now, I wonder, could unfold in song
> So many bitter things and diverse deaths and falls
> Of princes, over all the field
> By Turnus now despatched, now by the Trojan
>   hero . . .

When Aeneas despatches Turnus, the reader's task may seem to be at an end. The narrative is complete, the presented world of the Virgilian Iliad stops, with the death of Turnus as Hector and the triumph of Aeneas as Achilles. But the reader must also transform the narrative by including the process by which the presented world is offered, and make this a part of his understanding of the poem's total meaning. And for this there is the poem's other ending to be included: that is, the scene between Jupiter and Juno, and, behind that, the mirror scene between Jupiter and Venus, so that in a sense the poem's 'end' was written in book I. When the reader gets to the end of XII, images and motifs from book I remain in, or return to, his mind, a persistence more powerful than, and in a sense transcending, any specific reading: almost an independent life in the memory of the poem's meaning, a life independent, that is, of the actual 'text'. We may emphasise different parts of the poem with each reading, select this, exclude that, but our interaction with the poem will in the end be more than the sum of any particular passages read or translated, and will lead to the construction of an *Aeneid sine fine*, 'without end', the poem as a prelude to history and to the understanding of history.

Patterns of returning symmetry are found in a variety of narrative fictions from Homer onwards. For the reader of long works, these structures facilitate the construction of a total meaning: the sense of the ending involves a memory of the beginning: the true significance of the presented world of the fiction is perceived through the presentational process itself. When we first met Aeneas in *Aeneid* I, he was cold, tired, frightened and wishing he had died at Troy. 'His limbs were numb with cold', *soluuntur frigore membra* (1.92): the allusion here, and in the speech which follows, the *o terque quaterque beati*, 'o thrice and four times blessed . . .', is to *Odyssey* v, where Odysseus is also lost in a storm and far from the goal of his *nostos*. Odysseus wished he had died when the Trojans tried so hard to get him after Achilles' death. Aeneas wishes he had not survived Diomede's onslaught, and had died alongside Sarpedon and Hector, deaths closely linked with the saga of Achilles' wrath, deaths fated to be re-enacted in the Italian Iliad. Those words far away in book I, *soluuntur frigore membra*, recur in the last line but one of book XII: now they describe Turnus, and the cold is not that of the elements, or of a wished for and elusive death, but of the thing itself, inescapably there. In 1.97 Aeneas wished he had died at the right hand of Diomede, 'I wish I could have poured out this soul of mine': at the end of XII it is Aeneas's right hand which pours out Turnus's soul. The motif of Aeneas's preservation for posterity, first heard at the poem's outset, is heard again at its ending. It is for this he was spared. He has re-enacted the Iliadic vendetta, not just to avenge a personal loss (the

Pallas–Patroclus motif) but to secure the future 'so that the race of Dardanus might not perish', thus validating both Iliadic and Roman prophecy.

At the end of the *Aeneid*, Aeneas is nearly persuaded into an act of mercy which, had he managed it, would have perhaps changed the modern reader's sense of the entire text.

> et iam iamque magis cunctantem flectere sermo
> coeperat . . .
>
> *And now he hesitated, now Turnus's words nearly*
> *Turned him from his purpose . . .*

But the Iliadic motif of the armour of Patroclus is introduced, and Aeneas plunges in the sword, in a last access of that *furor* which in Homer's Achilles was by the last book of the *Iliad* spent: that same *furor* which Hercules, the type of culture hero and saviour hero, had shown in his killing of Cacus in book VIII, itself prefigurative of this last duel. Hercules in VIII is *furens animis*, he is *feruidus ira*. This is the model for Aeneas at the end of XII, *furiis accensus et ira | terribilis*. When he puts in the sword he is *feruidus*, in contrast to Turnus, on whom the cold of death has settled:

> '. . . Pallas te hoc uulnere, Pallas
> immolat et poenam scelerato ex sanguine sumit.'
> hoc dicens ferrum aduerso sub pectore condit
> feruidus; ast illi soluuntur frigore membra
> uitaque cum gemitu fugit indignata sub umbras.
>
> *'Pallas strikes you down, with this cut Pallas*
> *Takes this vengeance, sheds your evil blood.'*
> *Thus saying he buries his sword in the other's breast*
> *In the heat of the moment. But the other's limbs are cold,*
> *And his reluctant spirit, crying, vanishes to the dead.*

Structurally, the Iliadic revenge motif becomes a cover for the politically necessary elimination of a dangerous rival. (So too for Octavian the morally outrageous conduct of Antony with Cleopatra provided a cover for what was politically necessary.) At the end of the *Odyssey* no reader wants Odysseus to spare the suitors, and perhaps Virgil wanted his implied reader to take some of his sense of the ending of the *Aeneid* from the end of the *Odyssey*. But there is no psychological paradigm, and, for the modern, though perhaps not the implied Augustan reader, only a doubtful moral one. Despite the oracles, it is hard for the reader to feel much enthusiasm for Aeneas's claim to Lavinia or to see Turnus in the role of Paris rather than Menelaus. But for the implied reader Aeneas is Menelaus, who has traversed the sea to claim his lawful bride and secure the succession. The pattern of arrival, combat and victory (for the absence of Achilles is the crucial single element in the plot of the *Iliad*) seems peculiarly Homeric, and is common to both *Iliad* and *Odyssey*. Behind the despatching to the shades of Turnus's reluctant soul it is not easy, though, to detect the twittering shades of Penelope's suitors, down in Hades among the souls of Troy's greatest dead. It is to these great warrior ghosts that Turnus, in his self-proclaiming pride, descends.

Epic heroes may make the world a better place, albeit only for the time being. They cannot make it a good one. For Virgil all war is mad and one cannot conduct oneself morally on the battlefield. Only in an Odyssean sense can the killing of Turnus be morally acceptable, and then only if we import into our reading a sense that Aeneas's marriage to Lavinia was made in heaven long before her earthly betrothal to Turnus. This is a revenge killing, for Pallas–Patroclus; and for the killing in the *Iliad* of Trojan Hector, so that the reader may transfer to the furious Aeneas some of the anger he, the reader of the *Iliad* also, felt at the treatment of Hector by the furious Achilles. The foul deeds which Homer himself says Achilles devised for noble Hector are now requited.

Homer's Trojan war was fought for a domestic cause, yet clearly the deaths of so many great heroes and the ultimate destruction of the city of Troy, distantly descried within the poem yet lying, as an event, beyond it, gives the work a tragic grandeur and plenitude which transcends the story of Helen: transcends also the wrath theme. Virgil's Lavinia is much more of a minor character than the Helen of *Iliad* III, whom we see relating in such different ways to Priam, Aphrodite and Paris (let alone the Helen of *Odyssey* IV, reunited with Menelaus): indeed, Lavinia never speaks. It is not because of her that Aeneas is seized with that last cold fit of wrath. Turnus had not expected to be spared: he faced his destiny to the end. His request for decent burial follows that of Hector to Achilles. Aeneas does not echo Achilles' terrible rejection of that plea. Indeed, he goes much further than merely not rejecting the plea for burial: he nearly spared his life, *dextramque repressit*, 'stayed his hand'. Some critics have suggested that the final decision was a piece of covert political allegory, an encoded reference to acts of cruelty by Augustus against political rivals. But I know of no evidence for this. In *The Faerie Queene* Spenser has left the reader signs by which to construct from the narrative of Mercilla and Duessa an allegorical 'meaning' in terms of contemporary politics. There seems nothing comparable in the final scene of the *Aeneid*. What ought to surprise the reader, or so it seems to me, is not that Aeneas does not spare Turnus, but that he should have hesitated at all. The hesitation constitutes the surprise.

We know that Virgil abandoned the idea of an epic about Augustus in favour of a different kind of epic, a kind of synchronisation of the *Iliad* and Actium. The Homeric epics remain the principal ordering structure of the *Aeneid*. But this does not enclose readings of the poem within the confines, large and complex though they are, of the Homeric epics. It is unfortunate that some modern readings of the *Aeneid* take the poem's political and historical signs as propaganda, and there is sometimes a tendency to suppress these and see the poem 'without' or 'despite' this element. Or it is argued that Virgil himself lost faith in the Augustan dream, and wanted the poem destroyed not just because it had not been finally revised but because of some fancied 'philosophical' revulsion from

Realpolitik; and that Augustus's determination to have it published posthumously was a propagandist decision.

Augustus did not need propaganda. He had after Actium no rival, but what he did want was display, in various forms, in sculpture as well as poetry, of the values and virtues of the principate. Jupiter's first speech, for example, may be read like that. The benefits to Rome of the new régime flowed from the *princeps* downwards in a great expression of celebration. Virgil saw in the popular story of Aeneas a paradigm of those benefits, the story of the assumption, with some appropriate show of cautious reluctance, by one man of powers traditionally and destructively divided.

Virgil began his poetic career, in the first *Eclogue*, with an idealistic *Dankgesang* for the benefits, in *otium* and *libertas*, of the new leader, a saviour-hero for whom, as for Hercules, extravagantly figurative language was appropriate both in terms of literary tradition and as a political gesture. Between the pastoral poet's heartfelt thanksgiving for peace to write – *deus nobis haec otia fecit*, 'a god has made us this peace' – and the vision of the *pax Augusta* in Jupiter's speech, in *Aeneid* I, it is hard to register any falling-off of enthusiasm for the new order.

At the end of the *Odyssey*, Homer fulfilled, in another returning symmetry, the promise of Zeus to his daughter Athene in book I: Odysseus, a good man, who took heed of the gods, would come safe home, unlike Agamemnon, and despite the opposition of Poseidon. (The fulfilment of a divine promise thus provides the starting-point for Homer's two epics.) This structure is repeated in the *Aeneid*: Aeneas, a good man, made safe landfall, as promised by Jupiter to his daughter in book I, propitiated Juno and secured the Trojan succession by dynastic intermarriage. If Aeneas had not hesitated, there would be no problem at the end of the poem.

But he did. Would the implied reader, should he, have hesitated also, delaying assent to the final slaughter, the last piece of the Homeric jigsaw? It is an assent the modern reader, such is the nature of the poem, may continue to withhold. He may indeed want to 'lose' the poem after that *iam iamque magis*; to emphasise that moment, prolonged as though for ever, and skip the final act with its double Homeric allusion to Hector and the suitors ('noble Hector' and the suitors, more deplorable than Turnus). The combined tragic and moral strengths of the *Iliad* and the *Odyssey* could not provide Virgil with any other ending for his unendable poem. Where else could he have got another ending?

There was nowhere else. Aeneas's last act is an existential choice, terrible as such choices are; so it was also for the implied author, self-obliged to re-enact Homer in a historical context which lets in the reader's own doubts and insecurities.

Among all the burdens Aeneas carried – his father and his gods from Homeric Troy, the Shield bearing the fame and destiny of the future Rome – itself a model of the universe, which Atlas bore on his shoulders and which Hercules traversed in the cause of civilisation – the burden of Homeric epic was the greatest, for it was the poet's own. In the last lines of the poem he all but lays it aside – but not quite. The hero who turns his sword in Turnus's heart is the same man of whom, far back in book I, Virgil wrote: fate-driven, pursued by divine hatred, burdened, unlucky. His last words to his son in book XII are important now:

> Learn virtue and the truth about a hero's labours
> From me. But luck? Get that from others.

Of all Aeneas's burdens, this last killing is the heaviest, yet it always awaited him. The time that was foretold for Turnus was also his time, his *kairos*. He could not know, till the moment came, the doubts and hesitations it would involve. The hesitation at the end is the hero's and the reader's, for an existential choice is made for all, and sets a certain stamp upon humanity.

And perhaps that hesitation is also the poet's. His sense of having left the *Aeneid* unrevised, of being unable to complete a fully achieved text, are well authenticated. Thus there entered into the poem when it was published with its fifty-seven hemistichs (some of them editorially completed, though these completions have never entered the text), a sense of the finally unachieved.

Thus any reading of the poem will, even more than would be the case with a fully achieved work (for no finality is conceivable in any act of reading) produce a sense of having reached only one of many possible meanings. (*The Faerie Queene*, not merely unrevised but incomplete in terms of the poet's own published schema, is a more extreme example.) The very abruptness and, in a curious sense, the very finality of the ending of the *Aeneid* leaves the reader with a sense of uncertainty. The ending was foreseen and structurally 'given', and indeed in the scene on Olympus the reader has already gone past, overshot that narrative 'end': in its vaster perspective the death of Turnus seems almost like a flashback, although written in the historic present, 'narrative time'. Yet because the devices of prophecy had opened the poem up beyond its narrative end, the reader may wonder about the possibility of ending at all an epic whose revealed theme was *imperium sine fine*. And does not the uneasy 'end' imply for the modern reader doubts and ironies about *imperium sine fine* which, once read into the poem, seem to become Virgil's own? The splendours which the poem 'prophetically' opens up are now part of a past which for many readers exists now chiefly *in* the poem itself. The author and his implied (Augustan) reader had access to external referents, institutions, monuments, the living tissue of history, which he drew upon in the great visions of Rome in books I, VI and VIII. Now those descriptions often amount to all, or nearly all, we have. The rest has gone, or survives in material only the specialist can interpret. They have been superseded in our minds by a past Virgil could not imagine. Any reading of the *Aeneid*, then, will be coloured by insights and images to which Virgil had no access. And this too, in some unmistakable way, becomes part of the poem. The old idea of Virgil as *anima naturaliter Christiana*, poised uncertainly at the very end of the era of what Dante called the false and lying gods, unable to escape from the pagan world to whose values he seemed not wholly to assent, remains powerful. And we may recall other words of Dante, from the *Purgatorio*, the last words he wrote for Virgil to say in *his* epic:

> Expect no more signs from me . . .
> You are free to choose . . .[64]

I believe the peace and freedom, *otium* and *libertas*, with which Virgil hailed the Augustan settlement, remained for him the cornerstone of his creative career. I believe that in writing the *Aeneid*, his greatest work, and especially in writing the second half of it, *maius opus*, he found himself less free in his choices. As he went on, he created more and more signs to denote a hero for whom there simply did not exist enough freedom of choice. Dante perceived with love and reverence how close Virgil might have come to understanding the nature and value of freedom in choice and action. When he made Jupiter in book x detach himself from the action, he gave his heroes as much freedom as it was in his power to give them. The modern reader may invest Aeneas with a greater range of insight and choice than he could have possessed for his creator, and may also create an implied author with access to value-systems which lie in fact beyond the limits of the poem and of the pagan world. Yet the reader, importing these, is not, save in the narrowest and most scholastic sense, 'misinterpreting' the *Aeneid*. Indeed, he may be uncovering a more significant text, one that may be related to a greater range of insights into history and humanity.

[64] *Purgatorio* 27.139.

BIBLIOGRAPHY

Austin, R. G. (ed.) *Aeneid II*. Oxford 1964.
Barthes, R. *Introduction to the Structural Analysis of Narrative*. Birmingham 1966. (Translation of an essay first published in *Communications* 8 (1966).)
Bethell, S. L. *Essays on Literary Criticism and the English Tradition*. London 1969.
Booth, W. *The Rhetoric of Fiction*. Chicago 1961.
Bowra, C. M. *Homer*. London 1972.
Coleman, R. G. G. (ed.) *Vergil: Eclogues*. Cambridge 1977.
Conington, J. and Nettleship, H. (eds.) *The Works of Virgil, with a Commentary*, vol. III (*Aen.* VII–XII), rev. edn. London 1875.
Conway, R. S. (ed.) *Aeneid I*. Cambridge 1935.
Culler, J. *The Pursuit of Signs*. London 1981.
Eden, P. T. (ed.) *Aeneid VII*. Leiden 1975.
Ferrucci, F. *The Poetics of Disguise*. Cornell, Ithaca 1980.
Fordyce, C. J. (ed.) *Aeneid VII–VIII*. Oxford 1977.
Fowler, W. *Virgil's Gathering of the Clans*. Oxford 1918.
  The Death of Turnus. Oxford 1919.
Fraenkel, E. 'Some Aspects of the Structure of *Aeneid* VII', *JRS* 35 (1945) 1–14.
Gransden, K. W. (ed.) *Virgil: Aeneid VIII*. Cambridge 1976.
Griffin, J. *Homer on Life and Death*. Oxford 1980.
Highet, G. *The Speeches in Vergil's Aeneid*. Princeton 1972.
Johnson, W. R. *Darkness Visible*. Berkeley 1976.
Johnston, P. A. *Virgil's Agricultural Golden Age*. Leiden 1980.
Kermode, F. *The Sense of an Ending*. Oxford 1967.
Kirk, G. S. *Homer and the Oral Tradition*. Cambridge 1976.
Knauer, G. N. *Die Aeneis und Homer*. Göttingen 1964.
Lanham, R. 'Theory of the Λόγοι: the Speeches in Classical and Renaissance Narrative', in *To Tell a Story*, Clark Library Seminar Papers. Los Angeles 1973.
Macleod, C. W. (ed.) *Homer: Iliad Book XXIV*. Cambridge 1982.
Newman, J. K. *Augustus and the New Poetry*, Latomus 88. Brussels 1967.
Otis, B. *Virgil: a Study in Civilised Poetry*. Oxford 1964.
Oxford Latin Dictionary, ed. P. G. W. Glare. Oxford 1982.

Pöschl, V. *The Art of Virgil*. Ann Arbor 1962.
Richards, I. A. *The Philosophy of Rhetoric*. Oxford 1936.
Ruthrof, H. *The Reader's Construction of Narrative*. London 1981.
Syme, R. *The Roman Revolution*, 2nd edn. Oxford 1952.
Tolstoi, L. *War and Peace*, trans. N. L. and A. Maude. Oxford 1944.
West, D. 'Multiple Correspondence Similes in the *Aeneid*', *JRS* 59 (1969) 40–9.
West, D. and Woodman, T. *Creative Imitation and Latin Literature*. Cambridge 1979.
Willcock, M. M. *Companion to the Iliad*. Chicago 1976.
  (ed.) *The Iliad of Homer: Books I–XII*. London 1978.
  'Battle Scenes in the *Aeneid*', *PCPS* 87–99 (1983).
Williams, R. D. (ed.) *Aeneid I–VI*. London 1972.
  (ed.) *Aeneid VII–XII*. London 1973.
  (ed.) *Virgil: The Eclogues and Georgics*. London 1979.
Wilson, C. H. 'Jupiter and the Fates in the *Aeneid*', *CQ* 29 (1979) 361–71.

INDEXES

1 Names

Achilles, 11ff., 21ff., 58–60, 104–5, 113, 125–8, 136–8, 142–5, 162–3, 166, 192, 196ff.
Agamemnon, 13–17, 24–5, 172, 175, 177, 194, 196–7
Aineias (Homer's), 130, 135–7, 145–6, 175
Ajax, 124, 127, 166
Allecto, 55, 76–80
Amata, 76–80, 184
Antenor, 177
Antores, 152–3
Augustus, 57, 91–4, 128, 139

Briseis, 14, 25

Camilla, 3, 86–7, 183–90
Camillus, 188–90
Cleopatra, 3, 111

Dante, 34n., 39, 83, 149, 217
Dido, 3, 45, 60–1, 167–8, 187–8, 191
Diomede, 87, 174–7, 184
Drances, 167, 175, 177–83

Euphorbus, 115–16, 189
Euryalus, *see* Nisus and Euryalus
Evander, 56–7, 88–92, 143

Gorgythion, 115

Harpalyce, 189–90
Hector, 15–16, 113, 123–4, 142, 145–6, 159, 166, 170, 175, 192–3, 198ff.
Helen, 19–20, 85, 111, 171–3
Hera, 71–2, 133–4, 146–8
Heracles (Hercules), 38, 45, 51, 72, 91, 141, 167

Ilioneus, 60–2, 90

Juno, 36–9, 67–81, 146–9, 207–9
Jupiter, 36–7, 106–7, 130–8, 141, 146–9, 156

Latinus, 44–6, 55–62, 66–8, 174ff., 196ff.
Lausus, 105, 140, 152–3
Liger, 144
Lucretius, 63, 109, 138, 149–51
Lycaon, 104–5, 143–5

Marcellus, 105, 117, 194
Menelaus, 19, 44–5, 81, 173, 181, 194, 197–8, 212–13
Mercury, 49–56, 189
Mezentius, 86, 93–4, 151–5, 159–61, 196
Milton, 42–3, 50, 63, 65–6, 71, 133, 135–6, 167
Mnestheus, 123–4
Muses, 27, 39–43, 112, 203–4

Napoleon, 11, 24–5
Neptune, 55, 72–3
Nisus and Euryalus, 102–9, 162

Odysseus, 100, 102

Palinurus, 33
Pallas, 90–3, 104–6, 113, 116–17, 125–6, 140–3, 161ff., 179
Pandarus, 120–1
Patroclus, 27ff., 104, 113–14, 126–8, 138, 141–4, 162–3
Penthesilea, 3, 86, 186–7
Polydamas, 97, 176–7
Poseidon, 71–4, 99n., 135–6, 146
Priam, 19–21, 144, 196–7, 200–1

Sarpedon, 128, 141–2, 170
Saturn, 62–4
Sibyl, 88, 184–5

Thersites, 122, 177–8

INDEX OF PASSAGES

Thetis, 37, 97
Tiber (Tiberinus), 33, 88, 95, 124–5, 139
Tolstoi, 10–11, 15, 25ff., 41
Troilus, 104–5, 141
Turnus, 77–9, 98–9, 142–3, 150–2, 178–83, 191ff.

Venus, 36–8, 73, 131–3, 147–8
Virbius, 86, 189–90

Zeus, 11, 14–15, 17, 72, 97, 130, 135, 147–8, 175

2 Passages from the *Aeneid*

This index will enable the reader to identify passages from the *Aeneid* quoted in the book. The figures in brackets are line-references, the unbracketed figures page references.

Aen. I (3) 2, (488) 2, (565) 61, (459–60) 61, (36) 70, (126) 72, (4) 73, (11) 74, 202, (474–5) 103–4, 141, (257–96) 132–3, (479–82) 183, (490–3) 187, (487) 199, (254) 208, (92) 210, (97) 210
Aen. II (780–4) 60, (324–7) 173
Aen. III (375–6) 41, (163–6) 109–10
Aen. IV (129–278) 47–51, (1–2) 191
Aen. V (781–4) 73, (788) 73, (606) 84, 98
Aen. VI (900–1) 31, (869–70) 105, (759) 109, (93–4) 184–5
Aen. VII (1–7) 32, (9–10) 33, (37–44) 35, 39, 40, (45) 44, (70–1) 45, (96–101) 46, (116–18) 51, (120–2) 52, (170–2) 56, (251–8) 61, (239–40) 62, (259–60) 67, (286ff.) 68, (296–319) 74–5, (454–5) 78, (545) 80, (572) 80, (583–4) 80, (594–7) 80, (601ff.) 82–96, (623–5) 82, (285) 87, (813) 94, (641) 112, (805–11) 188
Aen. VIII (91–6) 34, (36–9) 53, 88, (626–9) 42, (592–3) 95, (71–2) 125, (515–17) 143
Aen. IX (2) 84, (2–5) 98, (12) 99–100, (12) 99, (130–53) 99–100, (166–7) 101, (430) 103, (184–5) 106, (188–96) 107, (205–6) 107, (446–9) 109, 113, (525–8) 112, (511) 119, (724–30) 120, (741–2) 121
Aen. X (8) 98, (467–9) 105, (163) 112, (792–3) 113, (501–8) 113, 142, 195, (118–19) 128, (1–4) 130–1, (244–5) 134, (105–13) 134–5, 156, (256–7) 138, (279–84) 140, (467–72) 141, (524–5) 143, (605–32) 146–9, (639–42) 150, (689) 151, (781–2) 153, (758–9) 152, 156, (885–6) 152, (900–9) 154–5, (1) 156, (861–2) 164
Aen. XI (182–3) 66, 169, (68–71) 117, (1–2) 159, (14–28) 160–1, (42–58) 162–4, (152) 163, (173–5) 165, (96–8) 165, (208–9) 170, (217–18) 170, (231–8) 174, (362–75) 181, (425–7) 182, (442) 182–3, (480) 184, (432–3) 186–7, (823–4) 190
Aen. XII (793) 39, (820–3) 54, (827) 67, (231–8) 174, (4–6) 191, (525–6) 195, 201, 204, (107–8) 195, 201, (197–211) 196–7, (311) 199, (190–3) 199, (427–9) 202, (503–4) 202, (500–3) 203–4, 209, (895) 206, (883–4) 206, (646–9) 207, (829) 208, (838–40) 209, (940ff.) 211ff., (435–6) 215